Life in Society

Second Edition

Life in Society

■■■■■■■■ ■■ ■ ■ ■■ ■ ■ ■ ■ ■ ■ ■ ■ ■ ■ ■ ■ ■

Readings to Accompany
SOCIOLOGY
A Down-to-Earth Approach
Eighth Edition

Edited by
James M. Henslin
Southern Illinois University, Edwardsville

PEARSON

Boston ■ New York ■ San Francisco
Mexico City ■ Montreal ■ Toronto ■ London ■ Madrid ■ Munich ■ Paris
Hong Kong ■ Singapore ■ Tokyo ■ Cape Town ■ Sydney

Senior Series Editor: Jeff Lasser
Series Editorial Assistant: Heather McNally
Senior Marketing Manager: Kelly May
Editorial Production Service: Omegatype Typography, Inc.
Composition Buyer: Linda Cox
Manufacturing Manager: Megan Cochran
Electronic Composition: Omegatype Typography, Inc.
Cover Administrator: Joel Gendron

For related titles and support materials, visit our online catalog at www.ablongman.com.

Between the time website information is gathered and then published, it is not unusual for some sites to have closed. Also, the transcriptions of URLs can result in typographical errors. The publisher would appreciate notification where these errors occur so that they may be requested in subsequent editions.

Library of Congress Cataloging-in-Publication Data

Life in society: readings to accompany Sociology, a down-to-earth approach, eighth
    edition / edited by James M. Henslin.—2nd.
        p.   cm.
    Includes bibliographical references and index.
    ISBN 0-205-49415-3
        1. Sociology.   I. Henslin, James M.   II. Henslin, James M. Sociology.

HM586.L54 2007
301—dc22

2005056637

Printed in the United States of America

10   9   8   7   6   5   4   3   2   1   11   10   09   08   07   06

Contents

Preface

It is gratifying to see that students and instructors alike have responded so favorably to *Sociology: A Down-to-Earth Approach*. Since many instructors want to give their students the opportunity to read original sociological research, I have designed this brief anthology as a companion for *Sociology*. Because the readings follow the text's outline chapter for chapter and I have chosen a single reading for each chapter, it is easy to incorporate these selections into the course. I have also included a reading on human sexuality for those who assign my online chapter.

As always, a selection may have several subthemes. This allows a reading to be incorporated into a different chapter than the one I have assigned it, or to be included in the course even though a particular chapter is not assigned. I have also written a short introduction to each selection and an introduction for each of the five parts.

If you have any suggestions for the next edition of this reader, please let me know. As always, I look forward to hearing from you.

Jim Henslin
henslin@aol.com

The Sociological Perspective

All of us, at least to some degree, want to understand social life. If nothing else, we want to understand why people react to us as they do. We may want to know why some people boast and tell lies, while others undergo personal hardship in order to tell the truth. These are important questions, and they affect our everyday lives. So do issues on a much broader scale, such as why certain types of jobs are drying up around us, why we need more and more education to get a good job, why so many marriages break up, why people are prejudiced, why people are marrying later, or why cohabitation—which most people used to consider shameful—is now so common. Then, too, there is the question of why nations go to war despite the common sentiment that war is evil and should be avoided.

The tool that sociology offers in our quest for understanding is called *the sociological perspective* (also known as *the sociological imagination*). Basically, the sociological perspective means that no behavior or event stands in isolation. Rather, it is connected to other events that surround it. To understand any particular behavior or event, we need to view it within the context in which it occurs. The sociological perspective sensitizes us to the need to uncover those connections.

Back in the 1950s and 1960s, sociologist C. Wright Mills noted that world events were coming to play an increasingly significant role in our personal lives. More than ever, this is so today. What transpires in other countries—even on the other side of the globe—has profound effects on our own lives. An economic downturn in Japan or Europe, for example, pinches our economy—and may force us to put our lives on hold. When a country such as China or India undergoes rapid industrialization, it changes the cost of the goods we buy and threatens domestic industries. When jobs are hard to get—or we can get only low-paying jobs—we may decide that it is better to postpone getting married, no matter how much we are in love. Very reluctantly, we may even determine that it is prudent to move back in with our parents. Similarly, if our country goes to war in some far-off region, perhaps in a country we hadn't even heard of before, many people's lives are disrupted, some even shattered.

Economies surge, then tumble. Empires grow to a peak of power, then overreach and decline. Wars come and go, not only leaving behind their dead and mutilated, but also becoming a strange and unwelcome intruder in our lives. The Internet appears, changing the way we do business, and even the way we communicate, do our homework, and, for some of us, how we make dates and meet our husbands and wives. What once were luxuries come to be considered as necessities. Even morals change, and what was once considered wrong comes to be accepted as an ordinary part of everyday life.

Such events form a shaping context that affects us profoundly. This context affects both the ways we look at the world and how we see ourselves. Our aspirations—and our other "innermost" desires—do not originate within us. Instead, if we view them from the sociological perspective, we see that they are transplanted inside us. The social origin of these transplantings, though, ordinarily remains beyond our field of vision. We tend to perceive only what we experience directly—our feelings, our interactions, our friendships, our problems. We perceive but dimly this vital context that underlies "who" and "what" we are.

In short, we cannot understand our lives merely by looking inside ourselves at our own abilities, emotions, desires, or aspirations. Nor is it sufficient to consider only our family, friends, associates, or even our neighborhood or the social institutions such as school and church that influence us. Though they are important, we have to also consider a world far beyond our immediate confines.

All these—our personal feelings, our everyday interactions, and events around the globe—come together in *the sociological perspective*. Learning to see ourselves and others from this perspective is a fascinating journey, perhaps the most promising aspect of our introduction to sociology.

To begin our journey, we open this anthology with a selection that has become a classic in sociology. Peter Berger invites you to consider the excitement of exploring social life and beginning to view it from the sociological perspective. We follow this with a reading by Napoleon Chagnon, who recounts his fascinating adventure with a tribe in South America. In the third selection, Gwynne Dyer examines techniques that the U.S. Marine Corps uses to turn ordinary boys into soldiers who will not hesitate to kill when the order is given. In the fourth article, John Coleman, a college president, introduces us to the world of the homeless in New York City, revealing how social structure influences social interaction. In the concluding selection, we follow Kathleen Blee as she does participant observation and interviewing of dangerous people. Her frank analysis of her research into racist organizations is a far cry from what can be a "dry" analysis of sociological methods.

Invitation to Sociology

Peter L. Berger

introduction

To grasp *the sociological perspective* is to see the world in a new light. It can even change the way you see your taken-for-granted world. If you peer beneath the surface of human relationships, for example, your angle of vision changes and other realities begin to emerge. Consider something as common and familiar as friendship. If you place the sociological lens on friendship, you find that it is far from a simple matter. The implicit understandings on which it is based begin to emerge, and you uncover a complex system of rights and obligations. As you probe beneath the surface, you expose friendship's reciprocal obligations—how, for example, you acquire a social debt when your friend does something for you, in what way you are expected to repay this debt, and what the consequences are if you fail to do so. Although seldom stated, such implicit understandings inhabit the taken-for-granted assumptions that rule relationships. Violate them, and you risk severing the friendship.

Uncovering realities that lie beneath the surface and attaining a different understanding of social life are part of the fascination of sociology. Regardless of a sociologist's topic—whether as comfortable as friendship or as jarring as the role of women in the organized hate movement (Reading 5)—as Berger points out in this selection, the sociologist's overriding motivation is curiosity, a desire to know more about some aspect of social life, to discover what is really going on in some setting.

Thinking Critically

As you read this selection, ask yourself:

1. What is the difference between a sociologist and a pollster?

2. What does Berger mean by this statement? "Statistical data by themselves do not make sociology."

3. What does Berger mean when he says that sociology is a game? If it is a game, can it be taken seriously?

It is gratifying from certain value positions (including some of this writer's) that sociological insights have served in a number of instances to improve the lot of groups of human beings by uncovering morally shocking conditions or by clearing away collective illusions or by showing that socially desired results could be obtained in more humane fashion. One might point, for example, to some applications of sociological knowledge in the penological practice of Western countries. Or one might cite the use made of sociological studies in the Supreme Court decision of 1954 on racial segregation in the public schools. Or one could look at the applications of other sociological studies to the humane planning of urban redevelopment. Certainly the sociologist who is morally and politically sensitive will derive gratification from such instances. But, once more, it will be well to keep in mind that what is at issue here is not sociological understanding as such but certain applications of this understanding. It is not difficult to see how the same understanding could be applied with opposite intentions. Thus the sociological understanding of the dynamics of racial prejudice can be applied effectively by those promoting intragroup hatred as well as by those wanting to spread tolerance. And the sociological understanding of the nature of human solidarity can be employed in the service of both totalitarian and democratic regimes. . . .

One image [of the sociologist is that of] a gatherer of statistics about human behavior. . . . He* goes out with a questionnaire, interviews people selected at random, then goes home [and] enters his tabulations [into computers]. . . . In all of this, of course, he is supported by a large staff and a very large budget. Included in this image is the implication that the results of all this effort are picayune, a pedantic restatement of what everybody knows anyway. As one observer remarked pithily, a sociologist is a fellow who spends $100,000 to find his way to a house of ill repute.

This image of the sociologist has been strengthened in the public mind by the activities of many agencies that might well be called parasociological, mainly agencies concerned with public opinion and market trends. The pollster has become a well-known figure in American life, inopportuning people about their views from foreign policy to toilet paper. Since the methods used in the pollster business bear close resemblance to sociological research, the growth of this image of the sociologist is understandable. . . . The fundamental sociological question, whether concerned with premarital petting or with Republican votes or with the incidence of gang knifings, is always presumed to be "how often?" or "how many?". . .

Now it must be admitted, albeit regretfully, that this image of the sociologist and his trade is not altogether a product of fantasy. . . . [A good] part of the sociological enterprise in this country continues to consist of little studies of obscure fragments of social life, irrelevant to any broader theoretical concern. One glance at

*Some classic articles in sociology that are reprinted in this anthology were written when "he" and "man" were generic, when they referred to both men and women. So it is with "his," "him," and so on. Although the writing style has changed, the sociological ideas have not.

the table of contents of the major sociological journals or at the list of papers read at sociological conventions will confirm this statement. . . .

Statistical data by themselves do not make sociology. They become sociology only when they are sociologically interpreted, put within a theoretical frame of reference that is sociological. Simple counting, or even correlating different items that one counts, is not sociology. There is almost no sociology in the Kinsey reports. This does not mean that the data in these studies are not true or that they cannot be relevant to sociological understanding. They are, taken by themselves, raw materials that can be used in sociological interpretation. The interpretation, however, must be broader than the data themselves. So the sociologist cannot arrest himself at the frequency tables of premarital petting or extramarital pederasty. These enumerations are meaningful to him only in terms of their much broader implications for an understanding of institutions and values in our society. To arrive at such understanding the sociologist will often have to apply statistical techniques, especially when he is dealing with the mass phenomena of modern social life. But sociology consists of statistics as little as philology consists of conjugating irregular verbs or chemistry of making nasty smells in test tubes.

Sociology has, from its beginnings, understood itself as a science. . . . [T]he allegiance of sociologists to the scientific ethos has meant everywhere a willingness to be bound by certain scientific canons of procedure. If the sociologist remains faithful to his calling, his statements must be arrived at through the observation of certain rules of evidence that allow others to check on or to repeat or to develop his findings further. It is this scientific discipline that often supplies the motive for reading a sociological work as against, say, a novel on the same topic that might describe matters in much more impressive and convincing language. . . .

The charge that many sociologists write in a barbaric dialect must . . . be admitted. . . . Any scientific discipline must develop a terminology. This is self-evident for a discipline such as, say, nuclear physics that deals with matters unknown to most people and for which no words exist in common speech. However, terminology is possibly even more important for the social sciences, just because their subject matter *is* familiar and just because words *do* exist to denote it. Because we are well acquainted with the social institutions that surround us, our perception of them is imprecise and often erroneous. In very much the same way most of us will have considerable difficulty giving an accurate description of our parents, husbands or wives, children or close friends. Also, our language is often (and perhaps blessedly) vague and confusing in its references to social reality. Take for an example the concept of *class,* a very important one in sociology: There must be dozens of meanings that this term may have in common speech—income brackets, races, ethnic groups, power cliques, intelligence ratings, and many others. It is obvious that the sociologist must have a precise, unambiguous definition of the concept if his work is to proceed with any degree of scientific rigor. In view of these facts, one can understand that some sociologists have been tempted to invent altogether new words to avoid the semantic traps of the vernacular usage.

Finally, we would look at an image of the sociologist not so much in his professional role as in his being, supposedly, a certain kind of person. This is the image of the sociologist as a detached, sardonic observer, and a cold manipulator of men. Where this image prevails, it may represent an ironic triumph of the sociologist's own efforts to be accepted as a genuine scientist. The sociologist here becomes the self-appointed superior man, standing off from the warm vitality of common existence, finding his satisfactions not in living but in coolly appraising the lives of others, filing them away in little categories, and thus presumably missing the real significance of what he is observing. Further, there is the notion that, when he involves himself in social processes at all, the sociologist does so as an uncommitted technician, putting his manipulative skills at the disposal of the powers that be.

This last image is probably not very widely held. . . . The problem of the political role of the social scientist is, nevertheless, a very genuine one. For instance, the employment of sociologists by certain branches of industry and government raises moral questions that ought to be faced more widely than they have been so far. These are, however, moral questions that concern all men in positions of responsibility. . . .

How then are we to conceive of the sociologist? The sociologist is someone concerned with understanding society in a disciplined way. The nature of this discipline is scientific. This means that what the sociologist finds and says about the social phenomena he studies occurs within a certain rather strictly defined frame of reference. One of the main characteristics of this scientific frame of reference is that operations are bound by certain rules of evidence. As a scientist, the sociologist tries to be objective, to control his personal preferences and prejudices, to perceive clearly rather than to judge normatively. This restraint, of course, does not embrace the totality of the sociologist's existence as a human being, but is limited to his operations *qua* sociologist. Nor does the sociologist claim that his frame of reference is the only one within which society can be looked at. For that matter, very few scientists in any field would claim today that one should look at the world only scientifically. The botanist looking at a daffodil has no reason to dispute the right of the poet to look at the same object in a very different manner. There are many ways of playing. The point is not that one denies other people's games but that one is clear about the rules of one's own. The game of the sociologist, then, uses scientific rules. As a result, the sociologist must be clear in his own mind as to the meaning of these rules. That is, he must concern himself with methodological questions. Methodology does not constitute his goal. The latter, let us recall once more, is the attempt to understand society. Methodology helps in reaching this goal. In order to understand society, or that segment of it that he is studying at the moment, the sociologist will use a variety of means. Among these are statistical techniques. Statistics can be very useful in answering certain sociological questions. But statistics does not constitute sociology. As a scientist, the sociologist will have to be concerned with the exact significance of the terms he is using. That is, he will have to be careful about terminology. This does not have to mean that he must invent a new language of his own, but it does mean that he cannot naively use the language of everyday discourse. Finally, the interest of the sociologist is primarily theoretical. That is, he is interested in understanding for its own sake. He may be aware of or even concerned with the practical applicability and consequences of his findings, but at that point he leaves the sociological frame of reference as such and moves into realms of values, beliefs and ideas that he shares with other men who are not sociologists. . . .

[W]e would like to go a little bit further here and ask a somewhat more personal (and therefore, no doubt, more controversial) question. We would like to ask not only what it is that the sociologist is doing but also what it is that drives him to it. Or, to use the phrase Max Weber used in a similar connection, we want to inquire a little into the nature of the sociologist's demon. In doing so, we shall evoke an image that is not so much ideal-typical in the above sense but more confessional in the sense of personal commitment. Again, we are not interested in excommunicating anyone. The game of sociology goes on in a spacious playground. We are just describing a little more closely those we would like to tempt to join our game.

We would say then that the sociologist (that is, the one we would really like to invite to our game) is a person intensively, endlessly, shamelessly interested in the doings of men. His natural habitat is all the human gathering places of the world, wherever men come together. The sociologist may be interested in many other things. But his consuming interest remains in the world of men, their institutions, their history, their passions. And since he is interested in men, nothing that men do can be altogether tedious for him. He will naturally be interested in the events that engage men's ultimate beliefs, their moments of tragedy and grandeur and ecstasy. But he will also be fascinated by the common place, the everyday. He will know reverence, but this reverence will not prevent him from wanting to see and to understand. He may sometimes feel revulsion or contempt. But this also will not deter him from wanting to have his questions answered. The sociologist, in his quest for understanding, moves through the world of men without respect for the usual lines of demarcation. Nobility and degradation, power and obscurity, intelligence and folly—these are equally *interesting* to him, however unequal they may be in his personal values or tastes. Thus his questions may lead him to all possible levels of society, the best and the least known places, the most respected and the most despised. And, if he is a good sociologist, he will find himself in all these places because his own questions have so taken possession of him that he has little choice but to seek for answers.

It would be possible to say the same things in a lower key. We could say that the sociologist, but for the grace of his academic title, is the man who must listen to gossip despite himself, who is tempted to look through keyholes, to read other people's mail, to open closed cabinets. Before some otherwise unoccupied psychologist sets out now to construct an aptitude test for sociologists on the basis of sublimated voyeurism, let us quickly say that we are speaking merely by way of analogy. Perhaps some little boys consumed with curiosity to watch their maiden aunts in the bathroom later become inveterate sociologists. This is quite uninteresting. What interests us is the curiosity that grips any sociologist in front of a closed door behind which there are human voices. If he is a good sociologist, he will want to open that door, to understand these voices. Behind each closed door he will anticipate some new facet of human life not yet perceived and understood.

The sociologist will occupy himself with matters that others regard as too sacred or as too distasteful for dispassionate investigation. He will find rewarding the company of priests or of prostitutes, depending not on his personal preferences but on the questions he happens to be asking at the moment. He will also concern himself with matters that others may find much too boring. He will be interested in the human interaction that goes with warfare or with great intellectual discoveries, but also in the relations between people employed in a restaurant or between a group of little girls playing with their dolls. His main focus of attention is not the ultimate significance of what men do, but the action in itself, as another example of the infinite richness of human conduct. So much for the image of our playmate.

In these journeys through the world of men the sociologist will inevitably encounter other professional Peeping Toms. Sometimes these will resent his presence, feeling that he is poaching on their preserves. In some places the sociologist will meet up with the economist, in others with the political scientist, in yet others with the psychologist or the ethnologist. Yet chances are that the questions that have brought him to these same places are different from the ones that propelled his fellow-trespassers. The sociologist's questions always remain essentially the same: "What are people doing with each other here?" "What are their relationships to each other?" "How are these relationships organized in institutions?" "What are the collective ideas that move men and institutions?" In trying to answer these questions in specific instances, the sociologist will, of course, have to deal with economic or political matters, but he will do so in a way rather different from that of the economist or the political scientist. The scene that he contemplates is the same human scene that these other scientists concern themselves with. But the sociologist's angle of vision is different. When this is understood, it becomes clear that it makes little sense to try to stake out a special enclave within which the sociologist will carry on business in his own right. There is, however, one traveler whose path the sociologist will cross more often than anyone else's on his journeys. This is the historian. Indeed, as soon as the sociologist turns from the present to the past, his preoccupations are very hard indeed to distinguish from those of the historian. However, we shall leave this relationship to a later part of our considerations. Suffice it to say here that the sociological journey will be much impoverished unless it is punctuated frequently by conversation with that other particular traveler.

Any intellectual activity derives excitement from the moment it becomes a trail of discovery. In some fields of learning this is the discovery of worlds previously unthought and unthinkable. This is the excitement of the astronomer or of the nuclear physicist on the antipodal boundaries of the realities that man is capable of conceiving. But it can also be the excitement of bacteriology or geology. In a different way it can be the excitement of the linguist discovering new realms of human expression or of the anthropologist exploring human customs in faraway countries. In such discovery, when undertaken with passion, a widening of awareness, sometimes a veritable transformation of consciousness, occurs. The universe turns out to be much more wonder-full than one had ever dreamed. The excitement of sociology is usually of a different sort. Sometimes, it is true, the sociologist penetrates into worlds that had previously been quite unknown to him—for instance, the world of crime, or the world of some bizarre religious sect, or the world fashioned by the exclusive concerns of some group such as medical specialists or military leaders or advertising executives. However, much of the time the sociologist moves in sectors of experience that are familiar to him and to most people in his society. He investigates communities, institutions and activities that one can read about every day in the newspapers. Yet there is another excitement of discovery beckoning in his investigations. It is not the excitement of coming upon the totally unfamiliar, but rather the excitement of finding the familiar becoming transformed in its meaning. The fascination of sociology lies in the fact that its perspective makes us see in a new light the very world in which we have lived all our lives. This also constitutes a transformation of consciousness. Moreover, this transformation is more relevant existentially than that of many other intellectual disciplines, because it is more difficult to segregate in some special compartment of the mind. The astronomer does not live in the remote galaxies, and the nuclear physicist can, outside his laboratory, eat and laugh and marry and vote without thinking about the insides of the atom. The geologist looks at rocks only at appropriate times, and the linguist speaks English with his wife. The sociologist lives in society, on the job and off it. His own life, inevitably, is part of his subject matter. Men being what they are, sociologists too manage to segregate their professional insights from their everyday affairs. But it is a rather difficult feat to perform in good faith.

The sociologist moves in the common world of men, close to what most of them would call real. The categories he employs in his analyses are only refinements of the categories by which other men live—power, class, status, race, ethnicity. As a result, there is a deceptive simplicity and obviousness about some sociological investigations. One reads them, nods at the familiar scene, remarks that one has heard all this before and don't people have better things to do than to waste their time on truisms—until one is suddenly brought up against an insight that radically questions everything one had previously assumed about this familiar scene. This is the point at which one begins to sense the excitement of sociology.

Let us take a specific example. Imagine a sociology class in a Southern college where almost all the students are white Southerners. Imagine a lecture on the subject of the racial system of the South. The lecturer is talking here of matters that have been familiar to his students from the time of their infancy. Indeed, it may be that they are much more familiar with the minutiae of this system than he is. They are quite bored as a result. It seems to them that he is only using more pretentious words to describe what they already know. Thus he may use the term "caste," one commonly used now by American sociologists to describe the Southern racial system. But in explaining the term he shifts to traditional Hindu society, to make it clearer. He then goes on to analyze the magical beliefs inherent in caste taboos, the social dynamics of commensalism and connubium, the economic interests concealed within the system, the way in which religious beliefs relate to the taboos, the effects of the caste system upon the industrial development of the society and vice versa—all in India. But suddenly India is not very far away at all. The lecture then goes back to its Southern theme. The familiar now seems not quite so familiar any more. Questions are raised that are new, perhaps raised angrily, but raised all the same. And at least some of the students have begun to understand that there are functions involved in this business of race that they have not read about in the newspapers (at least not those in their hometowns) and that their parents have not told them—partly, at least, because neither the newspapers nor the parents knew about them.

It can be said that the first wisdom of sociology is this—things are not what they seem. This too is a deceptively simple statement. It ceases to be simple after a while. Social reality turns out to have many layers of meaning. The discovery of each new layer changes the perception of the whole.

Anthropologists use the term "culture shock" to describe the impact of a totally new culture upon a newcomer. In an extreme instance such shock will be experienced by the Western explorer who is told, halfway through dinner, that he is eating the nice old lady he had been chatting with the previous day—a shock with predictable physiological if not moral consequences. Most explorers no longer encounter cannibalism in their travels today. However, the first encounters with polygamy or with puberty rites or even with the way some nations drive their automobiles can be quite a shock to an American visitor. With the shock may go not only disapproval or disgust but a sense of excitement that things can *really* be that different from what they are at home. To some extent, at least, this is the excitement of any first travel abroad. The experience of sociological discovery could be described as "culture shock" minus geographical displacement. In other words, the sociologist travels at home—with shocking results. He is unlikely to find that he is eating a nice old lady for dinner. But the discovery, for instance, that his own church has considerable money invested in the missile industry or that a few blocks from his home there are people who engage in cultic orgies may not be drastically different in emotional impact. Yet we would not want to imply that sociological discoveries are always or even usually outrageous to moral sentiment. Not at all. What they have in common with exploration in distant lands, however, is the sudden illumination of new and unsuspected facets of human existence in society. This is the excitement and, as we shall try to show later, the humanistic justification of sociology.

People who like to avoid shocking discoveries, who prefer to believe that society is just what they were taught in Sunday School, who like the safety of the rules and the maxims of what Alfred Schuetz has called the "world-taken-for-granted," should stay away from sociology. People who feel no temptation before closed doors, who have no curiosity about human beings, who are content to admire scenery without wondering about the people who live in those houses on the other side of that river, should probably also stay away from sociology. They will find it unpleasant or, at any rate, unrewarding. People who are interested in human beings only if they can change, convert or reform them should also be warned, for they will find sociology much less useful than they hoped. And people whose interest is mainly in their own conceptual constructions will do just as well to turn to the study of little white mice. Sociology will be satisfying, in the long run, only to those who can think of nothing more entrancing than to watch men and to understand things human. . . .

To be sure, sociology is an individual pastime in the sense that it interests some men and bores others. Some like to observe human beings, others to experiment with mice. The world is big enough to hold all kinds and there is no logical priority for one interest as against another. But the word "pastime" is weak in describing what we mean. Sociology is more like a passion. The sociological perspective is more like a demon that possesses one, that drives one compellingly, again and again, to the questions that are its own. An introduction to sociology is, therefore, an invitation to a very special kind of passion.

The Fierce People

Napoleon Chagnon

introduction ■ ■ ■ ■

The many cultures of humans are fascinating. Every human group has a culture, whether the group be an urban gang in the United States or a tribe in the jungles of South America. Like an envelope, our culture encloses us, exposing us to what is within the envelope and limiting us from seeing what lies beyond it. As our culture sets boundaries, it dictates what is significant and insignificant in life. It provides guidelines for how we should view the self and for how we should interact with one another. In short, culture provides the framework from which we view life. Understand a people's culture, and you come a long way toward understanding why they think and act the way they do.

Understanding and appreciation are quite different matters. To understand a group does not necessarily mean that you appreciate them. This distinction will become apparent as you read this selection by Chagnon, who recounts his harrowing stay with the Yanomamö, a tribe in South America. His account makes it apparent how uncomfortable he felt during his lengthy fieldwork.

Thinking Critically

As you read this selection, ask yourself:

1. Why didn't Chagnon develop an appreciation for the way of life of the Yanomamö?

2. Why was Chagnon so stingy with his food—and so reluctant to accept food from others?

3. How does the culture of the Yanomamö compare with your own culture? Look for both similarities and differences.

The Yanomamö Indians live in southern Venezuela and the adjacent portions of northern Brazil. Some 125 widely scattered villages have populations ranging from 40 to 250 inhabitants, with 75 to 80 people the most usual number. In total numbers their population probably approaches 10,000 people, but this is merely a guess. Many of the villages have not yet been contacted by outsiders, and nobody knows for sure exactly how many uncontacted villages there are, or how many people live in them. By comparison to African or Melanesian tribes, the Yanomamö population is small. Still, they are one of the largest unacculturated tribes left in all of South America.

But they have a significance apart from tribal size and cultural purity: The Yanomamö are still actively conducting warfare. It is in the nature of man to fight, according to one of their myths, because the blood of "Moon" spilled on this layer of the cosmos, causing men to become fierce. I describe the Yanomamö as "the fierce people" because that is the most accurate single phrase that describes them. That is how they conceive themselves to be, and that is how they would like others to think of them.

I spent nineteen months with the Yanomamö during which time I acquired some proficiency in their language and, up to a point, submerged myself in their culture and way of life. The thing that impressed me most was the importance of aggression in their culture. I had the opportunity to witness a good many incidents that expressed individual vindictiveness on the one hand and collective bellicosity on the other. These ranged in seriousness from the ordinary incidents of wife beating and chest pounding to dueling and organized raiding by parties that set out with the intention of ambushing and killing men from enemy villages. One of the villages was raided approximately twenty-five times while I conducted the fieldwork, six times by the group I lived among. . . .

This is not to state that primitive man everywhere is unpleasant. By way of contrast, I have also done limited fieldwork among the Yanomamö's northern neighbors, the Carib-speaking Makiritare Indians. This group was very pleasant and charming, all of them anxious to help me and honor bound to show any visitor the numerous courtesies of their system of etiquette. In short, they approached the image of primitive man that I had conjured up, and it was sheer pleasure to work with them. . . .

My first day in the field illustrated to me what my teachers meant when they spoke of "culture shock." I had traveled in a small, aluminum rowboat propelled by a large outboard motor for two and a half days. This took me from the Territorial capital, a small town on the Orinoco River, deep into Yanomamö country. On the morning of the third day we reached a small mission settlement, the field "headquarters" of a group of Americans who were working in two Yanomamö villages. The missionaries had come out of these villages to hold their annual conference on the progress of their mission work, and were conducting their meetings when I arrived. We picked up a passenger at the mission station, James P. Barker, the first non-Yanomamö to make a sustained, permanent contact with the tribe (in 1950). He had just returned from a year's furlough in the United States, where I had earlier visited him before leaving for Venezuela. He agreed to accompany me to the village I had selected for my base of operations to introduce me to the Indians. This village was also his own home base, but he had not been there for over a year and did not plan to join me for another three months. Mr. Barker had been living with this particular group about five years.

We arrived at the village, Bisaasi-teri, about 2:00 P.M. and docked the boat along the muddy bank at the terminus of the path used by the Indians to fetch their drinking water. It was hot and muggy, and my clothing was soaked with perspiration. It clung uncomfortably to my body, as it did thereafter for the remainder of the work. The small, biting gnats were out in astronomical numbers, for it was the beginning of the dry season. My face and hands were swollen from the venom of their numerous stings. In just a few moments I was to meet my first Yanomamö, my first primitive man. What would it be like? I had visions of entering the village and seeing 125 social facts running about calling each other kinship terms and sharing food, each waiting and anxious to have me collect his genealogy. I would wear them out in turn. Would they like me? This was important to me; I wanted them to be so fond of me that they would adopt me into their kinship system and way of life, because I had heard that successful anthropologists always get adopted by their people. I had learned during my seven years of anthropological training at the University of Michigan that kinship was equivalent to society in primitive tribes and that it was a moral way of life, "moral" being something "good" and "desirable." I was determined to work my way into their moral system of kinship and become a member of their society.

My heart began to pound as we approached the village and heard the buzz of activity within the circular compound. Mr. Barker commented that he was anxious to see if any changes had taken place while he was away and wondered how many of them had died during his absence. I felt into my back pocket to make sure that my notebook was there and felt personally more secure when I touched it. Otherwise, I would not have known what to do with my hands.

I looked up and gasped when I saw a dozen burly, naked, filthy, hideous men staring at us down the shafts of their drawn arrows! Immense wads of green tobacco were stuck between their lower teeth and lips making them look even more hideous, and strands of dark-green slime dripped or hung from their noses. We arrived at the village while the men were blowing a hallucinogenic drug up their noses. One of the side effects of the drug is a runny nose. The mucus is always saturated with the green powder and the Indians usually let it run freely from their nostrils. My next discovery was that there were a dozen or so vicious, underfed dogs snapping at my legs, circling me as if I were going to be their next meal. I just stood there holding my notebook, helpless and pathetic. Then the stench of the decaying vegetation and filth struck me and I almost got sick. I was horrified. What sort of a welcome was this for the person who came here to live with you and learn your way of life, to become friends with you? They put their weapons down when they recognized Barker and returned to their chanting, keeping a nervous eye on the village entrances.

We had arrived just after a serious fight. Seven women had been abducted the day before by a neighboring group, and the local men and their guests had just that morning recovered five of them in a brutal club fight that nearly ended in a shooting war. The abductors, angry because they lost five of the seven captives, vowed to raid the Bisaasi-teri. When we arrived and entered the village unexpectedly, the Indians feared that we were the raiders. On several occasions during the next two hours the men in the village jumped to their feet, armed themselves, and waited nervously for the noise outside the village to be identified. My enthusiasm for collecting ethnographic curiosities diminished in proportion to the number of times such an alarm was raised. In fact, I was relieved when Mr. Barker suggested that we sleep across the river for the evening. It would be safer over there.

As we walked down the path to the boat, I pondered the wisdom of having decided to spend a year and a half with this tribe before I had even seen what they were like. I am not ashamed to admit, either, that had there been a diplomatic way out, I would have ended my fieldwork then and there. I did not look forward to the next day when I would be left alone with the Indians; I did not speak a word of their language, and they were decidedly different from what I had imagined them to be. The whole situation was depressing, and I wondered why I ever decided to switch from civil engineering to anthropology in the first place. I had not eaten all day, I was soaking wet from perspiration, the gnats were biting me, and I was covered with red pigment, the result of a dozen or so complete examinations I had been given by as many burly Indians. These examinations capped an otherwise grim day. The Indians would blow their noses into their hands, flick as much of the mucus off that would separate in a snap of the wrist, wipe the residue into their hair, and then carefully examine my face, arms, legs, hair, and the contents of my pockets. I asked Mr. Barker how to say "Your hands are dirty"; my comments were met by the Indians in the following way: They would "clean" their hands by spitting a quantity of slimy tobacco juice into them, rub them together, and then proceed with the examination.

Mr. Barker and I crossed the river and slung our hammocks. When he pulled his hammock out of a rubber bag, a heavy, disagreeable odor of mildewed cotton came with it. "Even the missionaries are filthy," I thought to myself. Within two weeks everything I owned smelled the same way, and I lived with the odor for the remainder of the fieldwork. My own habits of personal cleanliness reached such levels that I didn't even mind being examined by the Indians, as I was not much cleaner than they were after I had adjusted to the circumstances.

So much for my discovery that primitive man is not the picture of nobility and sanitation I had conceived him to be. I soon discovered that it was an enormously time-consuming task to maintain my own body in the manner to which it had grown accustomed in the relatively antiseptic environment of the northern United States. Either I could be relatively well fed and relatively comfortable in a fresh change of clothes and do very little fieldwork, or, I could do considerably more fieldwork and be less well fed and less comfortable.

It is appalling how complicated it can be to make oatmeal in the jungle. First, I had to make two trips to the river to haul the water. Next, I had to prime my kerosene stove with alcohol and get it burning, a tricky procedure when you are trying to mix powdered milk and fill a coffee pot at the same time: the alcohol prime always burned out before I could turn the kerosene on, and I would have to start all over. Or, I would turn the kerosene on, hoping that the element was still hot enough to vaporize the fuel, and not start a small fire in my palm-thatched hut as the liquid kerosene squirted all over the table and walls and ignited. It was safer to start over with the alcohol. Then I had to boil the oatmeal and pick the bugs out of it. All my supplies, of course, were carefully stored in Indian- proof, ratproof, moisture-proof, and insect-proof containers, not one of which ever served its purpose adequately. Just taking things out of the multiplicity of containers and repacking them afterward was a minor project in itself. By the time I had hauled the water to cook with, unpacked my food, prepared the oatmeal, milk, and coffee, heated water for dishes, washed and dried the dishes, repacked the food in the containers, stored the containers in locked trunks and cleaned up my mess, the ceremony of preparing breakfast had brought me almost up to lunch time.

Eating three meals a day was out of the question. I solved the problem by eating a single meal that could be prepared in a single container, or, at most, in two containers, washed my dishes only when there were no clean ones left, using cold river water, and wore each change of clothing at least a week to cut down on my laundry problem, a courageous undertaking in the tropics. I was also less concerned about sharing my provisions with the rats, insects, Indians, and the elements, thereby eliminating the need for my complicated storage process. I was able to last most of the day on *café con leche,* heavily sugared espresso coffee diluted about five to one with hot milk. I would prepare this in the evening and store it in a thermos. Frequently, my single meal was no more complicated than a can of sardines and a package of crackers. But at least two or three times a week I would do something sophisticated, like make oatmeal or boil rice and add a can of tuna fish or tomato paste to it. I even saved time by devising a water system that obviated the trips to the river. I had a few sheets of zinc roofing brought in and made a rain-water trap. I caught the water on the zinc surface, funneled it into an empty gasoline drum, and then ran a plastic hose from the drum to my hut. When the drum was exhausted in the dry season, I hired the Indians to fill it with water from the river.

I ate much less when I traveled with the Indians to visit other villages. Most of the time my travel diet consisted of roasted or boiled green plantains that I obtained from the Indians, but I always carried a few cans of sardines with me in case I got lost or stayed away longer than I had planned. I found peanut butter and crackers a very nourishing food, and a simple one to prepare on trips. It was nutritious and portable, and only one tool was required to prepare the meal, a hunting knife that could be cleaned by wiping the blade on a leaf. More importantly, it was one of the few foods the Indians would let me eat in relative peace. It looked too much like animal feces to them to excite their appetites.

I once referred to the peanut butter as the dung of cattle. They found this quite repugnant. They did not know what "cattle" were, but were generally aware that I ate several canned products of such an animal. I perpetrated this myth, if for no other reason than to have some peace of mind while I ate. Fieldworkers develop strange defense mechanisms, and this was one of my own forms of adaptation. On another occasion I was eating a can of frankfurters and growing very weary of the demands of one of my guests for a share in my meal. When he asked me what I was eating, I replied: "Beef." He then asked, "What part of the animal are you eating?" to which I replied, "Guess!" He stopped asking for a share.

Meals were a problem in another way. Food sharing is important to the Ya-nomamö in the context of displaying friendship. "I am hungry," is almost a form of greeting with them. I could not possibly have brought enough food with me to feed the entire village, yet they seemed not to understand this. All they could see was that I did not share my food with them at each and every meal. Nor could I enter into their system of reciprocities with respect to food; every time one of them gave me something "freely," he would dog me for months to pay him back, not with food, but with steel tools. Thus, if I accepted a plantain from someone in a different vil-lage while I was on a visit, he would most likely visit me in the future and demand a machete as payment for the time that he "fed" me. I usually reacted to these kinds of demands by giving a banana, the customary reciprocity in their culture—food for food—but this would be a disappointment for the individual who had visions of that single plantain growing into a machete over time.

Despite the fact that most of them knew I would not share my food with them at their request, some of them always showed up at my hut during mealtime. I gradually became accustomed to this and learned to ignore their persistent demands while I ate. Some of them would get angry because I failed to give in, but most of them accepted it as just a peculiarity of the subhuman foreigner. When I did give in, my hut quickly filled with Indians, each demanding a sample of the food that I had given one of them. If I did not give all a share, I was that much more despicable in their eyes.

A few of them went out of their way to make my meals unpleasant, to spite me for not sharing; for example, one man arrived and watched me eat a cracker with honey on it. He immediately recognized the honey, a particularly esteemed Yanomamö food. He knew that I would not share my tiny bottle and that it would be futile to ask. Instead, he glared at me and queried icily, "Shaki![1] What kind of animal semen are you eating on that cracker?" His question had the desired effect, and my meal ended.

Finally, there was the problem of being lonely and separated from your own kind, especially your family. I tried to overcome this by seeking personal friendships among the Indians. This only complicated the matter because all my friends simply used my confidence to gain privileged access to my cache of steel tools and trade goods, and looted me. I would be bitterly disappointed that my "friend" thought no more of me than to finesse our relationship exclusively with the intention of getting at any locked up possessions, and my depression would hit new lows every time I discovered this. The loss of the possession bothered me much less than the shock that I was, as far as most of them were concerned, nothing more than a source of desirable items; no holds were barred in relieving me of these, since I was considered something sub-human, a non-Yanomamö.

The thing that bothered me most was the incessant, passioned, and aggressive demands the Indians made. It would become so unbearable that I would have to lock myself in my mud hut every once in a while just to escape from it: Privacy is one of Western culture's greatest achievements. But I did not want privacy for its own sake; rather, I simply had to get away from the begging. Day and night for the entire time I lived with the Yanomamö I was plagued by such demands as: "Give me a knife, I am poor!"; "If you don't take me with you on your next trip to Widokaiya-teri, I'll chop a hole in your canoe!"; "Don't point your camera at me or I'll hit you!"; "Share your food with me!"; "Take me across the river in your canoe and be quick about it!"; "Give me a cooking pot!"; "Loan me your flashlight so I can go hunting tonight!"; "Give me medicine . . . I itch all over!"; "Take us on a week-long hunting trip with your shotgun!"; and "Give me an axe, or I'll break into your hut when you are away visiting and steal one!" And so I was bombarded by such demands day after day, months on end, until I could not bear to see an Indian.

It was not as difficult to become calloused to the incessant begging as it was to ignore the sense of urgency, the impassioned tone of voice, or the intimidation and aggression with which the demands were made. It was likewise difficult to adjust to the fact that the Yanomamö refused to accept "no" for an answer until or unless it seethed with passion and intimidation—which it did after six months. Giving in to a demand always established a new threshold; the next demand would be for a bigger item or favor, and the anger of the Indians even greater if the demand was not met. I soon learned that I had to become very much like the Yanomamö to be able to get along with them on their terms: sly, aggressive, and intimidating.

Had I failed to adjust in this fashion I would have lost six months of supplies to them in a single day or would have spent most of my time ferrying them around in my canoe or hunting for them. As it was, I did spend a considerable amount of time doing these things and did succumb to their outrageous demands for axes and machetes, at least at first. More importantly, had I failed to demonstrate that I could not be pushed around beyond a certain point, I would have been the subject of far more ridicule, theft, and practical jokes than was the actual case. In short, I had to acquire a certain proficiency in their kind of interpersonal politics and to learn how to imply subtly that certain potentially undesirable consequences might follow if they did such and such to me. They do this to each other in order to establish precisely the point at which they cannot goad an individual any further without precipitating retaliation. As soon as I caught on to this and realized that much of their aggression was stimulated by their desire to discover my flash point, I got along much better with them and regained some lost ground. It was sort of like a political game that everyone played, but one in which each individual sooner or later had to display some sign that his bluffs and implied threats could be backed up. I suspect that the frequency of wife beating is a component of this syndrome, since men can display their ferocity and show others that they are capable of violence. Beating a wife with a club is considered to be an acceptable way of displaying ferocity and one that does not expose the male to much danger. The important thing is that the man has displayed his potential for violence and the implication is that other men better treat him with respect and caution.

After six months, the level of demand was tolerable in the village I used for my headquarters. The Indians and I adjusted to each other and knew what to expect with regard to demands on their part for goods, favors, and services. Had I confined my fieldwork to just that village alone, the field experience would have been far more enjoyable. But, as I was interested in the demographic pattern and social organization of a much larger area, I made regular trips to some dozen different villages in order to collect genealogies or to recheck those I already had. Hence, the intensity of begging and intimidation was fairly constant for the duration of the fieldwork. I had to establish my position in some sort of pecking order of ferocity at each and every village.

For the most part, my own "fierceness" took the form of shouting back at the Yanomamö as loudly and as passionately as they shouted at me, especially at first, when I did not know much of their language. As I became more proficient in their language and learned more about their political tactics, I became more sophisticated in the art of bluffing. For example, I paid one young man a machete to cut palm trees and make boards from the wood. I used these to fashion a platform in the bottom of my dugout canoe to keep my possessions dry when I traveled by river. That afternoon I was doing informant work in the village; the long-awaited mission supply boat arrived, and most of the Indians ran out of the village to beg goods from the crew. I continued to work in the village for another hour or so and went down to the river to say "hello" to the men on the supply boat. I was angry when I discovered that the Indians had chopped up all my palm boards and used them to paddle their own canoes across the river. I knew that if I overlooked this incident I would have invited them to take even greater liberties with my goods in the future. I crossed the river, docked amidst their dugouts, and shouted for the Indians to come out and see me. A few of the culprits appeared, mischievous grins on their faces. I gave a spirited lecture about how hard I had worked to put those boards in my canoe, how I had paid a machete for the wood, and how angry I was that they destroyed my work in their haste to cross the river. I then pulled out my hunting knife and, while their grins disappeared, cut each of their canoes loose, set them into the current, and let them float away. I left without further ado and without looking back.

They managed to borrow another canoe and, after some effort, recovered their dugouts. The headman of the village later told me with an approving chuckle that

I had done the correct thing. Everyone in the village, except, of course, the culprits, supported and defended my action. This raised my status.

Whenever I took such action and defended my rights, I got along much better with the Yanomamö. A good deal of their behavior toward me was directed with the forethought of establishing the point at which I would react defensively. Many of them later reminisced about the early days of my work when I was "timid" and a little afraid of them, and they could bully me into giving goods away.

Theft was the most persistent situation that required me to take some sort of defensive action. I simply could not keep everything I owned locked in trunks, and the Indians came into my hut and left at will. I developed a very effective means for recovering almost all the stolen items. I would simply ask a child who took the item and then take that person's hammock when he was not around, giving a spirited lecture to the others as I marched away in a faked rage with the thief's hammock. Nobody ever attempted to stop me from doing this, and almost all of them told me that my technique for recovering my possessions was admirable. By nightfall the thief would either appear with the stolen object or send it along with someone else to make an exchange. The others would heckle him for getting caught and being forced to return the item.

With respect to collecting the data I sought, there was a very frustrating problem. Primitive social organization is kinship organization, and to understand the Yanomamö way of life I had to collect extensive genealogies. I could not have deliberately picked a more difficult group to work with in this regard: They have very stringent name taboos. They attempt to name people in such a way that when the person dies and they can no longer use his name, the loss of the word in the language is not inconvenient. Hence, they name people for specific and minute parts of things, such as "toenail of some rodent," thereby being able to retain the words "toenail" and "(specific) rodent," but not being able to refer directly to the toenail of that rodent. The taboo is maintained even for the living: One mark of prestige is the courtesy others show you by not using your name. The sanctions behind the taboo seem to be an unusual combination of fear and respect.

I tried to use kinship terms to collect genealogies at first, but the kinship terms were so ambiguous that I ultimately had to resort to names. They were quick to grasp that I was bound to learn everybody's name and reacted, without my knowing it, by inventing false names for everybody in the village. After having spent several months collecting names and learning them, this came as a disappointment to me: I could not cross-check the genealogies with other informants from distant villages.

They enjoyed watching me learn these names. I assumed, wrongly, that I would get the truth to each question and that I would get the best information by working in public. This set the stage for converting a serious project into a farce. Each informant tried to outdo his peers by inventing a name even more ridiculous than what I had been given earlier, or by asserting that the individual about whom I inquired was married to his mother or daughter, and the like. I would have the informant whisper the name of the individual in my ear, noting that he was the father of such and such a child. Everybody would then insist that I repeat the name aloud, roaring in hysterics as I clumsily pronounced the name. I assumed that the laughter was in response to the violation of the name taboo or to my pronunciation. This was a reasonable interpretation, since the individual whose name I said aloud invariably became angry. After I learned what some of the names meant, I began to understand what the laughter was all about. A few of the more colorful examples are: "hairy vagina," "long penis," "feces of the harpy eagle," and "dirty rectum." No wonder the victims were angry.

I was forced to do my genealogy work in private because of the horseplay and nonsense. Once I did so, my informants began to agree with each other and I managed to learn a few new names, real names. I could then test any new informant by collecting a genealogy from him that I knew to be accurate. I was able to weed out the more mischievous informants this way. Little by little I extended the genealogies and learned the real names. Still, I was unable to get the names of the dead and extend the genealogies back in time, and even my best informants continued to deceive me about their own close relatives. Most of them gave me the name of a living man as the father of some individual in order to avoid mentioning that the actual father was dead.

The quality of a genealogy depends in part on the number of generations it embraces, and the name taboo prevented me from getting any substantial information about deceased ancestors. Without this information, I could not detect marriage patterns through time. I had to rely on older informants for this information, but these were the most reluctant of all. As I became more proficient in the language and more skilled at detecting lies, my informants became better at lying. One of them in particular was so cunning and persuasive that I was shocked to discover that he had been inventing his information. He specialized in making a ceremony out of telling me false names. He would look around to make sure nobody was listening outside my hut, enjoin me to never mention the name again, act very nervous and spooky, and then grab me by the head to whisper the name very softly into my ear. I was always elated after an informant session with him, because I had several generations of dead ancestors for the living people. The others refused to give me this information. To show my gratitude, I paid him quadruple the rate I had given the others. When word got around that I had increased the pay, volunteers began pouring in to give me genealogies.

I discovered that the old man was lying quite by accident. A club fight broke out in the village one day, the result of a dispute over the possession of a woman. She had been promised to Rerebawa, a particularly aggressive young man who had married into the village. Rerebawa had already been given her older sister and was enraged when the younger girl began having an affair with another man in the village, making no attempt to conceal it from him. He challenged the young man to a club fight, but was so abusive in his challenge that the opponent's father took offense and entered the village circle with his son, wielding a long club. Rerebawa swaggered out to the duel and hurled insults at both of them, trying to goad them into striking him on the head with their clubs. This would have given him the opportunity to strike them on the head. His opponents refused to hit him, and the fight ended.

Rerebawa had won a moral victory because his opponents were afraid to hit him. Thereafter, he swaggered around and insulted the two men behind their backs. He was genuinely angry with them, to the point of calling the older man by the name of his dead father. I quickly seized on this as an opportunity to collect an accurate genealogy and pumped him about his adversary's ancestors. Rerebawa had been particularly nasty to me up to this point, but we became staunch allies: We were both outsiders in the local village. I then asked about other dead ancestors and got immediate replies. He was angry with the whole group and not afraid to tell me the names of the dead. When I compared his version of the genealogies to that of the old man, it was obvious that one of them was lying. I challenged his information, and he explained that everybody knew that the old man was deceiving me and bragging about it in the village. The names the old man had given me were the dead ancestors of the members of a village so far away that he thought I would never have occasion to inquire about them. As it turned out, Rerebawa knew most of the people in that village and recognized the names.

I then went over the complete genealogical records with Rerebawa, genealogies I had presumed to be in final form. I had to revise them all because of the numerous lies and falsifications they contained. Thus, after five months of almost constant work on the genealogies of just one group, I had to begin almost from scratch!

Discouraging as it was to start over, it was still the first real turning point in my fieldwork. Thereafter, I began taking advantage of local arguments and animosities in selecting my informants, and used more extensively individuals who had married into the group. I began traveling to other villages to check the genealogies, picking villages that were on strained terms with the people about whom I wanted information. I would then return to my base camp and check with local informants the accuracy of the new information. If the informants became angry when I mentioned the new names I acquired from the unfriendly group, I was almost certain that the information was accurate. For this kind of checking I had to use informants whose genealogies I knew rather well: They had to be distantly enough related to the dead person that they would not go into a rage when I mentioned the name, but not so remotely related that they would be uncertain of the accuracy of the information. Thus, I had to make a list of names that I dared not use in the presence of each and every informant. Despite the precautions, I occasionally hit a name that put the informant into a rage, such as that of a dead brother or sister that other informants had not reported. This always terminated the day's work with that informant, for he would be too touchy to continue any further, and I would be reluctant to take a chance on accidentally discovering another dead kinsman so soon after the first.

These were always unpleasant experiences, and occasionally dangerous ones, depending on the temperament of the informant. On one occasion I was planning to visit a village that had been raided about a week earlier. A woman whose name I had on my list had been killed by the raiders. I planned to check each individual on the list one by one to estimate ages, and I wanted to remove her name so that I would not say it aloud in the village. I knew that I would be in considerable difficulty if I said this name aloud so soon after her death. I called on my original informant and asked him to tell me the name of the woman who had been killed. He refused, explaining that she was a close relative of his. I then asked him if he would become angry if I read off all the names on the list. This way he did not have to say her name and could merely nod when I mentioned the right one. He was a fairly good friend of mine, and I thought I could predict his reaction. He assured me that this would be a good way of doing it. We were alone in my hut so that nobody could overhear us. I read the names softly, continuing to the next when he gave a negative reply. When I finally spoke the name of the dead woman he flew out of his chair, raised his arm to strike me, and shouted: "You son-of-a-bitch![2] If you ever say that name again, I'll kill you!" He was shaking with rage, but left my hut quietly. I shudder to think what might have happened if I had said the name unknowingly in the woman's village. I had other, similar experiences in different villages, but luckily the dead person had been dead for some time and was not closely related to the individual into whose ear I whispered the name. I was merely cautioned to desist from saying any more names, lest I get people angry with me.

I had been working on the genealogies for nearly a year when another individual came to my aid. It was Kaobawa, the headman of Upper Bisaasi-teri, the group in which I spent most of my time. He visited me one day after the others had left the hut and volunteered to help me on the genealogies. He was poor, he explained, and needed a machete. He would work only on the condition that I did not ask him about his own parents and other very close kinsmen who were dead. He also added that he would not lie to me as the others had done in the past. This was perhaps the most important single event in my fieldwork, for out of this meeting evolved a very warm friendship and a very profitable informant-fieldworker relationship.

Kaobawa's familiarity with his group's history and his candidness were remarkable. His knowledge of details was almost encyclopedic. More than that, he was enthusiastic and encouraged me to learn details that I might otherwise have ignored. If there were things he did not know intimately, he would advise me to wait until he could check things out with someone in the village. This he would do clandestinely, giving me a report the next day. As I was constrained by my part of the bargain to avoid discussing his close dead kinsmen, I had to rely on Rerebawa for this information. I got Rerebawa's genealogy from Kaobawa.

Once again I went over the genealogies with Kaobawa to recheck them, a considerable task by this time: they included about two thousand names, representing several generations of individuals from four different villages. Rerebawa's information was very accurate, and Kaobawa's contribution enabled me to trace the genealogies further back in time. Thus, after nearly a year of constant work on genealogies, Yanomamö demography and social organization began to fall into a pattern. Only then could I see how kin groups formed and exchanged women with each other over time, and only then did the fissioning of larger villages into smaller ones show a distinct pattern. At this point I was able to begin formulating more intelligent questions because there was now some sort of pattern to work with. Without the help of Rerebawa and Kaobawa, I could not have made very much sense of the plethora of details I had collected from dozens of other informants.

Kaobawa is about 40 years old. I say "about" because the Yanomamö numeration system has only three numbers: one, two, and more-than-two. He is the headman of Upper Bisaasi-teri. He has had five or six wives so far and temporary affairs with as many more women, one of which resulted in a child. At the present time he has just two wives, Bahimi and Koamashima. He has had a daughter and a son by Bahimi, his eldest and favorite wife. Koamashima, about 20 years old, recently had her first child, a boy. Kaobawa may give Koamashima to his youngest brother. Even now the brother shares in her sexual services. Kaobawa recently gave his third wife to another of his brothers because she was beshi: "horny." In fact, this girl had been married to two other men, both of whom discarded her because of her infidelity. Kaobawa had one daughter by her; she is being raised by his brother.

Kaobawa's eldest wife, Bahimi, is about thirty-five years old. She is his first cross-cousin. Bahimi was pregnant when I began my fieldwork, but she killed the new baby, a boy, at birth, explaining tearfully that it would have competed with Ariwari, her nursing son, for milk. Rather than expose Ariwari to the dangers and uncertainty of an early weaning, she killed the new child instead. By Yanomamö standards, she and Kaobawa have a very tranquil household. He only beats her once in a while, and never very hard. She never has affairs with other men.

Kaobawa is quiet, intense, wise, and unobtrusive. He leads more by example than by threats and coercion. He can afford to be this way as he established his reputation for being fierce long ago, and other men respect him. He also has five mature brothers who support him, and he has given a number of his sisters to other men in the village, thereby putting them under some obligation to him. In short, his "natural" following (kinsmen) is large, and he does not have to constantly display his ferocity. People already respect him and take his suggestions seriously.

Rerebawa is much younger, only about twenty-two years old. He has just one wife by whom he has had three children. He is from Karohi-teri, one of the villages to which Kaobawa is allied. Rerebawa left his village to seek a wife in Kaobawa's group because there were no eligible women there for him to marry.

Rerebawa is perhaps more typical than Kaobawa in the sense that he is concerned about his reputation for ferocity and goes out of his way to act tough. He is, however, much braver than the other men his age and backs up his threats with action. Moreover, he is concerned about politics and knows the details of intervillage relationships over a large area. In this respect he shows all the attributes of a headman, although he is still too young and has too many competent older brothers in his own village to expect to move easily into the position of leadership there.

He does not intend to stay in Kaobawa's group and has not made a garden. He feels that he has adequately discharged his obligations to his wife's parents by providing them with fresh game for three years. They should let him take the wife and return to his own village with her, but they refuse and try to entice him to remain permanently in Bisaasi-teri to provide them with game when they are old. They have even promised to give him their second daughter if he will stay permanently.

Although he has displayed his ferocity in many ways, one incident in particular shows what his character is like. Before he left his own village to seek a wife, he had an affair with the wife of an older brother. When he was discovered, his brother attacked him with a club. Rerebawa was infuriated so he grabbed an axe and drove his brother out of the village after soundly beating him with the flat of the blade. The brother was so afraid that he did not return to the village for several days. I recently visited his village with him. He made a point to introduce me to this brother. Rerebawa dragged him out of his hammock by the arm and told me, "This is the brother whose wife I had an affair with," a deadly insult. His brother did nothing and slunk back into his hammock, shamed, but relieved to have Rerebawa release the vise-grip on his arm.

Despite the fact that he admires Kaobawa, he has a low opinion of the others in Bisaasi-teri. He admitted confidentially that he thought Bisaasi-teri was an abominable group: "This is a terrible neighborhood! All the young men are lazy and cowards and everybody is committing incest! I'll be glad to get back home." He also admired Kaobawa's brother, the headman of Monou-teri. This man was killed by raiders while I was doing my fieldwork. Rerebawa was disgusted that the others did not chase the raiders when they discovered the shooting: "He was the only fierce one in the whole group; he was my close friend. The cowardly Monou-teri hid like women in the jungle and didn't even chase the raiders!"

Even though Rerebawa is fierce and capable of being quite nasty, he has a good side as well. He has a very biting sense of humor and can entertain the group for hours on end with jokes and witty comments. And, he is one of few Yanomamö that I feel I can trust. When I returned to Bisaasi-teri after having been away for a year, Rerebawa was in his own village visiting his kinsmen. Word reached him that I had returned, and he immediately came to see me. He greeted me with an immense bear hug and exclaimed, "Shaki! Why did you stay away so long? Did you know that my will was so cold while you were gone that at times I could not eat for want of seeing you?" I had to admit that I missed him, too.

Of all the Yanomamö I know, he is the most genuine and the most devoted to his culture's ways and values. I admire him for that, although I can't say that I subscribe to or endorse these same values. By contrast, Kaobawa is older and wiser. He sees his own culture in a different light and criticizes aspects of it he does not like. While many of his peers accept some of the superstitions and explanatory myths as truth and as the way things ought to be, Kaobawa questions them and privately pokes fun at some of them. Probably, more of the Yanomamö are like Rerebawa, or at least try to be.

NOTES

1. "Shaki," or, rather, "Shakiwa," is the name they gave me because they could not pronounce "Chagnon." They like to name people for some distinctive feature when possible. *Shaki* is the name of a species of noisome bees; they accumulate in large numbers around ripening bananas and make pests of themselves by eating into the fruit, showering the people below with the debris. They probably adopted this name for me because I was also a nuisance,

continuously prying into their business, taking pictures of them, and, in general, being where they did not want me.

2. This is the closest English translation of his actual statement, the literal translation of which would be nonsensical in our language.

Anybody's Son Will Do

Gwynne Dyer

introduction ■ ■ ■ ■ ■

To understand the term *socialization*, substitute the word *learning*. Socialization does not refer only to children. All of us are being socialized all the time. Each time we are exposed to something new, we are being socialized. If we learn how to operate a new video control, play a new (or old) video game, watch a movie, read a book, or listen to a college lecture, we are being socialized. Even when we talk to a friend, socialization is taking place, for ideas and perspectives are being exchanged that become part of the way we view the world. And socialization doesn't stop when we reach a certain age. Even when we are old, we will be exposed to experiences that influence our viewpoints. Socialization, then, is a lifelong process. In this process, we are becoming more and more a part of our culture—or of our subculture.

From the examples just given, you can see that socialization is usually gentle, subtle, and gradual. But there are remarkable exceptions, such as the one analyzed in this selection. Dyer examines techniques by which the U.S. Marine Corps turns young men into killers—and how this organization is able to accomplish this remarkable transformation in just under 11 weeks. As you will see, the Marines' techniques are brutal, swift, and effective.

Thinking Critically

As you read this article, ask yourself:

1. How do the U.S. Marines socialize their recruits?

2. How do the socialization techniques used by the Marines compare with the socialization techniques that have been used to bring you to your current place in life?

3. Why are the socialization techniques of the Marines so effective?

You think about it and you know you're going to have to kill but you don't understand the implications of that, because in the society in which you've lived murder is the most heinous of crimes. . . and you are in a situation in which it's turned the other way round. . . . When you do actually kill someone the experience, my experience, was one of revulsion and disgust. . . .

I was utterly terrified—petrified—but I knew there had to be a Japanese sniper in a small fishing shack near the shore. He was firing in the other direction at Marines in another battalion, but I knew as soon as he picked off the people there—there was a window on our side—that he would start picking us off. And there was nobody else to go . . . and so I ran towards the shack and broke in and found myself in an empty room. . . .

There was a door which meant there was another room and the sniper was in that—and I just broke that down. I was just absolutely gripped by the fear that this man would expect me and would shoot me. But as it turned out he was in a sniper harness and he couldn't turn around fast enough. He was entangled in the harness so I shot him with a .45, and I felt remorse and shame. I can remember whispering foolishly, "I'm sorry" and then just throwing up. . . . I threw up all over myself. It was a betrayal of what I'd been taught since a child.

—William Manchester

Yet he did kill the Japanese soldier, just as he had been trained to—the revulsion only came afterward. And even after Manchester knew what it was like to kill another human being, a young man like himself, he went on trying to kill his "enemies" until the war was over. Like all the other tens of millions of soldiers who had been taught from infancy that killing was wrong, and had then been sent off to kill for their countries, he was almost helpless to disobey, for he had fallen into the hands of an institution so powerful and so subtle that it could quickly reverse the moral training of a lifetime.

The whole vast edifice of the military institution rests on its ability to obtain obedience from its members even unto death—and the killing of others. It has enormous powers of compulsion at its command, of course, but all authority must be based ultimately on consent. The task of extracting that consent from its members has probably grown harder in recent times, for the gulf between the military and the civilian worlds has undoubtedly widened: Civilians no longer perceive the threat of violent death as an everyday hazard of existence, and the categories of people whom it is not morally permissible to kill have broadened to include (in peacetime) the entire human race. Yet the armed forces of every country can still take almost any young male civilian and turn him into a soldier with all the right reflexes and attitudes in only a few weeks. Their recruits usually have no more than twenty years' experience of the world, most of it as children, while the armies have had all of history to practice and perfect their techniques.

Just think of how the soldier is treated. While still a child he is shut up in the barracks. During his training he is always being knocked about. If he makes the least mistake he is beaten, a burning blow on his body, another on his eye, perhaps his head is laid open with a wound. He is battered and bruised with flogging. On the march. . .they hang heavy loads round his neck like that of an ass.

—Egyptian, ca. 1500 B.C.

The moment I talk to the new conscripts about the homeland I strike a land mine. So I kept quiet. Instead, I try to make soldiers of them. I give them hell from morning to sunset. They begin to curse me, curse the army, curse the state.

Then they begin to curse together, and become a truly cohesive group, a unit, a fighting unit.

—Israeli, ca. A.D. 1970

All soldiers belong to the same profession, no matter what country they serve, and it makes them different from everybody else. They have to be different, for their job is ultimately about killing and dying, and those things are not a natural vocation for any human being. Yet all soldiers are born civilians. The method for turning young men into soldiers—people who kill other people and expose themselves to death—is basic training. It's essentially the same all over the world, and it always has been, because young men everywhere are pretty much alike.

Human beings are fairly malleable, especially when they are young, and in every young man there are attitudes for any army to work with: the inherited values and postures, more or less dimly recalled, of the tribal warriors who were once the model for every young boy to emulate. Civilization did not involve a sudden clean break in the way people behave, but merely the progressive distortion and redirection of all the ways in which people in the old tribal societies used to behave, and modern definitions of maleness still contain a great deal of the old warrior ethic. The anarchic machismo of the primitive warrior is not what modern armies really need in their soldiers, but it does provide them with promising raw material for the transformation they must work in their recruits.

Just how this transformation is wrought varies from time to time and from country to country. In totally militarized societies—ancient Sparta, the samurai class of medieval Japan, the areas controlled by organizations like the Eritrean People's Liberation Front today—it begins at puberty or before, when the young boy is immersed in a disciplined society in which only the military values are allowed to penetrate. In more sophisticated modern societies, the process is briefer and more concentrated, and the way it works is much more visible. It is, essentially, a conversion process in an almost religious sense—and as in all conversion phenomena, the emotions are far more important than the specific ideas. . . .

Armies know this. It is their business to get men to fight, and they have had a long time to work out the best way of doing it. All of them pay lip service to the symbols and slogans of their political masters, though the amount of time they must devote to this activity varies from country to country. . . . Nor should it be thought that the armies are hypocritical—most of their members really do believe in their particular national symbols and slogans. But their secret is that they know these are not the things that sustain men in combat.

What really enables men to fight is their own self-respect, and a special kind of love that has nothing to do with sex or idealism. Very few men have died in battle, when the moment actually arrived, for the United States of America or for the sacred cause of Communism, or even for their homes and families; if they had any choice in the matter at all, they chose to die for each other and for their own vision of themselves. . . .

The way armies produce this sense of brotherhood in a peacetime environment is basic training: a feat of psychological manipulation on the grand scale which has been so consistently successful and so universal that we fail to notice it as remarkable. In countries where the army must extract its recruits in their late teens, whether voluntarily or by conscription, from a civilian environment that does not share the military values, basic training involves a brief but intense period of indoctrination whose purpose is not really to teach the recruits basic military skills, but rather to change their values and their loyalties. "I guess you could say we brainwash them a little bit," admitted a U.S. Marine drill instructor, "but you know they're good people."

The duration and intensity of basic training, and even its major emphases, depend on what kind of society the recruits are coming from, and on what sort of military organization they are going to. It is obviously quicker to train men from a martial culture than from one in which the dominant values are civilian and commercial, and easier to deal with volunteers than with reluctant conscripts. Conscripts are not always unwilling, however; there are many instances in which the army is popular for economic reasons. . . .

It's easier if you catch them young. You can train older men to be soldiers; it's done in every major war. But you can never get them to believe that they like it, which is the major reason armies try to get their recruits before they are 20. There are other reasons too, of course, like the physical fitness, lack of dependents, and economic dispensability of teenagers, that make armies prefer them, but the most important qualities teenagers bring to basic training are enthusiasm and naiveté. Many of them actively want the discipline and the closely structured environment that the armed forces will provide, so there is no need for the recruiters to deceive the kids about what will happen to them after they join.

> *There is discipline. There is drill. . . . When you are relying on your mates and they are relying on you, there's no room for slackness or sloppiness. If you're not prepared to accept the rules, you're better off where you are.*
> —British army recruiting advertisement, 1976

> *People are not born soldiers, they become soldiers. . . . And it should not begin at the moment when a new recruit is enlisted into the ranks, but rather much earlier, at the time of the first signs of maturity, during the time of adolescent dreams.*
> —Red Star (Soviet army newspaper), 1973

Young civilians who have volunteered and have been accepted by the Marine Corps arrive at Parris Island, the Corps's East Coast facility for basic training, in a state of considerable excitement and apprehension: Most are aware that they are about to undergo an extraordinary and very difficult experience. But they do not make their own way to the base; rather, they trickle in to Charleston airport on various flights throughout the day on which their training platoon is due to form, and are held there, in a state of suppressed but mounting nervous tension, until late in the evening. When the buses finally come to carry them the seventy-six miles to Parris Island, it is often after midnight—and this is not an administrative oversight. The shock treatment they are about to receive will work most efficiently if they are worn out and somewhat disoriented when they arrive.

The basic training organization is a machine, processing several thousand young men every month, and every facet and gear of it has been designed with the sole purpose of turning civilians into Marines as efficiently as possible. Provided it can have total control over their bodies and their environment for approximately three months, it can practically guarantee converts. Parris Island provides that controlled environment, and the recruits do not set foot outside it again until they graduate as Marine privates eleven weeks later.

> *They're allowed to call home, so long as it doesn't get out of hand—every three weeks or so they can call home and make sure everything's all right, if they haven't gotten a letter or there's a particular set of circumstances. If it's a case of an emergency call coming in, then they're allowed to accept that call; if not, one of my staff will take the message. . . .*
>
> *In some cases I'll get calls from parents who haven't quite gotten adjusted to the idea that their son had cut the strings—and in a lot of cases that's what they're doing. The military provides them with an opportunity to leave home but they're still in a rather secure environment.*
>
> —Captain Brassington, USMC

For the young recruits, basic training is the closest thing their society can offer to a formal rite of passage, and the institution probably stands in an unbroken line of descent from the lengthy ordeals by which young males in precivilized groups were initiated into the adult community of warriors. But in civilized societies it is a highly functional institution whose product is not anarchic warriors, but trained soldiers.

Basic training is not really about teaching people skills; it's about changing them, so that they can do things they wouldn't have dreamt of otherwise. It works by applying enormous physical and mental pressure to men who have been isolated from their normal civilian environment and placed in one where the only right way to think and behave is the way the Marine Corps wants them to. The key word the men who run the machine use to describe this process is *motivation*.

> *I can motivate a recruit and in third phase, if I tell him to jump off the third deck, he'll jump off the third deck. Like I said before, it's a captive audience and I can train that guy; I can get him to do anything I want him to do. . . . They're good kids and they're out to do the right thing. We get some bad kids, but you know, we weed those out. But as far as motivation—here, we can motivate them to do anything you want, in recruit training.*
>
> —USMC drill instructor, Parris Island

The first three days the raw recruits spend at Parris Island are actually relatively easy, though they are hustled and shouted at continuously. It is during this time that they are documented and inoculated, receive uniforms, and learn the basic orders of drill that will enable young Americans (who are not very accustomed to this aspect of life) to do everything simultaneously in large groups. But the most important thing that happens in "forming" is the surrender of the recruits' own clothes, their hair—all the physical evidence of their individual civilian identities.

During a period of only 72 hours, in which they are allowed little sleep, the recruits lay aside their former lives in a series of hasty rituals (like being shaven to the scalp) whose symbolic significance is quite clear to them even though they are quite deliberately given absolutely no time for reflection, or any hint that they might have the option of turning back from their commitment. The men in charge of them know how delicate a tightrope they are walking, though, because at this stage the recruits are still newly caught civilians who have not yet made their ultimate inward submission to the discipline of the Corps.

> *Forming Day One makes me nervous. You've got a whole new mob of recruits, you know, 60 or 70 depending, and they don't know anything. You don't know what kind of a reaction you're going to get from the stress you're going to lay on them, and it just worries me the first day. . . .*
>
> *Things could happen, I'm not going to lie to you. Something might happen. A recruit might decide he doesn't want any part of this stuff and maybe take a poke at you or something like that. In a situation like that it's going to be a spur-of-the-moment thing and that worries me.*
>
> —USMC drill instructor

But it rarely happens. The frantic bustle of forming is designed to give the recruit no time to think about resisting what is happening to him. And so the recruits emerge from their initiation into the system, stripped of their civilian clothes, shorn of their hair, and deprived of whatever confidence in their own identity they may previously have had as 18-year-olds, like so many blanks ready to have the Marine identity impressed upon them.

The first stage in any conversion process is the destruction of an individual's former beliefs and confidence, and his reduction to a position of helplessness and need. It isn't really as drastic as all that, of course, for three days cannot cancel out 18 years; the inner thoughts and the basic character are not erased. But the recruits have already learned that the only acceptable behavior is to repress any unorthodox thoughts and to mimic the character the Marine Corps wants. Nor are they, on the whole, reluctant to do so, for they *want* to be Marines. From the moment they arrive at Parris Island, the vague notion that has been passed down for a thousand generations that masculinity means being a warrior becomes an explicit article of faith, relentlessly preached: To be a man means to be a Marine.

There are very few 18-year-old boys who do not have highly romanticized ideas of what it means to be a man, so the Marine Corps has plenty of buttons to push. And it starts pushing them on the first day of real training: The officer in charge of the formation appears before them for the first time, in full dress uniform with medals, and tells them how to become men.

> *The United States Marine Corps has 205 years of illustrious history to speak for itself. You have made the most important decision in your life. . . by signing your name, your life, pledge to the Government of the United States, and even more importantly, to the United States Marine Corps—a brotherhood, an elite unit. In 10.3 weeks you are going to become a member of that history, those traditions, this organization—if you have what it takes. . . .*
>
> *All of you want to do that by virtue of your signing your name as a man. The Marine Corps says that we build men. Well, I'll go a little bit further. We develop the tools that you have—and everybody has those tools to a certain extent right*

now. We're going to give you the blueprints, and we are going to show you how to build a Marine. You've got to build a Marine—you understand?
—Captain Pingree, USMC

The recruits, gazing at him with awe and adoration, shout in unison, "Yes, sir!" just as they have been taught. They do it willingly, because they are volunteers—but even conscripts tend to have the romantic fervor of volunteers if they are only 18 years old. Basic training, whatever its hardships, is a quick way to become a man among men, with an undeniable status, and beyond the initial consent to undergo it, it doesn't even require any decisions.

I had just dropped out of high school and I wasn't doing much on the street except hanging out, as most teenagers would be doing. So they gave me an opportunity— a recruiter picked me up, gave me a good line, and said that I could make it in the Marines, that I have a future ahead of me. And since I was living with my parents, I figured that I could start my own life here and grow up a little.
—USMC recruit

I like the hand-to-hand combat and . . . things like that. It's a little rough going on me, and since I have a small frame I would like to become deadly, as I would put it. I like to have them words, especially the way they've been teaching me here.
—USMC recruit (from Brooklyn), Parris Island

The training, when it starts, seems impossibly demanding physically for most of the recruits—and then it gets harder week by week. There is a constant barrage of abuse and insults aimed at the recruits, with the deliberate purpose of breaking down their pride and so destroying their ability to resist the transformation of values and attitudes that the Corps intends them to undergo. At the same time the demands for constant alertness and for instant obedience are continuously stepped up, and the standards by which the dress and behavior of the recruits are judged become steadily more unforgiving. But it is all carefully calculated by the men who run the machine, who think and talk in terms of the stress they are placing on the recruits: "We take so many c.c.'s of stress and we administer it to each man—they should be a little bit scared and they should be unsure, but they're adjusting." The aim is to keep the training arduous but just within most of the recruits' capability to withstand. One of the most striking achievements of the drill instructors is to create and maintain the illusion that basic training is an extraordinary challenge, one that will set those who graduate apart from others, when in fact almost everyone can succeed.

There has been some preliminary weeding out of potential recruits even before they begin training, to eliminate the obviously unsuitable minority, and some people do "fail" basic training and get sent home, at least in peacetime. The standards of acceptable performance in the U.S. armed forces, for example, tend to rise and fall in inverse proportion to the number and quality of recruits available to fill the forces to the authorized manpower levels. But there are very few young men who cannot be turned into passable soldiers if the forces are willing to invest enough effort in it.

Not even physical violence is necessary to effect the transformation, though it has been used by most armies at most times.

It's not what it was 15 years ago down here. The Marine Corps still occupies the position of a tool which the society uses when it feels like that is a resort that they have to fall to. Our society changes as all societies do, and our society felt that through enlightened training methods we could still produce the same product—and when you examine it, they're right. . . . Our 100 c.c.'s of stress is really all we need, not two gallons of it, which is what used to be. . . . In some cases with some of the younger drill instructors it was more an initiation than it was an acute test, and so we introduced extra officers and we select our drill instructors to "fine-tune" it.

—Captain Brassington, USMC

There is, indeed, a good deal of fine-tuning in the roles that the men in charge of training any specific group of recruits assume. At the simplest level, there is a sort of "good cop–bad cop" manipulation of the recruits' attitudes toward those applying the stress. The three younger drill instructors with a particular serial are quite close to them in age and unremittingly harsh in their demands for ever higher performance, but the senior drill instructor, a man almost old enough to be their father, plays a more benevolent and understanding part and is available for individual counseling. And generally offstage, but always looming in the background, is the company commander, an impossibly austere and almost godlike personage.

At least these are the images conveyed to the recruits, although of course all these men cooperate closely with an identical goal in view. It works: In the end they become not just role models and authority figures, but the focus of the recruits' developing loyalty to the organization.

I imagine there's some fear, especially in the beginning, because they don't know what to expect. . . . I think they hate you at first, at least for a week or two, but it turns to respect. . . . They're seeking discipline, they're seeking someone to take charge, 'cause at home they never got it. . . . They're looking to be told what to do and then someone is standing there enforcing what they tell them to do, and it's kind of like the father-and-son game, all the way through. They form a fatherly image of the DI whether they want to or not.

—Sergeant Carrington, USMC

Just the sheer physical exercise, administered in massive doses, soon has the recruits feeling stronger and more competent than ever before. Inspections, often several times daily, quickly build up their ability to wear the uniform and carry themselves like real Marines, which is a considerable source of pride. The inspections also help to set up the pattern in the recruits of unquestioning submission to military authority: Standing stock-still, staring straight ahead, while somebody else examines you closely for faults is about as extreme a ritual act of submission as you can make with your clothes on.

But they are not submitting themselves merely to the abusive sergeant making unpleasant remarks about the hair in their nostrils. All around them are deliberate reminders—the flags and insignia displayed on parade, the military music, the marching formations and drill instructors' cadenced calls—of the idealized organization, the "brotherhood" to which they will be admitted as full members if they submit and conform. Nowhere in the armed forces are the military courtesies so elaborately observed, the staffs' uniforms so immaculate (some DIs change several times a day), and the ritual aspects of military life so highly visible as on a basic training establishment.

Even the seeming inanity of close-order drill has a practical role in the conversion process. It has been over a century since mass formations of men were of any use on the battlefield, but every army in the world still drills its troops, especially during basic training, because marching in formation, with every man moving his body in the same way at the same moment, is a direct physical way of learning two things a soldier must believe: that orders have to be obeyed automatically and instantly, and that you are no longer an individual, but part of a group.

The recruits' total identification with the other members of their unit is the most important lesson of all, and everything possible is done to foster it. They spend almost every waking moment together—a recruit alone is an anomaly to be looked into at once—and during most of that time they are enduring shared hardships. They also undergo collective punishments, often for the misdeed or omission of a single individual (talking in the ranks, a bed not swept under during barracks inspection), which is a highly effective way of suppressing any tendencies toward individualism. And, of course, the DIs place relentless emphasis on competition with other "serials" in training: there may be something infinitely pathetic to outsiders about a marching group of anonymous recruits chanting, "Lift your heads and hold them high, 3313 is a-passin' by," but it doesn't seem like that to the men in the ranks.

Nothing is quite so effective in building up a group's morale and solidarity, though, as a steady diet of small triumphs. Quite early in basic training, the recruits begin to do things that seem, at first sight, quite dangerous: descend by ropes from fifty-foot towers, cross yawning gaps hand-over-hand on high wires (known as the Slide for Life, of course), and the like. The common denominator is that these activities are daunting but not really dangerous: the ropes will prevent anyone from falling to his death off the rappelling tower, and there is a pond of just the right depth—deep enough to cushion a falling man, but not deep enough that he is likely to drown—under the Slide for Life. The goal is not to kill recruits, but to build up their confidence as individuals and as a group by allowing them to overcome apparently frightening obstacles.

> *You have an enemy here at Parris Island. The enemy that you're going to have at Parris Island is in every one of us. It's in the form of cowardice. The most rewarding experience you're going to have in recruit training is standing on line every evening, and you'll be able to look into each other's eyes, and you'll be able to say to each other with your eyes: "By God, we've made it one more day! We've defeated the coward."*
>
> —Captain Pingree

> *Number on deck, sir, 45 . . . highly motivated, truly dedicated, rompin', stompin', bloodthirsty, kill-crazy United States Marine Corps recruits, SIR!*
>
> —Marine chant, Parris Island

If somebody does fail a particular test, he tends to be alone, for the hurdles are deliberately set low enough that most recruits can clear them if they try. In any large group of people there is usually a goat: someone whose intelligence or manner or lack of physical stamina marks him for failure and contempt. The competent drill instructor, without deliberately setting up this unfortunate individual for disgrace, will use his failure to strengthen the solidarity and confidence of the rest. When one hapless young man fell off the Slide for Life into the pond, for example, his drill instructor shouted the usual invective—"Well, get out of the water. Don't contaminate it all day"—and then delivered the payoff line: "Go back and change your clothes. You're useless to your unit now."

"Useless to your unit" is the key phrase, and all the recruits know that what it means is "useless in *battle*." The Marine drill instructors at Parris Island know exactly what they are doing to the recruits, and why. They are not rear-echelon people filling comfortable jobs, but the most dedicated and intelligent NCOs the Marine Corps can find; even now, many of them have combat experience. The Corps has a clear-eyed understanding of precisely what it is training its recruits for—combat— and it ensures that those who do the training keep that objective constantly in sight.

The DIs "stress" the recruits, feed them their daily ration of synthetic triumphs over apparent obstacles, and bear in mind all the time that the goal is to instill the foundations for the instinctive, selfless reactions and the fierce group loyalty that is what the recruits will need if they ever see combat. They are arch-manipulators, fully conscious of it, and utterly unashamed. These kids have signed up as Marines, and they could well see combat; this is the way they have to think if they want to live.

I've seen guys come to Vietnam from all over. They were all sorts of people that had been scared—some of them had been scared all their life and still scared. Some of them had been a country boy, city boys—you know, all different kinds of people—but when they got in combat they all reacted the same—99 percent of them reacted the same. . . . A lot of it is training here at Parris Island, but the other part of it is survival. They know if they don't conform—conform I call it, but if they don't react in the same way other people are reacting, they won't survive. That's just it. You know, if you don't react together, then nobody survives.
—USMC drill instructor, Parris Island

When I went to boot camp and did individual combat training they said if you walk into an ambush what you want to do is just do a right face—you just turn right or left, whichever way the fire is coming from, and assault. I said, "Man, that's crazy. I'd never do anything like that. It's stupid.". . .

The first time we came under fire, on Hill 1044 in Operation Beauty Canyon in Laos, we did it automatically. Just like you look at your watch to see what time it is. We done a right face, assaulted the hill—a fortified position with concrete bunkers emplaced, machine guns, automatic weapons—and we took it. And we killed—I'd estimate probably 35 North Vietnamese soldiers in the assault, and we only lost three killed. I think it was about two or three, and about eight or ten wounded. . . .

But you know, what they teach you, it doesn't faze you until it comes down to the time to use it, but it's in the back of your head, like, What do you do when you come to a stop sign? It's in the back of your head and you react automatically.
—USMC sergeant

Combat is the ultimate reality that Marines—or any other soldiers, under any flag—have to deal with. Physical fitness, weapons training, battle drills, are all indispensable elements of basic training, and it is absolutely essential that the recruits learn the attitudes of group loyalty and interdependency which will be their sole hope of survival and success in combat. The training inculcates or fosters all of those things, and even by the halfway point in the 11-week course, the recruits are generally responding with enthusiasm to their tasks. . . .

In basic training establishments,. . . the malleability is all one way: in the direction of submission to military authority and the internalization of military values. What a place like Parris Island produces when it is successful, as it usually is, is a soldier who will kill because that is his job.

4·····■

Diary of a Homeless Man

John R. Coleman

introduction ■ ■ ■ ■

When I was doing research on the homeless, I slept in homeless shelters across the nation—in about a dozen U.S. cities and one in Canada. The research was emotionally draining. I was challenged continuously to be alert to conduct the seemingly endless interviews and to watch out for danger that appeared to lurk around every comer. (I dictated one of my recordings squatted next to a building, describing the arrival of the police and medics to take a homeless man to the hospital. He had been attacked by another homeless man.)

I had built in a break with my brother and his family in California. When he and his wife went to work the day after I arrived, I was left alone in the house. It was at this point that I realized what a marvelous luxury a living room is. I could lie on the couch and flip TV channels to my heart's content. I had always taken the living room for granted, and only by being with the homeless who had no living rooms did the significance of "living room" hit me. The room actually took on a different meaning.

For thousands of people, the city street is their living room. These discards of the advanced technological society have been left behind in our culturally mandated frenetic pursuit for material wealth. Like others, John Coleman, the president of a small, private college, had seen these strange people on the streets of the city. Like others, he wondered what their life was like. And like a few of us—very few—he decided to find out first hand, by experiencing their world. He, too, left his comfortable, upper-middle-class home and joined the street people. This is his engrossing account of that experience.

Thinking Critically

As you read this article, ask yourself:

1. How do you think that the problem of homelessness can be solved? You must be practical; that is, you must try to come up with workable solutions.

2. Why do you think that the homeless are treated with such disdain (lack of respect)?

3. Assume that we will continue to have homeless people. How can we improve the way they are treated? Cite specific instances from the reading that you would try to solve.

■ ■ ■ WEDNESDAY, 1/19

Somehow, 12 degrees at 6 A.M. was colder than I had counted on. I think of myself as relatively immune to cold, but standing on a deserted sidewalk outside Penn Station with the thought of ten days ahead of me as a homeless man, the immunity vanished. When I pulled my collar closer and my watch cap lower, it wasn't to look the part of a street person; it was to keep the wind out.

My wardrobe wasn't much help. I had bought my "new" clothes—flannel shirt, baggy sweater, torn trousers, the cap and the coat—the day before on Houston Street for $19. "You don't need to buy shoes," the shop-keeper had said. "The ones you have on will pass for a bum's." I was hurt; they were shoes I often wore to the office.

Having changed out of my normal clothes in the Penn Station men's room and stowed them in a locker, I was ready for the street. Or thought so.

Was I imagining it, or were people looking at me in a completely different way? I felt that men, especially the successful-looking ones in their forties and over, saw me and wondered. For the rest, I wasn't there.

At Seventh Avenue and 35th Street, I went into a coffee shop. The counter-man looked me over carefully. When I ordered the breakfast special—99 cents plus tax—he told me I'd have to pay in advance. I did (I'd brought $40 to see me through the ten days), but I noticed that the other customers were given checks, and paid only when they left.

By 9:30, I had read a copy of the *Times* retrieved from a trash basket; I had walked most of the streets around the station; I had watched the construction at the new convention center. There was little else to do.

Later, I sat and watched the drug sales going on in Union Square. Then I went into the Income Maintenance Center on 14th Street and watched the people moving through the welfare lines. I counted the trucks on Houston Street.

I vaguely remembered a quote to the effect that "idleness is only enjoyable when you have a lot to do." It would help to be warm, too.

There was ample time and incentive to stare at the other homeless folk on the street. For the most part, they weren't more interesting than the typical faces on Wall Street or upper Madison Avenue. But the extreme cases caught and held the eye. On Ninth Avenue, there was a man on the sidewalk directing an imaginary (to me) flow of traffic. And another, two blocks away, tracing the flight of planes or birds—or spirits—in the winter sky. And there was a woman with gloves tied to her otherwise bare feet.

Standing outside the Port Authority Bus Terminal was a man named Howard. He was perhaps my age, but the seasons had left deeper marks on his face. "Come summertime, it's all going to be different," he told me. "I'm going to have a car to go to the beach. And I'm going to get six lemons and make me a jug of ice-cold lemonade to go with the car.

"This whole country's gone too far with the idea of one person being at the top. It starts with birthday parties. Who gets to blow out the candle? One person.

From *New York* Magazine, February 21, 1982. Reprinted by permission of the author.

And it takes off from there. If we're ever going to make things better, we gotta start with those candles."

Was there any chance of people like us finding work?

"Jobs are still out there for the young guys who want them," Howard said. "But there's nothing for us. Never again. No, I stopped dreaming about jobs a long time ago. Now I dream about cars. And lemonade."

Drugs and alcohol are common among the homeless. The damage done by them was evident in almost every street person I saw. But which was cause, and which was effect? Does it matter, once this much harm has been done?

My wanderings were all aimless. There was no plan, no goal, no reason to be anywhere at any time. Only hours into this role, I felt a useless part of the city streets. I wasn't even sure why I was doing this. . . .

A weathered drifter told me about a hideaway down in the bowels of the station, where it was warm and quiet. I found my way there and lay down on some old newspapers to sleep.

How long did I sleep? It didn't seem long at all. I was awakened by a flashlight shining in my eyes, and a voice, not an unkind one, saying, "You can't sleep here. Sorry, but you have to go outside."

I hadn't expected to hear that word "sorry." It was touching.

I left and walked up to 47th Street, between Fifth and Madison Avenues, where I knew there was a warm grate in the sidewalk. (I've been passing it every morning for over five years on my way to work.) One man was asleep there already. But there was room for two, and he moved over.

■ ■ ■ THURSDAY, 1/20

When you're spending the night on the street, you learn to know morning is coming by the kinds of trucks that roll by. As soon as there are other than garbage trucks— say, milk or bread trucks—you know the night will soon be over.

I went back to Penn Station to clean up in the washroom. The care with which some of the other men with me bathed themselves at the basins would have impressed any public-health officer. And I couldn't guess from the appearance of their clothes who would be the most fastidious.

I bought coffee and settled back to enjoy it out of the main traffic paths in the station. No luck. A cop found me and told me to take it to the street.

After breakfast ($1.31 at Blimpie), I walked around to keep warm until the public library opened. I saw in a salvaged copy of the *Times* that we had just had our coldest night of the year, well below zero with the windchill factor, and that a record 4,635 people had sought shelter in the city's hostels.

The library was a joy. The people there treated me the same as they might have had I been wearing my business suit. To pass the time, I got out the city's welfare reports for 50 years ago. In the winter of 1933, the city had 4,524 beds available for the homeless, and all were said to be filled every night. The parallel to 1983 was uncanny. But, according to the reports, the man in charge of the homeless program in 1933, one Joseph A. Manning, wasn't worried about the future. True, the country was in the midst of a depression. But there had been a slight downturn in the numbers served in the shelters in the two months immediately preceding his report. This meant, wrote Manning, that "the depression, in the parlance of the ring, is K.O.'d."

Already, I notice changes in me. I walk much more slowly. I no longer see a need to beat a traffic light or to be the first through a revolving door. Force of habit still makes me look at my wrist every once in a while. But there's no watch there, and it wouldn't make any difference if there were. The thermometer has become much more important to me now than any timepiece could be. . .

The temperature rose during the day. Just as the newspaper headlines seem to change more slowly when you're on the streets all day long, so the temperature seems to change more rapidly and tellingly.

At about 9 P.M., I went back to the heated grate on 47th Street. The man who had been there last night was already in place. He made it clear that there was again room for me.

I asked him how long he had been on the streets.

"Eleven years, going on twelve," he said.

"This is only my second night."

"You may not stick it out. This isn't for every man."

"Do you ever go into the shelters?"

"I couldn't take that. I prefer this anytime."

■ ■ ■ ■ FRIDAY, 1/21

When I left my grate mate—long before dawn—he wished me a good day. I returned the gesture: He meant his, and I meant mine.

In Manhattan's earliest hours, you get the feeling that the manufacture and removal of garbage is the city's main industry. So far, I haven't been lucky or observant enough to rescue much of use from the mounds of trash waiting for the trucks and crews. The best find was a canvas bag that will fit nicely over my feet at night.

I'm slipping into a routine: Washing up at the station. Coffee on the street. Breakfast at Blimpie. A search for the *Times* in the trash baskets. And then a leisurely stretch of reading in the park.

Some days bring more luck than others. Today I found 20 cents in a pay-phone slot and heard a young flutist playing the music of C.P.E. Bach on Sixth Avenue between 9th and 10th streets. A lot of people ignored her, even stepped over her flute case as if it were litter on the sidewalk. More often than not, those who put money in the case looked embarrassed. They seemed to be saying, "Don't let anyone see me being appreciative."

By nightfall, the streets were cruelly cold once again. . .

I headed for the 47th Street grate again but found my mate gone. There was no heat coming up through it. Do they turn it off on Friday nights? Don't we homeless have any rights?

On the northwest corner of Eighth Avenue and 33rd Street, there was a blocked-off subway entrance undergoing repair. I curled up against the wall there under some cardboard sheets. Rain began to fall, but I stayed reasonably dry and was able to get to sleep.

At some point, I was awakened by a man who had pulled back the upper piece of cardboard.

"You see my partner here. You need to give us some money."

I was still half-asleep. "I don't have any."

"You must have something, man."

"Would I be sleeping here in the rain if I did?"

His partner intervened. "C'mon. Leave the old bastard alone. He's not worth it."

"He's got something. Get up and give it to us."

I climbed to my feet and began fumbling in my pocket. Both men were on my left side. That was my chance. Suddenly I took off and ran along 33rd Street toward Ninth Avenue. They gave no chase. And a good thing, too, because I was too stiff with cold to run a good race.

■ ■ ■ ■ SATURDAY, 1/22

A man I squatted next to in a doorway on 29th Street said it all: "The onliest thing is to have a warm place to sleep. That and having somebody care about you. That'd be even onlier."

He had what appeared to be rolls of paper toweling wrapped around one leg and tied with red ribbon. But the paper, wet with rain by now, didn't seem to serve any purpose.

I slept little. The forecast was for more rain tomorrow, so why wish the night away?

The morning paper carried news of Mayor Koch's increased concern about the homeless.

But what can he do? He must worry that the more New York does to help, the greater the numbers will grow. At the moment he's berating the synagogues for not doing anything to take street people in.

Watching people come and go at the Volvo tennis tournament at Madison Square Garden, I sensed how uncomfortable they were at the presence of the homeless. Easy to love in the abstract, not so easy face to face.

It's no wonder that the railway police are under orders to chase us out of sight.

Perhaps a saving factor is that we're not individuals. We're not people anybody knows. So far I've had eye contact with only three people who know me in my other life. None showed a hint of recognition. One was the senior auditor at Arthur Andersen & Company, the accounting firm that handles the Clark Foundation, my employer. One was a fellow lieutenant in the Auxiliary Police Force, a man with whom I had trained for many weeks. And one was an owner in the cooperative apartment where I live. . . .

Early in the evening I fell asleep on the Seventh Avenue steps outside the Garden. Three Amtrak cops shook me awake to ask if two rather good-looking suitcases on the steps were mine. I said that I had never seen them.

One cop insisted that I was lying, but then a black man appeared and said they belonged to a friend of his. The rapid-fire questioning from two of the cops soon made that alibi rather unlikely. The third cop was going through the cases and spreading a few of the joints he found inside on the ground.

As suddenly as it had begun, the incident was over. The cops walked away, and the man retrieved the bags. I fell back to sleep. Some hours later when I woke up again, the black man was still there, selling.

■ ■ ■ ■ SUNDAY, 1/23

A new discovery of a warm and dry, even scenic, place to sit on a rainy day: the Staten Island Ferry.

For one 25-cent fare, I had four crossings of the harbor, read all I wanted of the copy of the Sunday *Times* I'd found, and finished the crossword puzzle.

When I got back to the Garden, where the tennis tournament was in its last hours, I found the police were being extra diligent in clearing us away from the departing crowds. One older woman was particularly incensed at being moved. "You're ruining my sex life," she shouted. "That's what you're doing. My sex life. Do you hear?"

A younger woman approached me to ask if I was looking for love. "No, ma'am. I'm just trying to stay out of the rain.". . .

So, back to the unused subway entrance, because there was still no heat across town on the 47th Street grate.

The night was very cold. Parts of me ached as I tried to sleep. Turning over was a chore, not only because the partially wet cardboard had to be re-arranged with such care, but also because the stiffer parts of my body seemed to belong to someone else. Whatever magic there was in those lights cutting down through the fog was gone by now. All I wanted was to be warm and dry once more. Magic could wait.

■ ■ ■ ■ MONDAY, 1/24

Early this morning I went to the warren of employment agencies on 14th Street to see if I could get a day's work. There was very little action at most of these last-ditch offices, where minimum wages and sub-minimum conditions are the rule.

But I did get one interview and thought I had a dishwashing job lined up. I'd forgotten one thing. I had no identification with me. No identification, no job.

There was an ageless, shaggy woman in Bryant Park this morning who delivered one of the more interesting monologues I've heard. For a full ten minutes, with no interruption from me beyond an occasional "Uh huh," she analyzed society's ills without missing a beat.

Beginning with a complaint about the women's and men's toilets in the park being locked ("What's a poor body to do?"), she launched into the strengths of the Irish, who, though strong, still need toilets more than others, and the weaknesses of the English and the Jews, the advantages of raising turkeys over other fowl, and the wickedness of Eleanor Roosevelt in letting the now Queen Mother and that stuttering king of hers rave so much about the hot dogs served at Hyde Park that we had no alternative but to enter World War II on their side. The faulty Russian satellite that fell into the Indian Ocean this morning was another example of shenanigans, she said. It turns out the Russians and Lady Diana, "that so-called Princess of Wales," are in cahoots to keep us so alarmed about such things far away from home that we don't get anything done about prayer in schools or the rest of it. But after all, what would those poor Protestant ministers do for a living if the children got some real religion in school, like the kind we got from the nuns, God bless them?

That at least was the gist of what she said. I know I've missed some of the finer points.

At 3:30 P.M., with more cold ahead, I sought out the Men's Shelter at 8 East 3rd Street. This is the principal entry point for men seeking the city's help. It provides meals for 1,300 or so people every day and beds for some few of those. I had been told that while there was no likelihood of getting a bed in this building I'd be given a meal here and a bed in some other shelter.

I've seen plenty of drawings of London's workhouses and asylums in the times of Charles Dickens. Now I've seen the real thing, in the last years of the twentieth century in the world's greatest city.

The lobby, and the adjacent "sitting room" were jammed with men standing, sitting, or stretched out in various positions on the floor. It was as lost a collection of souls as I could have imagined. Old and young, scarred and smooth, stinking and clean, crippled and hale, drunk and sober, ranting and still, parts of another world and parts of this one. The city promises to take in anyone who asks. Those rejected everywhere else find their way to East 3rd Street.

The air was heavy with the odors of Thunderbird wine, urine, sweat, and, above all, nicotine and marijuana. Three or four Human Resources Administration police officers seemed to be keeping the violence down to tolerable levels, but barely so.

After a long delay, I got a meal ticket for dinner and was told to come back later for a lodging ticket.

It was time to get in line to eat. This meant crowding into what I can only compare to a cattle chute in a stockyard. It ran along two walls of the sitting room and was already jammed. A man with a bullhorn kept yelling at us to stand up and stay in line. One very old and decrepit (or drunk?) man couldn't stay on his feet. He was helped to a chair, from which he promptly fell onto the floor. The bullhorn man had some choice obscenities for him, but they didn't seem to have any effect. The old man just lay there; and we turned our thoughts back to the evening meal.

I made a quick, and probably grossly unfair, assessment of the hundreds of men I could see in the room. Judging them solely by appearance, alertness, and body movements, I decided that one-quarter of them were perfectly able to work; they, more likely than not, were among the warriors who helped us win the battle against inflation by the selfless act of joining the jobless ranks. Another quarter might be brought back in time into job-readiness by some counseling and some caring for them as individuals. But the other half seemed so ravaged by illness, addiction, and sheer neglect that I couldn't imagine them being anything but society's wards from here on out to—one hopes—a peaceful end.

At the appointed hour, we were released in groups of twenty or thirty to descend the dark, filthy steps to the basement eating area. The man with the bullhorn was there again, clearly in charge and clearly relishing the extra power given to his voice by electric amplification. He insulted us collectively and separately without pause, but because his vocabulary was limited it tended to be the same four-letter words over and over.

His loudest attack on me came when I didn't move fast enough to pick up my meal from the counter. His analysis of certain flaws in my white ancestry wasn't hard to follow, even for a man in as much of a daze as I was.

The shouting and the obscenities didn't stop once we had our food. Again and again we were told to finish and get out. Eating took perhaps six minutes, but those minutes removed any shred of dignity a man might have brought in with him from the street.

Back upstairs, the people in charge were organizing the people who were to go to a shelter in Brooklyn. Few had volunteered, so there was more haranguing.

In the line next to the one where I was waiting for my lodging ticket a fight suddenly broke out. One man pulled a long knife from his overcoat pocket. The other man ran for cover, and a police officer soon appeared to remove the man with the knife from the scene. The issue, it seems, was one of proper places in the line.

There still weren't enough Brooklyn volunteers to suit the management, so they brought in their big gun: Mr. Bullhorn. "Now, listen up," he barked. "There aren't any buses going to Ft. Washington [another shelter] until 11:30, so if you want to get some sleep; go to Brooklyn. Don't ask me any questions. Just shut up and listen. It's because you don't listen up that you end up in a place like this."

I decided to ask a question anyway, about whether there would still be a chance for me to go Brooklyn once I got my lodging ticket. He turned on me and let me have the full force of the horn: "Don't ask questions, I said. You're not nobody."

The delays at the ticket-issuing window went on and on. Three staff members there seemed reasonably polite and even efficient. The fourth and heaviest one—I have no idea whether it was a man or woman—could not have moved more slowly without coming to a dead halt. The voice of someone who was apparently a supervisor came over the public-address system from time to time to apologize for the delay in going to the Ft. Washington shelter, which was in an armory, but any good he did from behind the scenes was undone by the staff out front and a "see-no-work, hear-no-work, do-no-work" attendant in the office.

As 11:30 approached, we crowded back into the sitting room to get ready to board the buses. A new martinet had appeared on the scene. He got as much attention through his voice, cane, and heavy body as Mr. Bullhorn had with his amplifying equipment. But this new man was more openly vile and excitable; he loved the power that went with bunching us all up close together and then ordering us to stretch out again in a thinner line. We practiced that routine several times. . . .

Long after the scheduled departure, the lines moved. We sped by school buses to the armory at Ft. Washington Avenue and 168th Street. There we were met, just before 2:30 A.M., by military police, social workers, and private guards. They marched us into showers (very welcome), gave us clean underwear, and sent us upstairs to comfortable cots arranged in long rows in a room as big as a football field.

There were 530 of us there for the night, and we were soon quiet.

■ ■ ■ TUESDAY, 1/25

We were awakened at 6 A.M. by whistles and shouting, and ordered to get back onto the buses for the return trip to lower Manhattan as soon as possible.

Back at 8 East 3rd Street, the worst of the martinets were off duty. So I thought breakfast might be a bit quieter than dinner had been. Still, by eight, I had seen three incidents a bit out of the ordinary for me.

A man waiting for breakfast immediately ahead of me in the cattle chute suddenly grabbed a chair from the adjoining area and prepared to break it over his neighbor's head. In my haste to get out of the way, I fell over an older man sleeping against the wall. After some shouts about turf, things cooled off between the fighters, and the old man forgave me.

In the stairwell leading down to the eating area, a young man made a sexual advance to me. When I withdrew from him and stupidly reached for my coat pocket, he thought I was going for a weapon. He at once pinned me against the wall and searched my pockets; there was nothing there.

As I came out of the building onto East 3rd Street, two black Human Resources Administration policemen were bringing two young blacks into the building. One officer had his man by the neck. The other officer had his man's hands cuffed behind his back and repeatedly kicked him hard in the buttocks.

My wanderings were still more aimless today. I couldn't get East 3rd Street out of my mind. What could possibly justify some of that conduct? If I were a staff member there, would I become part of the worst in that pattern? Or would I simply do as little, and think as little, as possible?

At day's end I can't recall much of where I went or why I went there.

Only isolated moments remain with me. Like. . .staring at the elegant crystal and silver in the shops just north of Madison Square Park and wondering what these windows say to the people I'd spent the night with.

Much too soon it was time to go back to the shelter for dinner and another night. At first I thought I didn't have the guts to do it again. Does one have to do *this* to learn who the needy are? I wanted to say, "Enough! There's only so much I need to see."

But I went back to the shelter anyway, probably because it took more guts to quit than it did to go ahead.

A man beside me in the tense dinner line drove one truth of this place home to me. "I never knew hell came in this color," he said.

I was luckier in my assignment for the night. I drew the Keener Building, on Wards Island, a facility with a capacity of 416 men. The building was old and neglected, and the atmosphere of a mental hospital, which it once was, still hung over it. But the staff was polite, the rooms weren't too crowded (there were only twelve beds in Room 326), the single sheet on each bed was clean, and there was toilet paper in the bathroom.

There were limits and guards and deprivations, but there was also an orderliness about the place. Here, at least, I didn't feel I had surrendered all of my dignity at the door.

■ ■ ■ ■ WEDNESDAY, 1/26

. . . Back to the shelter on East 3rd Street for dinner.

There is simply no other situation I've seen that is so devoid of any graces at all, so tense at every moment, or so empty of hope. The food isn't bad, and the building is heated; that's all it has going for it.

The only cutlery provided is a frail plastic spoon. With practice you can spread hard oleo onto your bread with the back of one. If there's liver or ham, you don't have to cut it; just put it between the two pieces of bread that go with each meal. Everything else—peas, collard greens, apple pudding, plums—can be managed with the spoon. And talk over dinner or sipping, rather than gulping, coffee isn't all that important.

What is hardest to accept is the inevitable jungle scene during the hour you stand in line waiting to eat. Every minute seems to be one that invites an explosion. You know instinctively that men can't come this often to the brink without someone going over. One person too many is going to try to jump ahead in line. One particular set of toes is going to be stepped on by mistake. And the lid is going to blow.

The most frightening people here are the many young, intensely angry blacks. Hatred pours out in all of their speech and some of their actions. I could spend a lot of time imagining how and why they became so completely angry—but if I were the major, the counselor, or the man with the bullhorn, I wouldn't know how to divert them from that anger any more. Hundreds and hundreds of men here have been destroyed by alcohol or drugs. A smaller, but for me more poignant, number are being destroyed by hate.

Their loudest message—and because their voices are so strong it is very loud indeed—is "Respect me, man." The constant theme is that someone or some group is putting them down, stepping on them, asking them to conform to a code they don't accept, getting in their way, writing them off.

So most of the fights begin over turf. A place in line. A corner to control. The have-nots scrapping with the have-nots. . . .

Tonight, I chose the Brooklyn shelter because I thought the buses going there would leave soonest. The shelter, a converted school, is on Williams Avenue and has about 400 beds.

We left in fairly good time but learned when we got to the shelter that no new beds would be assigned until after 11 P.M. We were to sit in the auditorium until then.

At about ten, a man herded as many of us newcomers as would listen to him into a corner of the auditorium. There he delivered an abusive diatribe outlining the horror that lay ahead for our possessions and our bodies during the night to come. It made the ranting at East 3rd Street seem tame.

It's illustrative of what the experience of homelessness and helplessness does to people that all of us—regardless of age, race, background, or health—listened so passively.

Only at midnight, when some other officials arrived, did we learn that this man had no standing whatsoever. He was just an underling who strutted for his time on the stage before any audience cowed enough to take what he dished out. . .

■ ■ ■ THURSDAY, 1/27

Back on the street this morning, I became conscious of how little time I had left to live this way. There seemed so much still to do, and so little time in which to do it.

One part of me tells me I have been fully a part of this. I know I walk with slower steps and bent shoulders. . . . I know I worry a lot more about keeping clean.

But then I recall how foolish that is, I'm acting. This will end tomorrow night. I can quit any time I want to. And unlike my mate from 47th Street, I haven't the slightest idea of what eleven years of sleeping on a grate amount to.

Early this afternoon, I went again to the Pavilion restaurant, where I had eaten five times before. I didn't recognize the man at the cash register.

"Get out," he said.

"But I have money."

"You heard me. Get out." His voice was stronger.

"That man knows me," I said, looking toward the owner in the back of the restaurant.

The owner nodded, and the man at the register said, "Okay, but sit in the back."

If this life in the streets had been real, I'd have gone out the door at the first "Get out." And the assessment of me as not worthy would have been self-fulfilling; I'd have lost so much respect for myself that I wouldn't have been worthy of being served the next time. The downward spiral would have begun.

Until now I haven't understood the extent of nicotine addiction. Dependencies on drugs and alcohol have been around me for a long time, but I thought before that smoking was a bad habit rather easy to overcome.

How many times have I, a nonsmoker, been begged for a cigarette in these days? Surely hundreds. Cigarettes are central. A few folks give them away, a small number sell them for up to 8 cents apiece, and almost all give that last pathetic end of a butt to the first man who asks for what little bit is left. I know addiction now as I didn't before.

Tonight, after a repeat of the totally degrading dinner-line scene at East 3rd Street, I signed up for Keener once again. No more Brooklyn for me.

Sitting upstairs with the other Keener-bound men, I carelessly put my left foot on the rung of the chair in front of me, occupied by a young black.

"Get your foot off, yo."

("Yo" means "Hey, there," "Watch yourself," "Move along," and much more.) I took it off. "Sorry," I said.

But it was too late. I had broken a cardinal rule. I had violated the man's turf. As we stood in the stairwell waiting for the buses, he told a much bigger, much louder, much angrier friend what I had done.

That man turned on me.

"Wait till we get you tonight, whitey. You stink. Bad. The worst I've ever smelled. And when you put your foot on that chair, you spread your stink around. You better get yourself a shower as soon as we get there, but it won't save you later on. . . . And don't sit near me or him on the bus. You hear, whitey?"

I didn't reply.

The bombardment went on as we mounted the bus. No one spoke up in my defense. Three people waved me away when I tried to sit next to them. The next person, black and close to my age, made no objection when I sat beside him.

The big man continued to tirade for a while, but he soon got interested in finding out from the driver how to go about getting a bus-driver's license. Perhaps he had come down from a high.

I admit I was scared. I wrote my name, address, and office telephone number on a piece of paper and slipped it into my pocket. At least someone would know where to call if the threats were real. I knew I couldn't and wouldn't defend myself in this setting.

While we stood in line on Wards Island waiting for our bed assignments, there were plenty of gripes about the man who was after me. But no one said anything directly to him. Somehow it didn't seem that this was the night when the meek would inherit the earth.

I slept fitfully. I don't like lying with the sheet hiding my face.

■ ■ ■ **FRIDAY, 1/28**

I was up and out of Keener as early as possible. That meant using some of my little remaining money for a city-bus ride back to Manhattan, but it was worth it to get out of there.

After breakfast on East 3rd Street, I was finished with the public shelters. That was an easy break for me to make, because I had choices and could run.

The day was cold and, for the early hours, clear. I washed the memory of the big man at 3rd Street out of my mind by wandering through the Fulton Fish Market. I walked across the Brooklyn Bridge and even sang as I realized how free I was to relax and enjoy its beauty.

With a cup of coffee and the *Times,* I sat on a cinder block by the river and read. In time, I wandered through the Wall Street district and almost learned the lay of some of the streets.

I walked up to the Quaker Meeting House at Rutherford Place and 15th Street. Standing on the porch outside, I tried hard to think how the doctrine that "there is that of God in every person" applied to that man last night and to some of the others I had encountered in these ten days. I still think it applies, but it isn't always easy to see how. . . .

Darkness came. I got kicked out of both the bus terminal and Grand Central. I got my normal clothes out of the locker at Penn Station, changed in the men's room, and rode the AA train home.

My apartment was warm, and the bed was clean.

That's the onliest thing.

Inside Organized Racism

Kathleen M. Blee

introduction ▪ ▪ ▪ ▪ ▪

In Chapter 5 of *Sociology*, we review the many ways that sociologists do research. Of those research methods, one of the most common is interviewing, which becomes more powerful when it is combined with participant observation. These two methods, interviewing and participant observation, fit together very well. Participant observation gives the researcher insight into the social dynamics of group members (such as their motivations, the group's hierarchy, and what the group members find rewarding). This, in turn, suggests areas to investigate and questions that should be asked. Similarly, what people talk about in response to open-ended questions cues the researcher into what to look for during participant observation.

In this selection, Blee discusses her research with women who are members of the organized hate movement. In what is one of the frankest discussions of methods by a sociologist, she takes us behind the scenes of her research. As you read her account, you will see how fearful she became. You will also see how her fears became a tool to sharpen her research skills and how they even helped her gain a better understanding of racist women.

As I have stated in *Sociology*, I admire the research that my fellow sociologists do, especially research that takes us behind the scenes of human groups to give us insight into why people in those groups think and behave as they do. I have special admiration for sociologists who do creative, risk-taking research, for it gives us understandings that cannot be gained in any other way. Blee's research is one such example. I think you will enjoy her account.

Thinking Critically

As you read this selection, ask yourself:

1. Why would a sociologist risk her life to do this kind of research? Why would people who lead such subterranean lives even talk to a researcher?

2. Blee used participant observation and interviews to study women in hate groups. Can you tell from this selection what types of information she was able to get that she could not have collected by other research methods?

3. Why do women (or men) join the organized hate movement?

At a racist gathering on the West Coast, Frank, a skinhead from Texas, sidled up to me to share his disgust at an event so mild it was "something you could see on the family channel." At his side, Liz echoed his sentiment, complaining that she felt trapped in a "Baptist church social." We chatted some more. Frank boasted that this was nothing like he expected. He made the long trip to "get his juices going," not to be part of something concocted by "wimps." Liz agreed, pointing with disdain to a group of women hauling boxes of hamburger buns over to a large grill.

I found their reactions baffling. To me, the scene was horrifying, anything but mundane. Frank's arms were covered with swastika tattoos. On his head was a baseball cap with a comic-like depiction of an African American man being lynched. Liz's black skirt, hose, and boots accentuated the small Klan cross embroidered on her white tailored shirt. The rituals of historical hatred being enacted in front of us seemed far from disappointingly "tame," as Frank and Liz's complaints suggested. A cross was doused with gasoline and set ablaze. People spoke casually of the need to "get rid" of African Americans, immigrants, Jews, gay men and lesbians, and Asian Americans, or exchanged historical trivia purporting to expose the Holocaust as a Zionist hoax. . . .

Only much later did I understand how Frank and Liz could compare a racist rally to a community social gathering. It was years before I could bring myself to read my notes on this rally, written on sheets of paper to which faint scents of smoke and kerosene still seemed to cling. Yet with time and psychic distance from my encounters with Frank, Liz, and others like them, I came to see that aspects of racist gatherings do mirror church socials or neighborhood picnics, albeit in a distorted, perverse fashion. I remember a card table piled high with racist children's books, bumper stickers, and index cards of "white power recipes"; sessions on self-help for disgruntled or substance-addicted members; hymns sung as background to speeches about strengthening the "racialist movement"; and the pancake breakfast and "social hour."

It was with an eerie sense of the familiar colliding with the bizarre that I crossed the boundary that divides the racist underground from the mainstream to write this book. Much about racist groups appears disturbingly ordinary, especially their evocation of community, family, and social ties. One woman gushed that a Ku Klux Klan rally "was a blast. I had fun. And it was just like a big family get-together. We played volleyball. And you had your little church thing on Sunday. For the longest time I thought I would be bored. But I wasn't bored at all.". . .

Some of the ideas voiced by racist groups can seem unremarkable, as evident in the scary similarity to mainstream right-wing stands on such issues as gun control. Still, the watershed that divides racist activism from the rest of society is striking. The beliefs of racist groups are not just extreme variants of mainstream racism, xenophobia, or anti-Semitism. Rather, their conspiratorial logic and zeal for activism separate members of racist groups from those on "the outside," as racist activists call it. By combining the aberrant with the ordinary, the peculiar with the prosaic, modern racist groups gain strength. To design effective strategies to combat racist groups, we must understand this combination. . . .

Women are the newest recruiting targets of racist groups, and they provide a key to these groups' campaign for racial supremacy. "We are very picky when we come to girls," one woman told me. "We don't like sluts. The girls must know their place but take care of business and contribute a lot too. Our girls have a clean slate. Nobody could disrespect us if they tried. We want girls [who are] well educated, the whole bit. And tough. . ."

The groups and networks that espouse and promote openly racist and anti-Semitic, and often xenophobic and homophobic, views and actions are what I call "organized racism." Organized racism is more than the aggregation of individual racist sentiments. It is a social milieu in which venomous ideas—about African Americans, Jews, Hispanics, Asians, gay men and lesbians, and others—take shape. Through networks of groups and activists, it channels personal sentiments of hatred into collective racist acts. . . .

Today, organized racism in the United States is rife with paradox. While racist groups are becoming more visible, their messages of racial hatred and white supremacy find little support in the rest of society. Racist groups increasingly have anti-Semitism as their core belief, though anti-Semitic attitudes in America as a whole are at their lowest ebb. Despite proclaiming bizarre and illogical views of race and religion, racist groups attract not only those who are ignorant, irrational, socially isolated, or marginal, but also intelligent, educated people, those with resources and social connections, those with something to lose. Organized racists trade in a currency of racist stereotyping little changed from the views of the nineteenth-century Klan and of anti-Semitism recycled from World War II–era Nazi propaganda, yet they recruit successfully among the young who have little or no knowledge of that history. They seize on racist rituals from the past to foment rage about the conditions of the present, appealing to teenagers whose lives are scarred by familial abuse and terror as well as the sons and daughters of stable and loving families, the offspring of privilege and the beneficiaries of parental attention. Racist groups project a sense of hypermasculinity in their militaristic swagger and tactics of bullying and intimidation, but they increasingly are able to bring women into their ranks.

When I began my research, I wanted to understand the paradoxes of organized racism. Were, I wondered, the increased numbers of women changing the masculine cast of racist groups? Why, I asked myself, did racist activists continue to see Jews, African Americans, and others as enemies, and why did they regard violence as a racial solution? Convinced that we can defeat organized racism only if we know how it recruits and retains its members, I also wanted to learn why people join organized racism and how being in racist groups affects them. . . .

■ ■ ■ FOCUSING ON RACIST WOMEN

To understand organized racism from the inside—from the experiences and beliefs of its members—I decided that I needed to talk with racist activists. I chose to interview women for a variety of reasons. On a practical level, I found that I could get access to women racists and develop some measure of rapport with them. More substantively, I wanted to study women racists because we know so little about them. Since 1980 women have been actively recruited by U.S. racist groups both because racist leaders see them as unlikely to have criminal records that would draw the attention of police and because they help augment membership rolls. Today, women are estimated to constitute nearly 50 percent of new members in some racist groups, leading some antiracist monitoring groups to claim that they are the "fastest growing part of the racist movement." Yet this new group of racist activists has been ignored, as researchers have tended to view racism as male-dominated and racist women as more interested in domestic and personal concerns than in its politics.

Eventually, I persuaded thirty-four women from a variety of racist and anti-Semitic groups across the country to talk to me at length about themselves and their racist activities. Fourteen women were in neo-Nazi but not skinhead groups, six were members of Ku Klux Klans, eight were white power skinheads, and six were in Christian Identity or related groups. What they told me shatters many common ideas about what racist activists are like.

Among the women I interviewed there was no single racist *type*. The media depict unkempt, surly women in faded T-shirts, but the reality is different. One of my first interviews was with Mary, a vivacious Klanswoman who met me at her door with a big smile and ushered me into her large, inviting kitchen. Her blond hair was pulled back into a long ponytail and tied with a large green bow. She wore dangling gold hoop earrings, blue jeans, a modest flowered blouse, and no visible tattoos or other racist insignia. Her only other jewelry was a simple gold-colored necklace. Perhaps sensing my surprise at her unremarkable appearance, she joked that her suburban appearance was her "undercover uniform."

Trudy, an elderly Nazi activist I interviewed somewhat later, lived in a one-story, almost shabby ranch house on a lower-middle-class street in a small town in the Midwest. Her house was furnished plainly. Moving cautiously with the aid of a walker, she brought out tea and cookies prepared for my visit. Meeting her reminded me of the phrase "old country women," which I had once heard from a southern policeman characterizing the rural Klanswomen in his area. . . .

My encounters with skinhead women were more guarded, although some were quite animated and articulate. Not one invited me into her home—all I got was a quick glance when I picked her up for an interview in some other location. Most seemed to live at or barely above the level of squatters, in dirty, poorly equipped spaces that were nearly uninhabitable. Their appearance varied. Molly sported five ear piercings that held silver hoops and a silver female sign, an attractive and professionally cut punk hairstyle, fine features, and intense eyes. Others were ghostly figures, with empty eyes and visible scars poorly hidden behind heavy makeup and garish lipstick.

Over a two-year period I spent considerable time with these women, talking to them about their racist commitments and getting them to tell me their life stories. Listening to them describe their backgrounds, I realized that many did not fit common stereotypes about racist women as uneducated, marginal members of society raised in terrible families and lured into racist groups by boyfriends and husbands. . . .

Why were these racist women willing to talk to me? They had a variety of reasons. Some hoped to generate publicity for their groups or themselves—a common motivation for granting interviews to the media. Many saw an opportunity to explain their racial politics to a white outsider, even one decidedly unsympathetic to their arguments. In a racist variant on the religious imperative to "bear witness" to the unconverted, they wanted the outside world to have an accurate (even if negative) account to counter superficial media reports. As one young woman put it, "I don't know what your political affiliations are, but I trust that you'll try to be as objective as possible." Others wished to support or challenge what they imagined I had been told in earlier interviews with racist comrades or competitors. And, despite their deep antagonism toward authority figures, some young women were flattered to have their opinions solicited by a university professor. They had rarely encountered someone older who talked with them without being patronizing, threatening, or directive.

From the beginning, when I asked women if I could interview them, I made it clear that I did not share the racial convictions of these groups. I explicitly said that my views were quite opposed to theirs, that they should not hope to convert me to their views, but that I would try to depict women racist activists accurately. I revealed my critical stance but made it clear that I had no intent to portray them as crazy and did not plan to turn them over to law enforcement or mental health agencies.

I was prepared to elaborate on my disagreements with organized racism in my interviews, but in nearly every case the women cut me short, eager to talk about themselves. Recognizing the extreme marginalization of the racist movement in the American political landscape, these women had no doubt that an ideological gulf divided them from me—it separates their beliefs from nearly all political ideas deemed acceptable in modern public life. They were accustomed to having people disagree with them, and they rarely tried to sway those who openly opposed their opinions. They were interested in me not as a potential convert, but rather as a recorder of their lives and thoughts. Their desire, at once personal and politically evangelical, was that someone outside the small racist groups to which they belong hear and record their words.

Indeed, such eagerness to talk underscores the ethical dilemma of inadvertently providing a platform for racist propaganda. Studies on racist extremists have the power to publicize even as they scrutinize. The problem was brought to the fore as I considered the issue of anonymity for my interviewees. Although the inclusion of more biographical details about the racist women activists I interviewed would be useful, I decided that doing so would unavoidably reveal their identities and thus give further publicity to them and their groups. For this reason, I have used pseudonyms for interviewees and their groups and changed all identifying details, while rendering quotations verbatim. Most people interviewed by scholars desire to remain anonymous, but these women wanted to be known. Some tried to demand that I use their names or the names of their groups. When an older Ku Klux Klan woman thanked me "for writing an article that might inspire others," however, I was convinced that my decision to disguise identities was correct. . . .

Walking a tightrope in my interviews, I kept a balance between maintaining enough distance to make it clear that I rejected their ideas and creating sufficient rapport to encourage women to talk to me. A successful interview needs some conversational common ground. Each party needs to feel understood, if not entirely accepted, by the other. These racist women were unlikely to reveal much about themselves if they did not have some trust in me, if I could not manage to express interest in their lives and refrain from repeatedly condemning them.

Usually a researcher can establish rapport with interviewees by proffering details of his or her personal life or expressing agreement with their choices and beliefs. Because I was unwilling to do either, I was forced to rely on more indirect and fragile measures. Like those at family gatherings and office parties who strain toward congeniality across known lines of disagreement, I seized on any experiences or values that we shared, no matter how trivial. When they expressed dissatisfaction with their bodies, I let them know that I had the same concerns. I commented positively when they talked of their children in parental rather than political terms—for example, when they worried about having enough time to be good mothers—and hoped that my sympathy would lead them to overlook my silence when they discussed such things as the "racial education" they planned for their children. . . .

A researcher can be simultaneously an "insider" and an "outsider" to the culture of those being studied. As a white person I had access that no nonwhite researcher could enjoy. As a woman, I had a store of shared experiences that could support a stream of conversational banter about bodies, men, food, and clothing in which a male researcher would be unlikely to engage. Certainly, both I and the women I interviewed realized that I was an outsider to the world of organized racism. But even the obvious barriers between us gave me insight into their convoluted racial beliefs. For example, my contradictory status as both a racial outsider (to their politics) and an apparent racial insider (as white) helped me understand their ambivalent descriptions of their racial and racist identities.

Yet a reliance on rapport is problematic when scholars do not share a worldview with those they study. Trying to understand the world through the eyes of someone for whom you have even a little sympathy is one thing, but the prospect of developing empathy for a racist activist whose life is given meaning and purpose by the desire to annihilate you or others like you is a very different matter. . . .

There are uncomfortable emotional complexities to this kind of research. Interviewing members of racist groups is dangerous but also intriguing, even offering a voyeuristic thrill. Though I'm embarrassed to admit it, I found meeting racist activists to be exciting as well as horrifying. The ethnographer Barrie Thorne captures this sense of fieldwork as adventure: it consists of "venturing into exciting, taboo, dangerous, perhaps enticing social circumstances; getting the flavor of participation, living out moments of high drama; but in some ultimate way having a cop-out, a built-in escape, a point of outside leverage that full participants lack."[1]

Fieldwork with "unloved groups" also poses the problem of seduction. As Antonius Robben, an anthropologist of Argentinean fascism, notes, even when researchers and interviewees begin as wary opponents, scholars can be drawn into "trad[ing] our critical stance as observers for an illusion of congeniality with cultural insiders."[2] Indeed, others who study loathsome political groups cite the pain of discovering that participants in some of history's most dreadful social movements can be charming and engaging in interviews.[3]

My time with Linda, a white power skinhead from the West, illustrates one instance of emotional seduction. Before our formal interview, our relationship was tense. With every phone call Linda insisted on changing the place and conditions of the interview, demanding ever more evidence that I was not with the police. She repeatedly threatened to bring her boyfriend and a gun to the interview, in violation of our agreement. Each of her demands required more negotiation and gave Linda another opportunity to remind me that she would not hesitate to hurt anyone who betrayed her or her group. Indeed, I had ample reason to take her threats seriously: both Linda and her boyfriend had served prison sentences for assault, selling drugs, and other offenses. I came to the interview frightened and prepared for hostile confrontation. In person, however, Linda confounded my expectations. She was charming, soft-spoken, and concerned for my comfort during the interview. Although quite willing to express appalling attitudes, Linda prefaced many of her statements by apologizing for what I might find offensive. My fear eased, replaced by a seductive, false rapport as Linda set the parameters of our interaction and I responded to her. Off-guard, I pressed Linda less aggressively than the other women to explain contradictions in the chronology and logic of her story. In retrospect, the field notes that I taped immediately after the interview make me uneasy. They show how disarming emotional manipulation can be, even when one is on guard against it:

> I found the [negotiation and preparation for the] interview with Linda to be the most emotionally stressful, maybe with the exception of [another] interview during which I was fearing for my life. Actually with Linda and [her boyfriend] there was no indication that they might try to harm me at all. In fact, quite the contrary. I actually was afraid of that before they came because they both have very violent reputations, but in person they were extremely cordial and very friendly, not trying to intimidate me in any way. Perhaps trying to cultivate me.

Researchers often talk informally about the emotional side of doing fieldwork, but it is a subject rarely discussed in print. Pondering one's own emotional state may seem narcissistic—yet it also can be analytically revealing. In the early stages of this research, I experienced a great deal of fear. The violent reputations of some of the women I wanted to interview, including the skinhead organizer whose comrades referred to her as "Ms. Icepick," did little to dispel my concerns. As I got to know some people in the racist world, I became somewhat less afraid. As I began to see them in more complicated, less stereotyped ways, I no longer worried that every interaction would end in disaster. It also became clear that as a woman in that male-dominated world I was safer because I seemed to pose little threat: male researchers were seen as more personally challenging to male racists and more likely to be covert police operatives.

But in other respects, I grew more afraid as I became less naive. For one thing, I came to realize that my white skin color would provide me little protection. Many racist activists who have faced criminal charges were turned in by other whites, sometimes even members of their own groups. Moreover . . . some racists see race as determined by commitment to white power politics rather than by genetics. I could not assume that those I interviewed would view me either as white or as nonhostile. I could not count on racial immunity from violence.

As I was contacting and interviewing racist women, the structure of the racist movement also changed in two ways that increased my risk. First, the 1995 bombing of the Alfred P. Murrah Federal Building in Oklahoma City occurred midway through my interviewing. In its wake, the racist movement went further underground. Racist groups were subject to investigation and members became increasingly sensitive to the possibility of police informants and infiltrators. Second, as a result of the heightened scrutiny of hate groups after the Oklahoma City bombing, the racist movement became less organized. Some adopted a strategy known as "leaderless resistance," which was designed to make the racist movement less vulnerable to investigation and prosecution. Racist activists began to operate in small units or cells, sometimes in pairs or even alone, to avoid detection by authorities. While adhering to a common agenda of Aryan supremacism, they were able to develop their own strategies, even select enemies, without answering to formal leaders; they used the Internet or other anonymous means to disseminate their ideas rather than relying on organized groups.

Leaderless resistance makes studying the racist movement scarier because it reduces the accountability of individual racists. When I attended a racist rally in the later stages of my research, I came with the permission of the rally's leader. I felt, or at least hoped, that his invitation would ensure my safety. Yet a significant number of those in attendance felt no allegiance to him; they did not care whether their words or actions might reflect on the group or implicate its leader. The *organization* of organized racism, I realized, was double-pronged. It channeled the racist beliefs of members into collective strategies of terrorism, building an agenda of racist practices that could be catastrophic. But it could also curb the violence of particular individuals, unruly members whose actions could bring the collective and its leaders to the attention of the authorities. Without leaders, such restraints do not exist.

My fear was caused by more than simple proximity to racist groups. It was deliberately fed by the women I interviewed, who hoped to limit the scope of my study and shape my analysis. . . . The racist women constantly drew attention to my vulnerability to them, asking whether I was afraid to come see them, whether I was afraid to be in their homes. . . . Even a woman in prison on death row, who was brought to our interview in handcuffs, found a way to undermine any power I had over her by noting that she could call on gangs of allies in and outside the prison walls. "I'm not scared of anybody," she told me, "so I'm not gonna worry about it. I'll say what I got to say . . . 'cause I got the Jamaican Posse and the Cuban Posse all behind me, they gonna kick ass."

Some women were more indirect in their intimidation. Many bragged of their group's violence, making it clear that they treated enemies harshly. An Aryan supremacist boasted that the racist movement attracted people who were "totally messed up and totally mindless," people who were prone to "fight and kill, rip off armored cars, get guns.". . . Even now, years after completing the interviews, I receive signed and anonymous letters warning that they "are watching" me, that I had better tell "the truth" about them and their movement.

Often the women saw even the selection of where we would conduct the interview as an opening to use intimidation. Usually, I asked each woman to choose a place where she would feel comfortable, although I reminded her that I did not want to be interrupted by family members or racist group comrades. Several suggested their homes, saying that they would be most at ease there but also warning that their houses contained weapons and that other comrades (presumably less trustworthy than themselves) might appear at the house during the interview. Others picked a public place but indicated that they would station armed comrades nearby in case the interview did not "proceed as planned." On only two occasions did I refuse a suggestion for an interview site, both for safety reasons. One woman wanted me to be blindfolded and transported to an unknown destination in the back of a truck. Another proposed a meeting in a very remote racist compound to which I would have to be driven by a racist group member. And even in these cases, when my concerns for personal safety denied them their choice, they continued the implicit threats. For example, after the woman who had wanted me to be blindfolded agreed on a more visible site, she assured me that I should not be concerned for my safety there because "men with guns" would be hidden along the street "in case of a police raid.". . .

But fear went both ways. These women were afraid of me. I could betray their confidences to the police, to enemies, or to family members who were not aware of their activities. Telling me about their journey into organized racism could feel empowering to them, but it could also expose them to retribution. One Washington racist skinhead worried that I might secretly funnel information to violent gangs of antiracist skinheads about buildings occupied by racist skinheads: "[After you leave], well, uh, I wonder if some skin's house is gonna get Molotov-cocktailed and the [antiracist skinheads] are doing this in retaliation." An older neo-Nazi was concerned that my tape recording of her interview "could be used against me in a court of law." Many expressed suspicions about how I had found them at all. Throughout the interview a woman from the East repeatedly asked, "Just how did you become aware of the group that I'm in?" Worried that such fears could derail the interview, I assured each woman that her interview would be confidential and that I would not ask questions about illegal activities. . . . [Yet] I had to interrupt several of these women to keep them from telling me about their illegal activities or plans. A young Nazi activist in California, for example, deflected nearly all my inquiries about her family by saying that she was being constantly watched by the police, who could use such information against her, yet she repeatedly returned to an unsolicited story about her friends who "buried their guns in oil drums up in the hills for when the race war comes."

Racists also used their own fear to create rapport to keep the interview moving. Usually the task of creating rapport falls to the researcher, who generally has the most to gain from a successful interview. But many of these women were highly motivated to have me hear their stories. Thus, even as they tried to make me more afraid, they often pointed to their vulnerability to me; a woman might emphasize my exposure in the well-guarded living room of a racist leader, and at the same time observe that I probably had "really good connections to the police." At times, this tempering became nearly comical; one interviewee repeatedly made note of the guns and sketches of lynchings that lay around her living room but then sought to assure me that although "the average person has an idea that the Klan is very military [violent] and they're afraid," she was no threat, because she "wasn't aware of [that reputation] until just recently." But fear did help bring our sense of risk to the same level, making plain the stalemate in which we at least seemed to be equally unsafe.

Although the danger of engaging with racist activists actually increased while I was interviewing these women, I became less afraid over time, for reasons that are disturbing. The first interviews, conducted largely with members of the Ku Klux Klan, left me nearly paralyzed with fear. My field journal is full of notes on how to increase my own safety. Before each interview, I made elaborate preparations, giving friends instructions on what to do if I did not return on schedule. Yet my field notes on the last interviews, conducted largely with neo-Nazis and white power skinheads—members of groups that in recent years have been more likely than the Klan to engage in overt violence—show that my fears had largely abated. I took personal risks that earlier I would have found unthinkable. I had become more numb to tales of assaults and boasts of preparing for "race war."

It is terrifying to realize that you find it difficult to be shocked. But gradually my dealings with racist women became like a business transaction, with both parties parrying for favorable terms. I was not unafraid, but I took fewer precautions based on fear. Perhaps this change in attitude explains why my later interviews were less productive. In the earlier interviews, the tension created by fear made me think hard. As it subsided, some of my analytical edge slipped away as well. I was becoming anesthetized to the horrors of organized racism, a numbness that was personally dismaying and that also signaled my need to regain emotional distance from this research before writing about it—a process that took years. . . .

My experience suggests something about what it must feel to be inside a racist group: how the bizarre begins to feel normal, taken-for-granted, both unquestioned and unquestionable; how Jews or African Americans or gay men might come to seem so demonic and so personally threatening that group members could be moved to actions that seem incomprehensible to those on the outside. This state of mind results from a perceptual contraction that is all but imperceptible to the actor.

My feelings of fear also provide insight into the internal workings of racist groups. Fear is highly salient in the racist movement. Since they are greatly outnumbered by the racial, sexual, religious, and political groups they seek to destroy, organized racists use physical intimidation and the threat of violence to gain power over their opponents. Demonstrations, marches, violent propaganda, cross burnings, and terroristic actions are meant to demonstrate the strength of the racial movement and induce fear among enemies. So are the shocking cartoons and graphics that are the mainstay of racist propaganda. Racists pay close attention to their opponents' reactions, noting with glee any indication that they are feared by other groups or by the public. And fear is wielded within their groups as well. Members are warned repeatedly of the dire consequences that might befall them if they defect, particularly if they betray the group to the outside. These are not idle threats, as those who leave racist groups often risk violence at the hands of their former comrades. While I was doing these interviews, police on the East Coast were investigating the chilling abduction, assault, and near-murder of a young girl by a mixed- sex gang of skinheads who feared that she would defect from the group. . . .

The emotional world of organized racism becomes clearer when I consider the emotional work I needed to do to study racist groups. In the course of interviewing, I constantly sensed the need to display certain feelings. Sometimes I mimicked what I did not feel, forcing myself to laugh along with the more innocuous comments, hoping to establish rapport and fend off anecdotes that might be more offensive. At other times I withheld the emotions I did feel, maintaining a blank and studied expression when confronted with cross burnings or propaganda that glorified Nazi atrocities or even the interviewee's warped take on current events. In an interview done right after the Oklahoma City bombing, as the sickening images of the bombing were still in the newspapers and fresh in my mind, a woman told me that the people in her group "were happy about what happened in Oklahoma. There's a lot of anger out there. The people, some felt sorry for the [white] children but the rest of them got what they deserved, the government deserved. The government provoked this. . . . It's like in Germany when the skinheads went on the streets and burned down the refugee centers and the townspeople poured out and applauded. It could reach that point here." Throughout, I had to feign interest in the women's intricate stories of hatred, to ask questions in a neutral tone, and to be responsive when I wanted to flee or scream. But by examining my emotional work, I gained some insight into how the racist movement manipulates the emotions of its members, evoking not just fear but also awe.

Individual and political needs collide in writing about racism. As we acknowledge the rationality of racist women, we must never forget the evil they do. Yet writing from, and about, the stories of racist women runs the risk of personalizing them too much, making their ideas more sympathetic or less odious. It may subtly lend an academic gloss to the importance of racist activists, empowering them to work harder on behalf of their beliefs. These are dangerous outcomes—but the consequences of not learning from and about racists are worse.

If we stand too far back from racist groups and fail to look carefully at the women and men in organized racism, we are likely to draw politically misleading conclusions. Superficial studies simply caricature racist activists and make organized racism a foil against which we see ourselves as righteous and tolerant. We cannot simply comb the backgrounds of racist activists in search of a flaw—an absent parent, childhood victimization, or economic hard times—that "explains" their racist commitment. Moreover, we cannot use Germany in the 1930s as a prototype for all movements of the extreme right. Economic distress and social dislocation may explain the rise of such large-scale, powerful movements as the German Nazis or earlier American racist organizations, but such factors play only a small role in the tiny and politically marginal racist movement in the United States today.

We gain far more by taking a direct, hard look at the members of modern racist groups, acknowledging the commonalities between them and mainstream groups as well as the differences. In this book I tell the story of modern organized racism from the inside, focusing on how racist activists understand themselves and their worldviews. . . .

REFERENCES

1. Barrie Thorne, "Political Activist as Participant Observer: Conflicts of Commitment in a Study of the Draft Resistance Movement of the 1960s." In *Contemporary Field Research: A Collection of Readings,* Robert M. Emerson, ed. Prospect Heights, Ill: Waveland Press, 1983:235–252.

2. Antonius C. G. M. Robben, "The Politics of Truth and Emotion among Victims and Perpetrators of Violence." In *Fieldwork Under Fire: Contemporary Studies of Violence and Survival.* Canolyn Nordstrom and Antonius C. G. M. Robben, eds. Berkeley: University of California Press, 1995:81–104.

3. See Claudia Koonz, *Mothers in the Fatherland: Women, Family Life, and Nazi Politics.* New York: St. Martin's Press, 1987; and Robben, "Politics of Truth and Emotion."

II Social Groups and Social Control

It is easy to lose sight of the significance that our birth ushers us into a world that already exists. For the most part, we yawn at such a statement. It seems to be one of those "of course, we all know that" types of observations, and we ordinarily fail to grasp its profound implications for our lives. That the world we enter is already constructed means that we join a human group that has established ways of "doing social life." Our group lays out for us an arbitrary system of norms that it expects us to follow. Although these norms (along with statuses and roles) may pinch, we are expected to conform to them. In effect, the expectations that the group has set for us form a structure within which we are supposed to live our lives.

Social life is like a game, for it consists of rules and penalties for violating them. The game is in progress when we are born, and because it is the only game in town, we have little choice but to play it. Our life consists of learning how to play the game set out for us—but also of learning that there are subgames and how we can escape into them.

For social life to exist, there is no question that rules are necessary. If you can't depend on people to do things, everything falls apart. For social groups to function, to do whatever they have set out to do, they must be able to depend on their members to fulfill the tasks assigned them. This applies to all social groups, whether they be as small as our family or as large as a multinational corporation. It applies both to groups that are part of the mainstream society and to those that are part of the underworld.

As inevitable as norms are, so is deviance. Where there are rules, there will be rule breakers. *All* of us violate some of our group's many rules; that is, all of us fail to meet some of the expectations that others have of us. In sociological terms, we all become deviants. *Deviant*, in sociology, simply means someone who has deviated from the rules, someone who has wandered from the path that they were expected to follow. Deviant does *not* necessarily mean a horrible person—although horrible people are included in the term. *Deviant* is an inclusive term. It refers not only to killers and rapists, but also to people who tell white lies and to drivers who go over the speed limit.

It has been said that the first rule of sociology is that nothing is as it appears. In other words, behind the scenes of the reality that people (groups and organizations) put forward for others to view lies a hidden reality. It is a goal of sociology to peer beneath the surface and to expose this hidden reality.

Sociologists do not take for granted the views that groups put forward for public consumption; rather, they peer beneath this surface so they can analyze what lies behind these images that people so carefully construct.

Sociologists have found that participant observation (reviewed in Chapter 5 of *Sociology* and in the fifth reading in this book) is a good way of peering behind the scenes. This method helps us to explore the reality that is usually open only to insiders. In the first article in this part, William Thompson does just this. As he takes us behind the scenes of a meat-packing plant, not only do we learn about violations of hygiene in the processing of our food but also we get to see how workers become trapped in a way of life that they dislike. In the second selection, also written by Thompson, we are taken behind the scenes of mortuaries. Not only do we look over the shoulder of morticians as they sell caskets, but we also get to see how morticians handle the stigma of handling the dead, and how, despite this stigma, they are able to construct and maintain solid views of the self. In the third and concluding selection, Ayres Boswell and Joan Spade analyze the *social* bases of rape. To do this, they take us into two different types of frat houses, where we can see why some fraternities have higher or lower risks of abusing women.

Hanging Tongues:
A Sociological Encounter
with the Assembly Line

William E. Thompson

introduction

Few of us are born so wealthy that we do not have to work for a living. Some jobs seem to be of little importance, as with those we take during high school and college. We simply accept work that is available, looking at the job as a temporary activity to help us get by for the time being. When its time is up, we discard the job as we would a worn-out shirt or blouse. In contrast, the jobs we take after we have completed our education—those full-time, more or less permanent endeavors at which we labor so long and hard—in these we invest much of ourselves. In turn, as our schedules come to revolve around their demands, we become aware of how central these jobs are to our lives.

All jobs, however, whether full-time and permanent or temporary and discarded, are significant for our lives. Each contributes in its own way to our thinking and attitudes, becoming a part of the general stockpile of experiences that culminates in our basic orientations to life. Because of the significance of work for our lives, then, sociologists pay a great deal of attention to the work setting.

Of all jobs, one of the most demanding, demeaning, and demoralizing is that of the assembly line. Those of us who have worked on assembly lines have shared a work experience unlike any other, and for many of us education was the way by which we escaped from this modern slavery. As Thompson examines the assembly line in the meat-packing industry, he makes evident how this job affects all aspects of the workers' lives. His analysis provides a framework that you can use in reflecting on your own work experiences.

Thinking Critically

As you read this selection, ask yourself:

1. How does work at the meat-packing plant affect the lives of the workers? When they face such rigorous, demanding work, why don't they simply quit?

2. How have jobs influenced your orientations to life and the work that you are preparing for? (You may want to apply the concept of reference groups, discussed in Chapter 6 of *Sociology*.)

3. Why would anyone engage in sabotage at work?

This qualitative sociological study analyzes the experience of working on a modern assembly line in a large beef plant. It explores and examines a special type of assembly line work which involves the slaughtering and processing of cattle into a variety of products intended for human consumption and other uses.

Working in the beef plant is "dirty work," not only in the literal sense of being drenched with perspiration and beef blood, but also in the figurative sense of performing a low-status, routine, and demeaning job. Although the work is honest and necessary in a society which consumes beef, slaughtering and butchering cattle is generally viewed as an undesirable and repugnant job. In that sense, workers at the beef plant share some of the same experiences as other workers in similarly regarded occupations (for example, ditch-diggers, garbage collectors, and other types of assembly line workers). . . .

■ ■ ■ ■ THE SETTING

The setting for the field work was a major beef processing plant in the Midwest. At the time of the study, the plant was the third largest branch of a corporation which operated ten such plants in the United States. . . .

The beef plant was organizationally separated into two divisions: Slaughter and Processing. This study focused on the Slaughter division in the area of the plant known as the *kill floor.* A dominant feature of the kill floor was the machinery of the assembly line itself. The line was composed of an overhead stainless steel rail which began at the slaughter chute and curved its way around every work station in the plant. Every work station contained specialized machinery for the job performed at that place on the line. Dangling from the rail were hundreds of stainless steel hooks pulled by a motorized chain. Virtually every part of the line and all of the implements (tubs, racks, knives, etc.) were made of stainless steel. The walls were covered with a ceramic tile and the floor was made of sealed cement. There were floor drains located at every work station, so that at the end of each work segment (at breaks, lunch, and shift's end) the entire kill floor could be hosed down and cleaned for the next work period.

From William E. Thompson, "Hanging Tongues: A Sociological Encounter with the Assembly Line." *Qualitative Sociology,* 1983, Vol. 6, No. 3, pp. 215–237. Reprinted with kind permission from Springer Science and Business Media.

Another dominant feature of the kill floor was the smell. Extremely difficult to describe, yet impossible to forget, this smell combined the smells of live cattle, manure, fresh beef blood, and internal organs and their contents. This smell not only permeated the interior of the plant, but was combined on the outside with the smell of smoke from various waste products being burned and could be smelled throughout much of the community. This smell contributed greatly to the general negative feelings about work at the beef plant, as it served as the most distinguishable symbol of the beef plant to the rest of the community. The single most often asked question of me, during the research by those outside the beef plant was, "How do you stand the smell?" In typical line workers' fashion, I always responded, "What smell? All I smell at the beef plant is money.". . .

■ ■ ■ METHOD

The method of this study was nine weeks of full-time participant observation as outlined by Schatzman and Strauss (1973) and Spradley (1979; 1980). To enter the setting, the researcher went through the standard application process for a summer job. No mention of the research intent was made, though it was made clear that I was a university sociology professor. After initial screening, a thorough physical examination, and a helpful reference from a former student and part-time employee of the plant, the author was hired to work on the *Offal* crew in the Slaughter division of the plant. . . .

■ ■ ■ THE WORK

. . . The line speed on the kill floor was 187. That means that 187 head of cattle were slaughtered per hour. At any particular work station, each worker was required to work at that speed. Thus, at my work station, in the period of one hour, 187 beef tongues were mechanically pulled from their hooks; dropped into a large tub filled with water; had to be taken from the tub and hung on a large stainless steel rack full of hooks; branded with a "hot brand" indicating they had been inspected by a USDA inspector, and then covered with a small plastic bag. The rack was taken to the cooler, replaced with an empty one, and the process began again.

It would be logical to assume that if a person worked at a steady, continuous pace of handling 187 tongues per hour, everything would go smoothly; not so. In addition to hanging, branding, and bagging tongues, the worker at that particular station also cleaned the racks and cleaned out a variety of empty stainless steel tubs used to hold hearts, kidneys, and other beef organs. Thus, in order to be free to clean the tubs when necessary, the "tongue-hanger" had to work at a slightly faster pace than the line moved. Then, upon returning from cleaning the tubs, the worker would be behind the line (*in a hole*) and had to work much faster to catch up with the line. Further, one fifteen-minute break and a thirty-minute lunch break were scheduled for an eight-hour shift. Before the "tongue-hanger" could leave his post for one of these, all tongues were required to be properly disposed of, all tubs washed and stored, and the work area cleaned.

My first two nights on the job, I discovered the consequences of working at the line speed (hanging, branding, and bagging each tongue as it fell in the tub). At the end of the work period when everybody else was leaving the work floor for break or lunch, I was furiously trying to wash all the tubs and clean the work area. Consequently, I missed the entire fifteen minute break and had only about ten minutes for lunch. By observing other workers, I soon caught on to the system. Rather than attempting to work at a steady pace consistent with the line speed, the norm was to work sporadically at a very frenzied pace, actually running ahead of the line and plucking tongues from the hooks before they got to the station. With practice, I learned to hang two or three tongues at a time, perform all the required tasks, and then take an unscheduled two or three minute break until the line caught up with me. Near break and lunch everybody worked at a frantic pace, got ahead of the line, cleaned the work areas, and even managed to add a couple of minutes to the scheduled break or lunch.

Working ahead of the line seems to have served as more than merely a way of gaining a few minutes of extra break time. It also seemed to take on a symbolic meaning. The company controlled the speed of the line. Seemingly, that took all element of control over the work process away from the workers. . . . However, when the workers refused to work at line speed and actually worked faster than the line, they not only added a few minutes of relaxation from the work while the line caught up, but they symbolically regained an element of control over the pace of their own work. . . .

▪ ▪ ▪ COPING

One of the difficulties of work at the beef plant was coping with three aspects of the work: monotony, danger, and dehumanization. While individual workers undoubtedly coped in a variety of ways, some distinguishable patterns emerged.

Monotony

The monotony of the line was almost unbearable. At my work station, a worker would hang, brand, and bag between 1,350 and 1,500 beef tongues in an eight-hour shift. With the exception of the scheduled fifteen-minute break and a thirty-minute lunch period (and sporadic brief gaps in the line), the work was mundane, routine, and continuous. As in most assembly line work, one inevitably drifted into daydreams (e.g., Garson, 1975; King, 1978; Linhart, 1981). It was not unusual to look up or down the line and see workers at various stations singing to themselves, tapping their feet to imaginary music, or carrying on conversations with themselves. I found that I could work with virtually no attention paid to the job, with my hands and arms automatically performing their tasks. In the meantime, my mind was free to wander over a variety of topics, including taking mental notes. In visiting with other workers, I found that daydreaming was the norm. Some would think about their families, while others fantasized about sexual escapades, fishing, or anything unrelated to the job. One individual who was rebuilding an antique car at home in his spare time would meticulously mentally rehearse the procedures he was going to perform on the car the next day.

Daydreaming was not inconsequential, however. During these periods, items were most likely to be dropped, jobs improperly performed, and accidents incurred. Inattention to detail around moving equipment, stainless steel hooks, and sharp knives invariably leads to dangerous consequences. Although I heard rumors of drug use to help fight the monotony, I never saw any workers take any drugs nor saw any drugs in any worker's possession. It is certainly conceivable that some workers might have taken something to help them escape the reality of the line, but the nature of the work demanded enough attention that such a practice could be ominous.

Danger

The danger of working in the beef plant was well known. Safety was top priority (at least in theory) and management took pride in the fact that only three employee on-the-job deaths had occurred in twelve years. Although deaths were uncommon, serious injuries were not. The beef plant employed over 1,800 people. Approximately three-fourths of those employed had jobs which demanded the use of a knife honed to razor-sharpness. Despite the use of wire-mesh aprons and gloves, serious cuts were almost a daily occurrence. Since workers constantly handled beef blood, danger of infection was ever present. As one walked along the assembly line, a wide assortment of bandages on fingers, hands, arms, necks, and faces could always be seen.

In addition to the problem of cuts, workers who cut meat continuously sometimes suffered muscle and ligament damage to their fingers and hands. In one severe case, I was told of a woman who worked in processing for several years who had to wear splints on her fingers while away from the job to hold them straight. Otherwise, the muscles in her hand would constrict her fingers into the grip position, as if holding a knife. . . .

When I spoke with fellow workers about the dangers of working in the plant, I noticed interesting defense mechanisms. . . . After a serious accident, or when telling about an accident or death which occurred in years past, the workers would almost immediately dissociate themselves from the event and its victim. Workers tended to view those who suffered major accidents or death on the job in much the same way that nonvictims of crime often view crime victims as either partially responsible for the event, or at least as very different from themselves (Barlow, 1981). "Only a part-timer," "stupid," "careless" or something similar was used, seemingly to reassure the worker describing the accident that it could not happen to him. The reality of the situation was that virtually all the jobs on the kill floor were dangerous, and any worker could have experienced a serious injury at any time. . . .

Dehumanization

Perhaps the most devastating aspect of working at the beef plant (worse than the monotony and the danger) was the dehumanizing and demeaning elements of the job. In a sense, the assembly line worker became a part of the assembly line. The assembly line is not a tool used by the worker, but a machine which controls him/her. A tool can only be productive in the hands of somebody skilled in its use, and hence becomes an extension of the person using it. A machine, on the other hand, performs specific tasks; thus its operator becomes an extension of it in the production process. . . . When workers are viewed as mere extensions of the machines with which they work, their human needs become secondary in importance to the smooth mechanical functioning of the production process. In a bureaucratic structure, when "human needs collide with systems needs, the individual suffers" (Hummel, 1977:65).

Workers on the assembly line are seen as interchangeable as the parts of the product on the line itself. An example of one worker's perception of this phenomenon at the beef plant was demonstrated the day after a fatal accident occurred. I asked the men in our crew what the company did in the case of an employee death (I wondered if there was a fund for flowers, or if the shift was given time off to go to the funeral, etc.). One worker's response was: "They drag off the body, take the hard hat and boots and check 'em out to some other poor sucker, and throw him in the guy's place." While employee death on the job was not viewed quite that coldly by the company, the statement fairly accurately summarized the overall result of a fatal accident, and importance of any individual worker to the overall operation of the production process. It accurately summarized the workers' perceptions about management's attitudes toward them. . . .

■ ■ ■ SABOTAGE

It is fairly common knowledge that assembly line work situations often led to employee sabotage or destruction of the product or equipment used in the production process (Garson, 1975; Balzer, 1976; Shostak, 1980). This is the classic experience of alienation as described by Marx (1964a,b). . . . At the beef plant I quickly learned that there was an art to effective sabotage. Subtlety appeared to be the key. "The art lies in sabotaging in a way that is not immediately discovered," as a Ford worker put it (King, 1978:202). This seemed to hold true at the beef plant as well. . . .

The greatest factor influencing the handling of beef plant products was its status as a food product intended for human consumption. . . . Though not an explicitly altruistic group, the workers realized that the product would be consumed by people (even family, relatives, and friends), so consequently, they rarely did anything to actually contaminate the product.

Despite formal norms against sabotage, some did occur. It was not uncommon for workers to deliberately cut chunks out of pieces of meat for no reason (or for throwing at other employees). While regulations required that anything that touched the floor had to be put in tubs marked "inedible," the informal procedural norms were otherwise. When something was dropped, one usually looked around to see if an inspector or foreman noticed. If not, the item was quickly picked up and put back on the line.

Several explanations might be offered for this type of occurrence. First, since the company utilized a profit-sharing plan, when workers damaged the product, or had to throw edible pieces into inedible tubs (which sold for pet food at much lower prices), profits were decreased. A decrease in profits to the company ultimately led to decreased dividend checks to employees. Consequently, workers were fairly careful not to actually ruin anything. Second, when something was dropped or mishandled and had to be rerouted to "inedible," it was more time-consuming than if the product had been handled properly and kept on the regular line. In other words, if no inspector noticed, it was easier to let it go through on the line. There was a third, and seemingly more meaningful, explanation for this behavior, however. It was against the rules to do it, it was a challenge to do it, and thus it was fun to do it.

The workers practically made a game out of doing forbidden things simply to see if they could get away with it. . . . New workers were routinely socialized into the subtle art of rulebreaking as approved by the line workers. At my particular work station, it was a fairly common practice for other workers who were covered with beef blood to come over to the tub of swirling water designed to clean the tongues, and as soon as the inspector looked away, wash their hands, arms, and knives in the tub. This procedure was strictly forbidden by the rules. If witnessed by a foreman or inspector, the tub had to be emptied, cleaned, and refilled, and all the tongues in the tub at the time had to be put in the "inedible" tub. All of that would be a time-consuming and costly procedure, yet the workers seemed to absolutely delight in successfully pulling off the act. As Balzer (1976:90) indicates:

> Since a worker often feels that much if not all of what he does is done in places designated by the company, under company control, finding ways to express personal freedom from this institutional regimentation is important.

Thus, artful sabotage served as a symbolic way in which the workers could express a sense of individuality, and hence, self-worth.

■ ■ ■ ■ **THE FINANCIAL TRAP**

Given the preceding description and analysis of work at the beef plant, why did people work at such jobs? Obviously, there are a multitude of plausible answers to that question. Without doubt, however, the key is money. The current economic situation, the lack of steady employment opportunities (especially for the untrained and poorly educated), combined with the fact that the beef plant's starting wage exceeded the minimum wage by approximately $5.50 per hour emerge as the most important reasons people went to work there.

Despite the high hourly wage and fringe benefits, however, the monotony, danger, and hard physical work drove many workers away in less than a week. During my study, I observed much worker turnover. Those who stayed displayed an interesting pattern which helps explain why they did not leave. Every member of my work crew answered similarly my questions about why they stayed at the beef plant. Each of them took the job directly after high school, because it was the highest-paying job available. Each of them had intended to work through the summer and then look for a better job in the fall. During that first summer on the job they fell victim to what I label the "financial trap."

The "financial trap" was a spending pattern which demanded the constant weekly income provided by the beef plant job. This scenario was first told to me by an employee who had worked at the plant for over nine years. He began the week after his high school graduation, intending only to work that summer in order to earn enough money to attend college in the fall. After about four weeks' work he purchased a new car. He figured he could pay off the car that summer and still save enough money for tuition. Shortly after the car purchase, he added a new stereo sound system to his debt; next came a motorcycle; then the decision to postpone school for one year in order to continue working at the beef plant and pay off his debts. A few months later he married; within a year purchased a house; had a child; and bought another new car. Nine years later, he was still working at the beef plant, hated every minute of it, but in his own words "could not afford to quit." His case was not unique. Over and over again, I heard stories about the same process of falling into the "financial trap." The youngest and newest of our crew had just graduated from high school and took the job for the summer in order to earn enough money to attend welding school the following fall. During my brief tenure at the beef plant, he purchased a new motorcycle, a new stereo, and a house trailer. When I left, he told me he had decided to postpone welding school for one year in order "to get everything paid for." I saw the financial trap closing in on him fast; he did, too. . . .

■ ■ ■ **SUMMARY AND CONCLUSIONS**

There are at least three interwoven phenomena in this study which deserve further comment and research.

First is the subtle sense of unity which existed among the line workers. . . . The line both symbolically and literally linked every job, and consequently every worker, to each other. . . . A system of "uncooperative teamwork" seemed to combine simultaneously a feeling of "one for all, all for one, and every man for himself." Once a line worker made it past the first three or four days on the job which "weeded out" many new workers, his status as a *beefer* was assured and the sense of unity was felt as much by the worker of nine weeks as it was by the veteran of nine years. Because the workers maintained largely secondary relationships, this feeling of unification is not the same as the unity typically found on athletic teams, in fraternities, or among various primary groups. Yet it was a significant social force which bound the workers together and provided a sense of meaning and worth. Although their occupation might not be highly respected by outsiders, they derived mutual self-respect from their sense of belonging.

A second important phenomenon was the various coping methods . . . the beef plant line workers developed and practiced . . . for retaining their humanness. Daydreaming, horseplay, and occasional sabotage protected their sense of self. Further, the prevailing attitude among workers that it was "us" against "them" served as a reminder that, while the nature of the job might demand subjugation to bosses, machines, and even beef parts, they were still human beings. . . .

A third significant finding was that consumer spending patterns among the beefers seemed to "seal their fate" and make leaving the beef plant almost impossible. A reasonable interpretation of the spending patterns of the beefers is that having a high-income/low-status job encourages a person to consume conspicuously. The prevailing attitude seemed to be "I may not have a nice job, but I have a nice home, a nice car, etc." This conspicuous consumption enabled workers to take indirect pride in their occupations. One of the ways of overcoming drudgery and humiliation on the job was to surround oneself with as many desirable material things as possible off the job. These items (cars, boats, motorcycles, etc.) became tangible rewards for the sacrifices endured at work.

The problem, of course, is that the possession of these expensive items required the continual income of a substantial paycheck which most of these men could only obtain by staying at the beef plant. These spending patterns were further complicated by the fact that they were seemingly "contagious." Workers talked to each other on breaks about recent purchases, thus reinforcing the norm of immediate gratification. A common activity of a group of workers on break or lunch was to run to the parking lot to see a fellow worker's new truck, van, car, or motorcycle. Even the seemingly more financially conservative were usually caught up in this activity and often could not wait to display their own latest acquisitions. Ironically, as the workers cursed their jobs, these expensive possessions virtually destroyed any chance of leaving them.

Working at the beef plant was indeed "dirty work." It was monotonous, difficult, dangerous, and demeaning. Despite this, the workers at the beef plant worked hard to fulfill employer expectations in order to obtain financial rewards. Through a variety of symbolic techniques, they managed to overcome the many negative aspects of their work and maintain a sense of self-respect about how they earned their living.

REFERENCES

Balzer, Richard (1976). *Clockwork: Life In and Outside an American Factory.* Garden City, NY: Doubleday.

Barlow, Hugh (1981). *Introduction to Criminology.* 2d ed. Boston: Little, Brown.

Garson, Barbara (1975). *All the Livelong Day: The Meaning and Demeaning of Routine Work.* Garden City, NY: Doubleday.

Hummel, Ralph P. (1977). *The Bureaucratic Experience.* New York: St. Martin's Press.

King, Rick (1978). "In the sanding booth at Ford," Pp. 199–205 in John and Erna Perry (eds.), *Social Problems in Today's World.* Boston: Little, Brown.

Linhart, Robert (translated by Margaret Crosland) (1981). *The Assembly Line.* Amherst: University of Massachusetts Press

Marx, Karl (1964a). *Economic and Philosophical Manuscripts of 1844.* New York International Publishing (1844).

———— (1964b). *The Communist Manifesto.* New York: Washington Square Press (1848).

Schatzman, Leonard, and Anselm L. Strauss (1973). *Field Research.* Englewood Cliffs, NJ: Prentice-Hall.

Shostak, Arthur (1980). *Blue Collar Stress.* Reading, MA: Addison-Wesley.

Spradley, James P. (1979). *The Ethnographic Interview.* New York: Holt, Rinehart & Winston.

———— (1980). *Participant Observation.* New York: Holt, Rinehart & Winston.

Handling the Stigma
of Handling the Dead

William E. Thompson

introduction ▪ ▪ ▪ ▪ ▪

Life expectancy used to be much shorter than it is now. A hundred years ago, the average American died before the age of 50. Back then, death was also a family affair. Not only did people die at home, but also their mothers, wives, and sisters washed and dressed the body. Wakes (grieving ceremonies) were held at home, with the body put on display in the parlor, where family, friends, and neighbors "paid their last respects." After the wake, the men transported the body in a coffin they had made and lowered it into a grave they had dug.

In today's world, formal organizations have replaced many family functions, including those of handling death. People die in hospitals, attended by strangers. Other strangers deliver the body to a funeral home. There, still more strangers prepare the body for burial by draining its blood and replacing it with embalming fluids. Afterward, strangers dress the body in clothing selected by relatives, comb the hair, put makeup on the face, and place the body on display in a room reserved for this purpose (sometimes called "the eternal slumber room"). The family participates by arranging a ceremony to be held in this room (or at a religious site) and by appointing friends to carry the body from this room to a vehicle whose only purpose is to transport dead bodies. Strangers drive this specialized vehicle to the graveyard. Who are these "death specialists" who handle dead bodies, and how do they handle the stigma that comes from handling the dead? This is the focus of Thompson's analysis.

Thinking Critically

As you read this selection, ask yourself:

1. Why have formal organizations taken over such a previously intimate function of the family as taking care of the dead? How would you feel about taking care of a dead family member? What is the origin of your feelings? (Don't say they are natural. They are not.)

2. How do society's "death specialists" handle the stigma of handling the dead?

3. If you have ever been to a funeral, compare what you experienced with what you read in this selection.

In a complex, industrialized society a person's occupation or profession is central to his or her personal and social identity. As Pavalko (1988) pointed out, two strangers are quite ". . . likely to 'break the ice' by indicating the kind of work they do." As a result, individuals often made a number of initial judgments about others based on preconceived notions about particular occupations.

This study examines how morticians and funeral directors handle the stigma associated with their work. Historically, stigma has been attached to those responsible for caring for the dead, and the job typically was assigned to the lower classes (e.g., the Eta of Japan and the Untouchables in India), and in some cases, those who handled the dead were forbidden from touching the living.

Morticians and funeral directors are fully aware of the stigma associated with their work, so they continually strive to enhance their public image and promote their social credibility. They must work to shift the emphasis on their work from the dead to the living, and away from sales and toward service. As Aries (1976, 99) noted:

> In order to sell death, it had to be made friendly . . . since 1885 . . . [funeral directors have] presented themselves not as simple sellers of services, but as "doctors of grief" who have a mission . . . [which] consists in aiding the mourning survivors to return to normalcy.

Couched within the general theoretical framework of symbolic interactionism, there are a variety of symbolic and dramaturgical methods whereby morticians and funeral directors attempt to redefine their occupations and minimize and/or neutralize negative attitudes toward them and what they do.

■ ■ ■ METHOD

This study reflects over 2 years of qualitative fieldwork. Extensive ethnographic interviews were conducted with 19 morticians and funeral directors in four states: Kansas, Missouri, Oklahoma, and Texas. The funeral homes included both privately owned businesses and branches of large franchise operations.

Interviewees included people from different age groups, both sexes, and both whites and nonwhites. There were 16 males and 3 females interviewed for this study, ranging in age from 26 to 64 years.

■ ■ ■ THE STIGMA OF HANDLING THE DEAD

Until [about 1900] in this country, people died at home and friends and family members prepared the bodies for burial (Lesy, 1987). As medical knowledge and technology progressed and became more specialized, more and more deaths occurred outside the home—usually in hospitals. Death became something to be handled by a select group of highly trained professionals—doctors, nurses, and hospital staff. As fewer people witnessed death firsthand, it became surrounded with more mystery, and physically handling the dead became the domain of only a few.

Members or friends of the family relinquished their role in preparing bodies for disposal to an *undertaker*, ". . . a special person who would 'undertake' responsibility for the care and burial of the dead" (Amos, 1983, 2). Most states began licensing embalmers around the end of the nineteenth century (Amos, 1983). These licensed embalmers were viewed as unusual, if not downright weird. They were not family members or friends of the deceased faced with the unsavory but necessary responsibility for disposing of a loved one's body, but strangers who *chose* to work with dead bodies—for compensation. Although most welcomed the opportunity to relinquish this chore they also viewed those who willingly assumed it with some skepticism and even disdain.

Sudnow (1967, 51–64) underscored the negative attitudes toward people who work with the dead in describing how those who work in a morgue, for example, are "death-tainted" and work very hard to rid themselves of the social stigma associated with their jobs. Morticians and funeral directors cannot escape from this "taint of death" and they must constantly work to "counteract the stigma" directed at them and their occupations.

Are morticians and funeral directors really that stigmatized? After all, they generally are well-known and respected members of their communities. In small communities and even many large cities, local funeral homes have been owned and operated by the same family for several generations. These people usually are members of civic organizations, have substantial incomes, and live in nice homes and drive nice automobiles. Most often they are viewed as successful business people. On the other hand, their work is surrounded by mystery, taboos, and stigma, and they often are viewed as cold, detached, and downright morbid for doing it. All the respondents in this study openly acknowledged that stigma was associated with their work. Some indicated that they thought the stigma primarily came from the "misconception" that they were "getting rich" off other people's grief; others believed it simply came from working with the dead. Clearly these two aspects of their work—handling the dead and profiting from death and grief—emerged as the two most stigmatizing features of the funeral industry according to respondents.

■ ■ ■ MANAGING STIGMA

Erving Goffman wrote the most systematic analysis of how individuals manage a "spoiled" social identity in his classic work, *Stigma* (1963). He described several techniques, such as "passing," "dividing the social world," "mutual aid," "physical distance," "disclosure," and "covering," employed by the *discredited* and *discreditable* to manage information and conceal their stigmatizing attributes (41–104). Although these techniques work well for the physically scarred, blind, stammerers, bald, drug addicted, ex-convicts, and many other stigmatized categories of people, they are less likely to be used by morticians and funeral directors.

Except perhaps when on vacation, it is important for funeral directors to be known and recognized in their communities and to be associated with their work. Consequently, most of the morticians and funeral directors studied relied on other strategies for reducing the stigma associated with their work. Paramount among these strategies were: symbolic redefinition of their work, role distance, professionalism, emphasizing service, and enjoying socioeconomic status over occupational prestige. This was much less true for licensed embalmers who worked for funeral directors, especially in chain-owned funeral homes in large cities. In those cases the author found that many embalmers concealed their occupation from their neighbors and others with whom they were not intimately acquainted.

Symbolic Redefinition

One of the ways in which morticians and funeral directors handle the stigma of their occupations is through symbolically negating as much of it as possible. Woods and Delisle (1978, 98) revealed how sympathy cards avoid the use of the terms "dead" and "death" by substituting less harsh words such as "loss," "time of sorrow," and "hour of sadness." This technique is also used by morticians and funeral directors to reduce the stigma associated with their work.

Words that are most closely associated with death are rarely used, and the most harsh terms are replaced with less ominous ones. The term *death* is almost never used by funeral directors; rather, they talk of "passing on," "meeting an untimely end," or "eternal slumber." There are no *corpses* or *dead bodies,* they are referred to as "remains," "the deceased," "loved one," or more frequently, by name (e.g., "Mr. Jones"). Use of the term *body* is almost uniformly avoided around the family. Viewing rooms (where the embalmed body is displayed in the casket) usually are given serene names such as "the sunset room," "the eternal slumber room," or, in one case, "the guest room." Thus, when friends or family arrive to view the body, they are likely to be told that "Mr. Jones is lying in repose in the eternal slumber room." This language contrasts sharply with that used by morticians and funeral directors in "backstage" areas (Goffman, 1959, 112) such as the embalming room where drowning victims often are called "floaters," burn victims are called "crispy critters," and others are simply referred to as "bodies" (Turner and Edgley, 1976).

All the respondents indicated that there was less stigma attached to the term *funeral director* than *mortician* or *embalmer,* underscoring the notion that much of the stigma they experienced was attached to physically handling the dead. Consequently, when asked what they do for a living, those who acknowledge that they are in the funeral business (several indicated that they often do not) referred to themselves as "funeral directors" even if all they did was the embalming. *Embalming* is referred to as "preservation" or "restoration," and in order to be licensed, one must have studied "mortuary arts" or "mortuary science." Embalming no longer takes place in an *embalming room,* but in a "preparation room," or in some cases the "operating room."

Coffins are now "caskets," which are transported in "funeral coaches" (not *hearses*) to their "final resting place" rather than to the *cemetery* or worse yet, *graveyard,* for their "interment" rather than *burial.* Thus, linguistically, the symbolic redefinition is complete, with death verbally redefined during every phase, and the stigma associated with it markedly reduced.

All the morticians and funeral directors in this study emphasized the importance of using the "appropriate" terms in referring to their work. Knowledge of the stigma attached to certain words was readily acknowledged, and all indicated that the earlier terminology was stigma-laden, especially the term "undertaker," which they believed conjured up negative images in the mind of the public. For example, a 29-year-old male funeral director indicated that his father still insisted on calling himself an "undertaker." "He just hasn't caught up with [modern times]," the son remarked. Interestingly, when asked why he did not refer to himself as an undertaker, he replied "It just sounds so old-fashioned [pause] plus, it sounds so morbid."

In addition to using language to symbolically redefine their occupations, funeral directors carefully attempt to shift the focus of their work away from the care of the dead (especially handling the body), and redefine it primarily in terms of caring for the living. The dead are deemphasized as most of the funeral ritual is orchestrated for the benefit of the friends and family of the deceased (Turner and Edgley, 1976). By redefining themselves as "grief therapists" or "bereavement counselors" their primary duties are associated with making funeral arrangements, directing the services, and consoling the family in their time of need.

Role Distance

Because a person's sense of self is so strongly linked to occupation, it is common practice for people in undesirable or stigmatized occupations to practice role distance. Although the specific role-distancing techniques vary across different occupations and among different individuals within an occupation, they share the common function of allowing individuals to violate some of the role expectations associated with the occupation, and express their individuality within the confines of the occupational role. Although the funeral directors and morticians in this study used a variety of role-distancing techniques, three common patterns emerged: emotional detachment, humor, and countering the stereotype.

Emotional Detachment.   One of the ways that morticians and funeral directors overcome their socialization regarding death taboos and the stigma associated with handling the dead is to detach themselves from the body of the work. Charmaz (1980) pointed out that a common technique used by coroners and funeral directors to minimize the stigma associated with death work is to routinize the work as much as possible. When embalming, morticians focus on the technical aspects of the job rather than thinking about the person they are working on. One mortician explained:

> When I'm in the preparation I never think about the who *who* I'm working on, I only think about what has to be done next. When I picked up the body, it was a person. When I get done, clean and dress the body, and place it in the casket, it becomes a

person again. But in here it's just something to be worked on. I treat it like a mechanic treats an automobile engine—with respect, but there's no emotion involved. It's just a job that has to be done.

Another mortician described his emotional detachment in the embalming room:

You can't think too much about this process [embalming], or it'll really get to you. For example, one time we brought in this little girl. She was about four years old—the same age as my youngest daughter at the time. She had been killed in a wreck; had gone through the windshield; was really a mess.

At first, I wasn't sure I could do this one—all I could think about was my little girl. But when I got her in the prep room, my whole attitude changed. I know this probably sounds cold, and hard I guess, but suddenly I began to think of the challenge involved. This was gonna be an open-casket service, and while the body was in pretty good shape, the head and face were practically gone. This was gonna take a lot of reconstruction. Also, the veins are so small on children that you have to be a lot more careful.

Anyway, I got so caught up in the job, that I totally forgot about working on a little girl. I was in the room with her about six hours when—[his wife] came in and reminded me that we had dinner plans that night. I washed up and went out to dinner and had a great time. Later that night, I went right back to work on her without even thinking about it.

It wasn't until the next day when my wife was dressing the body, and I came in, and she was crying, that it hit me. I looked at the little girl, and I began crying. We both just stood there crying and hugging. My wife kept saying "I know this was tough for you," and "yesterday must have been tough." I felt sorta guilty, because I knew what she meant, and it should've been tough for me, real tough emotionally, but it wasn't. The only "tough" part had been the actual work, especially the reconstruction—I had totally cut off the emotional part.

It sometimes makes you wonder. Am I really just good at this, or am I losing something. I don't know. All I know is, if I'd thought about the little girl the way I did that next day, I never could have done her. It's just part of this job—you gotta just do what has to be done. If you think about it much, you'll never make it in this business.

Humor. Many funeral directors and morticians use humor to detach themselves emotionally from their work. The humor, of course, must be carefully hidden from friends and relatives of the deceased, and takes place in backstage areas such as the embalming room, or in professional group settings such as at funeral directors' conventions.

The humor varies from impromptu comments while working on the body to standard jokes told over and over again. Not unexpectedly, all the respondents indicated a strong distaste for necrophilia jokes. One respondent commented, "I can think of nothing less funny—the jokes are sick, and have done a lot of damage to the image of our profession."

Humor is an effective technique of diffusing the stigma associated with handling a dead body, however, and when more than one person is present in the embalming room, it is common for a certain amount of banter to take place, and jokes or comments are often made about the amount of body fat or the overendowment, or lack thereof, of certain body parts. For example, one mortician indicated that a common remark made about the males with small genitalia is, "Well, at least he won't be missed."

As with any occupation, levels of humor varied among the respondents. During an interview one of the funeral directors spoke of some of the difficulties in advertising the business, indicating that because of attitudes toward death and the funeral business, he had to be sure that his newspaper advertisements did not offend anyone. He reached into his desk drawer and pulled out a pad with several "fake ads" written on it. They included:

> "Shake and Bake Special—Cremation with No Embalming"
> "Business Is Slow, Somebody's Gotta Go"
> "Try Our Layaway Plan—Best in the Business"
> "Count on Us, We'll Be the Last to Let You Down"
> "People Are Dying to Use Our Services"
> "Pay Now, Die Later"
> "The Buck Really Does Stop Here"

He indicated that he and one of his friends had started making up these fake ads and slogans when they were doing their mortuary internships. Over the years, they occasionally corresponded by mail and saw each other at conventions, and they would always try to be one up on the other with the best ad. He said, "Hey, in this business, you have to look for your laughs where you can find them."

Countering the Stereotype.   Morticians and funeral directors are painfully aware of the common negative stereotype of people in their occupations. The women in this study were much less concerned about the stereotype, perhaps because simply being female shattered the stereotype anyway. The men, however, not only acknowledged that they were well aware of the public's stereotypical image of them, but also indicated that they made every effort *not* to conform to it.

One funeral director, for instance, said:

> People think we're cold, unfriendly, and unfeeling. I always make it a point to be just the opposite. Naturally, when I'm dealing with a family I must be reserved and show the proper decorum, but when I am out socially, I always try to be very upbeat—very alive. No matter how tired I am, I try not to show it.

Another indicated that he absolutely never wore gray or black suits. Instead, he wore navy blue and usually with a small pinstripe. "I might be mistaken for the minister or a lawyer," he said, "but rarely for an undertaker."

The word *cold,* which often is associated with death came up in a number of interviews. One funeral director was so concerned about the stereotype of being "cold," that he kept a handwarmer in the drawer of his desk. He said, "My hands tend to be cold and clammy. It's just a physical trait of mine, but there's no way that I'm going to shake someone's hand and let them walk away thinking how cold it was." Even on the warmest of days, he indicated that during services, he carried the handwarmer in his right-hand coat pocket so that he could warm his hand before shaking hands with or touching someone.

Although everyone interviewed indicated that he or she violated the public stereotype, each one expressed a feeling of being atypical. In other words, although they believed that they did not conform to the stereotype, they felt that many of their colleagues did. One funeral director was wearing jeans, a short-sleeved sweatshirt and a pair of running shoes during the interview. He had just finished mowing the lawn at the funeral home. "Look at me," he said, "Do I look like a funeral director? Hell, _____ [the funeral director across the street] wears a suit and tie to mow his grass!—or, at least he would if he didn't hire it done."

Others insisted that very few funeral directors conform to the public stereotype when out of public view, but feel compelled to conform to it when handling funeral arrangements, because it is an occupational role requirement. "I always try to be warm and upbeat," one remarked, "But, let's face it, when I'm working with a family, they're experiencing a lot of grief—I have to respect that, and act accordingly." Another indicated that he always lowered his voice when talking with family and friends of the deceased, and that it had become such a habit, that he found himself speaking softly almost all the time. "One of the occupational hazards, I guess," he remarked.

The importance of countering the negative stereotype was evident, when time after time, persons being interviewed would pause and ask "I'm not what you expected, am I?" or something similar. It seemed very important for them to be reassured that they did not fit the stereotype of funeral director or mortician.

Professionalism

Another method used by morticians and funeral directors to reduce occupational stigma is to emphasize professionalism. Amos (1983, 3) described embalming as:

> . . . an example of a vocation in transition from an occupation to a profession. Until mid-nineteenth century, embalming was not considered a profession and this is still an issue debated in some circles today.

Most morticians readily admit that embalming is a very simple process and can be learned very easily. In all but two of the funeral homes studied, the interviewees admitted that people who were not licensed embalmers often helped with the embalming process. In one case, in which the funeral home was owned and operated by two brothers, one of the brothers was a licensed funeral director and licensed embalmer. The other brother had dropped out of high school and helped their father with the funeral business while his brother went to school to meet the educational requirements for licensure. The licensed brother said:

> By the time I got out of school and finished my apprenticeship, _____ [his brother] had been helping Dad embalm for over three years—and he was damned good at it. So when I joined the business, Dad thought it was best if I concentrated on handling the funeral arrangements and pre-service needs. After Dad died, I was the only licensed embalmer, so "officially" I do it all—all the embalming and the funeral arrangements. But, to tell you the truth, I only embalm every now and then when we have several to do, 'cause _____ usually handles most of it. He's one of the best—I'd match him against any in the business.

Despite the relative simplicity of the embalming process and the open admission by morticians and funeral directors that "almost anyone could do it with a little practice," most states require licensure and certification for embalming. The four states represented in this study (Kansas, Oklahoma, Missouri, and Texas) have similar requirements for becoming a licensed certified embalmer. They include a minimum of 60 college hours with a core of general college courses (English, mathematics, social studies, etc.) plus 1 year of courses in the "mortuary sciences" or "mortuary arts." These consist of several courses in physiology and biology, and a 1-year apprenticeship under a licensed embalmer. To become a licensed funeral director requires the passing of a state board examination, which primarily requires a knowledge of state laws related to burial, cremation, disposal of the body, and insurance.

Although the general consensus among them was that an individual did not need a college education to become a good embalmer, they all stressed the importance of a college education for being a successful funeral director. Most thought that some basic courses in business, psychology, death and dying, and "bereavement counseling" were valuable preparation for the field. Also, most of the funeral directors were licensed insurance agents, which allowed them to sell burial policies.

Other evidence of the professionalization of the funeral industry includes state, regional, and national professional organizations that hold annual conventions and sponsor other professional activities; professional journals; state, regional, and national governing and regulating boards; and a professional code of ethics. Although the funeral industry is highly competitive, like most other professions, its members demonstrate a strong sense of cohesiveness and in-group identification.

One of the married couples in this study indicated that it was reassuring to attend national conventions where they met and interacted with other people in the funeral industry because it helps to "reassure us that we're not weird." The wife went on to say:

> A lot of people ask us how we can stand to be in this business—especially because he does all of the embalming. They act like we must be strange or something. When we go to the conventions and meet with all of the other people there who are just like us—people who like helping other people—I feel normal again.

All these elements of professionalization—educational requirements, exams, boards, organizations, codes of ethics, and the rest—lend an air of credibility and dignity to the funeral business while diminishing the stigma associated with it. Although the requirements for licensure and certification are not highly exclusive, they still represent forms of boundary maintenance, and demand a certain level of commitment from those who enter the field. Thus, professionalization helped in the transition of the funeral business from a vocation that can be pursued by virtually anyone to a profession that can be entered only by those with the appropriate qualifications. As Pine (1975, 28) indicated:

> Because professionalization is highly respected in American society, the word . . . "profession". . . tends to be used as a symbol by occupations seeking to improve or enhance the lay public's conception of that occupation, and funeral directing is no exception. To some extent, this appears to be because the funeral director hopes to overcome the stigma of "doing death work."

"By claiming professional status, funeral directors claim prestige and simultaneously seek to minimize the stigma they experience for being death workers involved in 'dirty work.'"

The Shroud of Service

One of the most obvious ways in which morticians and funeral directors neutralize the stigma associated with their work is to wrap themselves in a "shroud of service." All the respondents emphasized their service role over all other aspects of their jobs. Although their services were not legally required in any of the four states included in this study, all the respondents insisted that people desperately needed them. As one funeral director summarized, "Service, that's what we're all about—we're there when people need us the most."

Unlike the humorous fantasy ads mentioned earlier, actual advertisements in the funeral industry focus on service. Typical ads for the companies in this study read:

> "Our Family Serving Yours for Over 60 Years"
> "Serving the Community for Four Generations"
> "Thoughtful Service in Your Time of Need"

The emphasis on service, especially on "grief counseling" and "bereavement therapy," shifts the focus away from the two most stigmatizing elements of funeral work: the handling and preparation of the body, which already has been discussed at length; and retail sales, which are widely interpreted as profiting from other people's grief. Many of the funeral directors indicated that they believed the major reason for negative public feelings toward their occupation was not only that they handled dead bodies, but the fact that they made their living off the dead, or at least, off the grief of the living.

All admitted that much of their profit came from the sale of caskets and vaults, where markup is usually a minimum of 100%, and often 400–500%, but all played down this aspect of their work. The Federal Trade Commission requires that funeral directors provide their customers with itemized lists of all charges. The author was provided with price lists for all merchandise and services by all the funeral directors in this study. When asked to estimate the "average price" of one of their funerals, respondents' answers ranged from $3,000 to $4,000. Typically, the casket accounted for approximately half of the total expense. Respondents indicated that less than 5% of their business involved cremations, but that even then they often encouraged the purchase of a casket. One said, "A lot of people ask about cremation, because they think it's cheaper, but I usually sell them caskets even for cremation; then, if you add the cost of cremation and urn, cremation becomes more profitable than burial."

Despite this denial of the retail aspects of the job, trade journals provide numerous helpful hints on the best techniques for displaying and selling caskets, and great care is given to this process. In all the funeral homes visited, one person was charged with the primary responsibility for helping with "casket selection." In smaller family-operated funeral homes, this person usually was the funeral director's wife. In the large chain-owned companies, it was one of the "associate funeral directors." In either case, the person was a skilled salesperson.

Nevertheless, the sales pitch is wrapped in the shroud of service. During each interview, the author asked to be shown the "selection room," and to be treated as if he were there to select a casket for a loved one. All the funeral directors willingly complied, and most treated the author as if he actually were there to select a casket. Interestingly, most perceived this as an actual sales opportunity and mentioned their "pre-need selection service" and said that if the author had not already made such arrangements, they would gladly assist him with the process. The words "sell," "sales," "buy," and "purchase" were carefully avoided.

Also, although by law the price for each casket must be displayed separately, most funeral homes also displayed a "package price" that included the casket and "full services." If purchased separately, the casket was always more expensive than if it was included in the package of services. This gave the impression that a much more expensive casket could be purchased for less money if bought as part of a service package. It also implied that the services provided by the firm were of more value than the merchandise.

The funeral directors rationalized the high costs of merchandise and funerals by emphasizing that they were a small price to pay for the services performed. One insisted, "We don't sell merchandise, we sell service!" Another asked "What is peace of mind worth?" and another "How do you put a price on relieving grief?"

Another rationalization for the high prices was the amount involved in arranging and conducting funeral services. When asked about the negative aspects of their jobs, most emphasized the hard work and long hours involved. In fact, all but two of the interviewees said that they did not want their children to follow in their footstep, because the work was largely misunderstood (stigmatized), too hard, the hours too long, and "the income not nearly as high as most people think."

In addition to emphasizing the service aspect of their work, funeral directors also tend to join a number of local philanthropic and service organizations (Pine, 1975, 49). Although many businessmen find that joining such organizations is advantageous for making contacts, Stephenson (1985, 223) contended that the small-town funeral director "may be able to counter the stigma of his or her occupation by being active in the community, thereby counteracting some of the negative images associated with the job of funeral directing."

Socioeconomic Status versus Occupational Prestige

It seems that what funeral directors lack in occupational prestige, they make up for in socioeconomic status. Although interviewees were very candid about the number of funerals they performed every year and the average costs per funeral, most were reluctant to disclose their annual incomes. One exception was a 37-year-old funeral home owner, funeral director, and licensed embalmer in a community of approximately 25,000 who indicated that in the previous year he had handled 211 funerals and had a gross income of just under $750,000. After deducting overhead (three licensed embalmers on staff, a receptionist, a gardener, a student employee, insurance costs, etc.), he estimated his net income to have been "close to $250,000." He quickly added, however, that he worked long hours, had his 5-day vacation cut to two (because of a "funeral call that he had to handle personally") and despite his relatively high income (probably one of the two or three highest incomes in the community), he felt morally, socially, and professionally obligated to hide his wealth in the community. "I have to walk a fine line," he said, "I can live in a nice home, drive a nice car, and wear nice suits, because people know that I am a successful businessman—but, I have to be careful not to flaunt it."

One of the ways he reconciles this dilemma was by enjoying "the finer things in life" outside the community. He owned a condominium in Vail where he took ski trips and kept his sports car. He also said that none of his friends or neighbors there knew that he was in the funeral business. In fact, when they inquired about his occupations he told them he was in insurance (which technically was true because he also was a licensed insurance agent who sold burial policies). When asked why he did not disclose his true occupational identity, he responded:

> When I tell people what I really do, they initially seem "put off," even repulsed. I have literally had people jerk their hands back during a handshake when somebody introduces me and then tells them what I do for a living. Later, many of them become very curious and ask a lot of questions. If you tell people you sell insurance, they usually let the subject drop.

Although almost all the funeral directors in this study lived what they characterized as fairly "conservative lifestyles," most also indicated that they enjoyed many of the material things that their jobs offered them. One couple rationalized their recent purchase of a very expensive sailboat (which both contended they "really couldn't afford"), by saying, "Hey, if anybody knows that you can't take it with you, it's us—we figured we might as well enjoy it while we can." Another commented, "Most of the people in this community would never want to do what I do, but most of them would like to have my income."

■ ■ ■ SUMMARY AND CONCLUSION

This study describes and analyzes how people in the funeral industry attempt to reduce and neutralize the stigma associated with their occupations. Morticians and funeral directors are particularly stigmatized, not only because they perform work that few others would be willing to do (preparing dead bodies for burial), but also because they profit from death. Consequently, members of the funeral industry consciously work at stigma reduction.

Paramount among their strategies are symbolically redefining their work. This especially involves avoiding all language that reminds their customer of death, the body, and retail sales; morticians and funeral directors emphasize the need for their professional services of relieving family grief and bereavement counseling. They also practice role distance, emphasize their professionalism, wrap themselves in a "shroud of service," and enjoy their relatively high socioeconomic status rather than lament their lower occupational prestige.

REFERENCES

Amos, E. P. 1983. *Kansas Funeral Profession Through the Years.* Topeka: Kansas Funeral Directors' Association.

Aries, P. 1976. *Western Attitudes Toward Death: From the Middle Ages to the Present.* Trans. P. M. Ranum. Baltimore: Johns Hopkins University Press, p. 99.

Charmaz, K. 1980. *The Social Reality of Death: Death in Contemporary America.* Reading, MA: Addison-Wesley.

Goffman, E. 1959. *The Presentation of Self in Everyday Life.* Garden City, NY: Anchor Doubleday.

Lesy, M. 1987. *The Forbidden Zone.* New York: Farrar, Straus & Giroux.

Pavalko, R. M. 1988. *Sociology of Occupations and Profession,* 2nd ed. Itasca, IL: Peacock.

Pine, V. R. 1975. *Caretaker of the Dead: The American Funeral Director.* New York: Irvington.

Stephenson, J. S. 1985. *Death, Grief and Mourning: Individual and Social Realities.* New York: Free Press.

Sudnow, D. 1967. *Passing On: The Social Organization of Dying.* Englewood Cliffs, NJ: Prentice-Hall.

urner, R. E., and D. Edgley. 1976. "Death as Theater: A Dramaturgical Analysis of the American Funeral." *Sociology and Social Research,* 60 (July): 377–392.

Woods, A. S., and R. G. Delisle. 1978. "The Treatment of Death in Sympathy Cards." Pp. 95–103 in C. Winick (ed.), *Deviance and Mass Media.* Beverly Hills, CA: Sage.

Fraternities and Rape Culture

A. Ayres Boswell and Joan Z. Spade

introduction ▪ ▪ ▪ ▪ ▪

College certainly is a varied experience: challenging, with its many assignments, higher academic standards, and new vocabularies; frustrating, when concepts don't seem to sink in and instructors seem too demanding; fulfilling, with the satisfactions that come from forming new friendships and the sense of accomplishment that comes with passing courses and mastering new ideas; and, at the end, threatening, when the world of work and careers looms and, by comparison, college life suddenly appears so comfortable and inviting.

On many campuses, fraternities are part of college life, a welcome respite from onerous classroom demands. They provide friendships, fun, and an escape from responsibilities with like-minded, compatible people who share your sentiments. In some cases, bonds forged in fraternities become significant foundations for successful careers. Some fraternities have a darker side, however: a definition of masculinity that includes a calculated exploitation that destroys people. Not all fraternities are the same, though, and this selection exposes cultural elements that minimize or maximize the exploitation of women.

Thinking Critically

As you read this selection, ask yourself:

1. Based on this article, what *social* factors produce rape?

2. Compare the characteristics of the high-risk and low-risk fraternities analyzed in this selection. Why do you think that fraternities differ so greatly?

3. How do the findings reported in this selection support or detract from the main sociological principle emphasized in *Sociology*—that even our intensely personal characteristics (our attitudes, self-evaluations, and points of view) have *social* origins and are *socially* maintained?

Date rape and acquaintance rape on college campuses are topics of concern to both researchers and college administrators. . . . Although considerable attention focuses on the incidence of rape, we know relatively little about the context or the *rape culture* surrounding date [and] acquaintance rape. Rape culture is a set of values and beliefs that provide[s] an environment conducive to rape. The term applies to a generic culture surrounding and promoting rape, not the specific settings in which rape is likely to occur. We believe that the specific settings also are important in defining relationships between men and women.

Some have argued that fraternities are places where rape is likely to occur on college campuses and that the students most likely to accept rape myths and be more sexually aggressive are more likely to live in fraternities and sororities, consume higher doses of alcohol and drugs, and place a higher value on social life at college. Others suggest that sexual aggression is learned in settings such as fraternities and is not part of predispositions or preexisting attitudes. To prevent further incidences of rape on college campuses, we need to understand what it is about fraternities in particular and college life in general that may contribute to the maintenance of a rape culture on college campuses.

Our approach is to identify the social contexts that link fraternities to campus rape and promote a rape culture. Instead of assuming that all fraternities provide an environment conducive to rape, we compare the interactions of men and women at fraternities identified on campus as being especially *dangerous* places for women, where the likelihood of rape is high, to those seen as *safer* places, where the perceived probability of rape occurring is lower. . .

■ ■ ■ ■ METHOD

We observed social interactions between men and women at a private coeducational school in which a high percentage (49.4 percent) of students affiliate with Greek organizations. The university has an undergraduate population of approximately 4,500 students, just more than one third of whom are women; the students are primarily from upper-middle-class families. . . .

We used a variety of data collection approaches: observations of interactions between men and women at fraternity parties and bars, formal interviews, and informal conversations. The first author, a former undergraduate at this school and a graduate student at the time of the study, collected the data. She knew about the social life at the school and had established rapport and trust between herself and undergraduate students as a teaching assistant in a human sexuality course.

. . . In our study, 40 women students identified fraternities that they considered to be high risk, or to have more sexually aggressive members and higher incidence of rape, as well as fraternities that they considered to be safe houses. The women represented all four years of undergraduate college and different living groups (sororities,

From A. Ayres Boswell and Joan Z. Spade, "Fraternities and Collegiate Rape Culture: Why Are Some Fraternities More Dangerous Places for Women?" *Gender & Society,* April 1996, Vol. 10, No. 2: 133–147. © 1996 Sociologists for Women in Society. Reprinted with permission of Sage Publications, Inc.

residence halls, and off-campus housing). Observations focused on the four fraterni-ties named most often by these women as high-risk houses and the four identified as low-risk houses.

Throughout the spring semester, the first author observed at two fraternity parties each weekend at two different houses (fraternities could have parties only on weekends at this campus). . . . The observer focused on the social context as well as interaction among participants at each setting. In terms of social context, she observed the following: ratio of men to women, physical setting such as the party decor and theme, use and control of alcohol and level of intoxication, and explicit and implicit norms. She noted interactions between men and women (i.e., physical contact, conversational style, use of jokes) and the relations among men (i.e., their treatment of pledges and other men at fraternity parties). . . .

■ ■ ■ ■ RESULTS

The Settings

Fraternity Parties.   We observed several differences in the quality of the interaction of men and women at parties at high-risk fraternities compared to those at low-risk houses. A typical party at a low-risk house included an equal number of women and men. The social atmosphere was friendly, with considerable interaction between women and men. Men and women danced in groups and in couples, with many of the couples kissing and displaying affection, toward each other. Brothers explained that, because many of the men in these houses had girlfriends, it was normal to see couples kissing on the dance floor. Coed groups engaged in conversations at many of these houses, with women and men engaging in friendly exchanges, giving the im-pression that they knew each other well. Almost no cursing and yelling was observed at parties in low-risk houses; when pushing occurred, the participants apologized. Respect for women extended to the women's bathrooms, which were clean and well supplied.

At high-risk houses, parties typically had skewed gender ratios, sometimes involving more men and other times involving more women. Gender segregation also was evident at these parties, with the men on one side of a room or in the bar drinking while women gathered in another area. Men treated women differently in the high-risk houses. The women's bathrooms in the high-risk houses were filthy, including clogged toilets and vomit in the sinks. When a brother was told of the mess in the bathroom at a high-risk house, he replied, "Good, maybe some of these beer wenches will leave so there will be more beer for us."

Men attending parties at high-risk houses treated women less respectfully, en-gaging in jokes, conversations, and behaviors that degraded women. Men made a display of assessing women's bodies and rated them with thumbs up or thumbs down for the other men in the sight of the women. One man attending a party at a high-risk fraternity said to another, "Did you know that this week is Women's Awareness

Week? I guess that means we get to abuse them more this week." Men behaved more crudely at parties at high-risk houses. At one party, a brother dropped his pants, including his underwear, while dancing in front of several women. Another brother slid across the dance floor completely naked.

The atmosphere at parties in high-risk fraternities was less friendly overall. With the exception of greetings, men and women rarely smiled or laughed and spoke to each other less often than was the case at parties in low-risk houses. The few one-on-one conversations between women and men appeared to be strictly flirtatious (lots of eye contact, touching, and very close talking). It was rare to see a group of men and women together talking. Men were openly hostile, which made the high-risk parties seem almost threatening at times. For example, there was a lot of touching, pushing, profanity, and name calling, some done by women.

Students at parties at the high-risk houses seemed self-conscious and aware of the presence of members of the opposite sex, an awareness that was sexually charged. Dancing early in the evening was usually between women. Close to midnight, the sex ratio began to balance out with the arrival of more men or more women. Couples began to dance together but in a sexual way (close dancing with lots of pelvic thrusts). Men tried to pick up women using lines such as "Want to see my fish tank?" and "Let's go upstairs so that we can talk; I can't hear what you're saying in here."

Although many of the same people who attended high-risk parties also attended low-risk parties, their behavior changed as they moved from setting to setting. Group norms differed across contexts as well. At a party that was held jointly at a low-risk house with a high-risk fraternity, the ambience was that of a party at a high-risk fraternity with heavier drinking, less dancing, and fewer conversations between women and men. The men from both high- and low-risk fraternities were very aggressive; a fight broke out, and there was pushing and shoving on the dance floor and in general.

As others have found, fraternity brothers at high-risk houses on this campus told about routinely discussing their sexual exploits at breakfast the morning after parties and sometimes at house meetings. During these sessions, the brothers we interviewed said that men bragged about what they did the night before with stories of sexual conquests often told by the same men, usually sophomores. The women involved in these exploits were women they did not know or knew but did not respect, or faceless victims. Men usually treated girlfriends with respect and did not talk about them in these storytelling sessions. Men from low-risk houses, however, did not describe similar sessions in their houses. . . .

Gender Relations

Relations between women and men are shaped by the contexts in which they meet and interact. As is the case on other college campuses, *hooking up* has replaced dating on this campus, and fraternities are places where many students hook up. Hooking up is a loosely applied term on college campuses that had different meanings for men and women on this campus.

Most men defined hooking up similarly. One man said it was something that happens

> when you are really drunk and meet up with a woman you sort of know, or possibly don't know at all and don't care about. You go home with her with the intention of getting as much sexual, physical pleasure as she'll give you, which can range any-where from kissing to intercourse, without any strings attached.

The exception to this rule is when men hook up with women they admire. Men said they are less likely to press for sexual activity with someone they know and like be-cause they want the relationship to continue and be based on respect.

Women's version of hooking up differed. Women said they hook up only with men they cared about and described hooking up as kissing and petting but not sexual intercourse. Many women said that hooking up was disappointing because they wanted longer-term relationships. First-year women students realized quickly that hook-ups were usually one-night stands with no strings attached, but many contin-ued to hook up because they had few opportunities to develop relationships with men on campus. One first-year woman . . . said, "It was fun in the beginning. You get a lot of attention and kiss a lot of boys and think this is what college is about, but it gets tiresome fast."

Whereas first-year women get tired of the hook-up scene early on, many men do not become bored with it until their junior or senior year. As one upperclassman said, "The whole game of hooking up became really meaningless and tiresome for me during my second semester of my sophomore year, but most of my friends didn't get bored with it until the following year."

In contrast to hooking up, students also described monogamous relationships with steady partners. Some type of commitment was expected, but most people did not anticipate marriage. The term *seeing each other* was applied when people were sexually involved but free to date other people. This type of relationship involved less commitment than did one of boyfriend/girlfriend but was not considered to be a hook-up.

The general consensus of women and men interviewed on this campus was that the Greek system, called "the hill," set the scene for gender relations. The predomi-nance of Greek membership and subsequent living arrangements segregated men and women. During the week, little interaction occurred between women and men after their first year in college because students in fraternities or sororities live and dine in separate quarters. In addition, many non-Greek upper-class students move off campus into apartments. Therefore, students see each other in classes or in the library, but there is no place where students can just hang out together.

Both men and women said that fraternities dominate campus social life, a situ-ation that everyone felt limited opportunities for meaningful interactions. One senior Greek man said,

> This environment is horrible and so unhealthy for good male and female relationships and interactions to occur. It is so segregated and male dominated. . . . It is our party,

with our rules and our beer. We are allowing these women and other men to come to our party. Men can feel superior in their domain.

Comments from a senior woman reinforced his views: "Men are dominant; they are the kings of the campus. It is their environment that they allow us to enter; therefore, we have to abide by their rules." A junior woman described fraternity parties as

> good for meeting acquaintances but almost impossible to really get to know anyone. The environment is so superficial, probably because there are so many social cliques due to the Greek system. Also, the music is too loud and the people are too drunk to attempt to have a real conversation, anyway.

Some students claim that fraternities even control the dating relationships of their members. One senior woman said, "Guys dictate how dating occurs on this campus, whether it's cool, who it's with, how much time can be spent with the girlfriend and with the brothers." Couples either left campus for an evening or hung out separately with their own same-gender friends at fraternity parties, finally getting together with each other at about 2 A.M. Couples rarely went together to fraternity parties. Some men felt that a girlfriend was just a replacement for a hook-up. According to one junior man, "Basically a girlfriend is someone you go to at 2 A.M. after you've hung out with the guys. She is the sexual outlet that the guys can't provide you with."

Some fraternity brothers pressure each other to limit their time with and commitment to their girlfriends. One senior man said, "The hill [fraternities] and girlfriends don't mix." A brother described a constant battle between girlfriends and brothers over who the guy is going out with for the night, with the brothers usually winning. Brothers teased men with girlfriends with remarks such as "whipped" or "where's the ball and chain?" A brother from a high-risk house said that few brothers at his house had girlfriends; some did, but it was uncommon. One man said that from the minute he was a pledge he knew he would probably never have a girlfriend on this campus because "it was just not the norm in my house. No one has girlfriends; the guys have too much fun with [each other]."

The pressure on men to limit their commitment to girlfriends, however, was not true of all fraternities or of all men on campus. Couples attended low-risk fraternity parties together, and men in the low-risk houses went out on dates more often. A [man] in one low-risk house said that about 70 percent of the members of his house were involved in relationships with women, including the pledges (who were sophomores).

Treatment of Women

Not all men held negative attitudes toward women that are typical of a rape culture, and not all social contexts promoted the negative treatment of women. When men were asked whether they treated the women on campus with respect, the most common response was "On an individual basis, yes, but when you have a group of men together, no." Men said that, when together in groups with other men, they sensed a pressure to be disrespectful toward women. A first-year man's perception of the treatment of women was that "they are treated with more respect to their faces, but behind closed doors, with a group of men present, respect for women is not an issue." One senior man stated, "In general, college-aged men don't treat women their age with respect because 90 percent of them think of women as merely a means to sex." Women reinforced this perception. A first-year woman stated, "Men here are more interested in hooking up and drinking beer than they are in getting to know women as real people." Another woman said, "Men here use and abuse women."

Characteristic of rape culture, a double standard of sexual behavior for men versus women was prevalent on this campus. As one Greek senior man stated, "Women who sleep around are sluts and get bad reputations; men who do are champions and get a pat on the back from their brothers." Women also supported a double standard for sexual behavior by criticizing sexually active women. A first-year woman spoke out against women who are sexually active: "I think some girls here make it difficult for the men to respect women as a whole."

One concrete example of demeaning sexually active women on this campus is the "walk of shame." Fraternity brothers come out on the porches of their houses the night after parties and heckle women walking by. It is assumed that these women spent the night at fraternity houses and that the men they were with did not care enough about them to drive them home. Although sororities now reside in former fraternity houses, this practice continues and sometimes the victims of hecklings are sorority women on their way to study in the library. . . .

Fraternity men most often mistreated women they did not know personally. Men and women alike reported incidents in which brothers observed other brothers having sex with unknown women or women they knew only casually. A sophomore woman's experience exemplifies this anonymous state: "I don't mind if 10 guys were watching or it was videotaped. That's expected on this campus. It's the fact that he didn't apologize or even offer to drive me home that really upset me." Descriptions of sexual encounters involved the satisfaction of men by nameless women. A brother in a high-risk fraternity, described a similar occurrence:

> A brother of mine was hooking up upstairs with an unattractive woman who had been pursuing him all night. He told some brothers to go outside the window and watch. Well, one thing led to another and they were almost completely naked when the woman noticed the brothers outside. She was then unwilling to go any further, so the brother went outside and yelled at the other brothers and then closed the shades. I don't know if he scored or not, because the woman was pretty upset. But he did win the award for hooking up with the ugliest chick that weekend. . . .

■ ■ ■ DISCUSSION AND CONCLUSION

These findings describe the physical and normative aspects of one college campus as they relate to attitudes about and relations between men and women. Our findings suggest that an explanation emphasizing rape culture also must focus on those characteristics of the social setting that play a role in defining heterosexual relationships on college campuses. The degradation of women as portrayed in rape culture was not found in all fraternities on this campus. Both group norms and individual behavior changed as students went from one place to another. Although individual men are the ones who rape, we found that some settings are more likely places for rape than are others. Our findings suggest that rape cannot be seen only as an isolated act and blamed on individual behavior and proclivities, whether it be alcohol consumption or attitudes. We also must consider characteristics of the settings that promote the behaviors that reinforce a rape culture.

Relations between women and men at parties in low-risk fraternities varied considerably from those in high-risk houses. Peer pressure and situational norms influenced women as well as men. Although many men in high- and low-risk houses shared similar views and attitudes about the Greek system, women on this campus, and date rape, their behaviors at fraternity parties were quite different. . . .

The social scene on this campus, and on most others, offers women and men few other options to socialize. Although there may be no such thing as a completely safe fraternity party for women, parties at low-risk houses . . . encouraged men and women to get know each other better and decreased the probability that women would become faceless victims. Although both men and women found the social scene on this campus demeaning, neither demanded different settings for socializing, and attendance at fraternity parties is a common form of entertainment.

These findings suggest that a more conducive environment for conversation can promote more positive interactions between men and women. Simple changes would provide the opportunity for men and women to interact in meaningful ways such as adding places to sit and lowering the volume of music at fraternity parties or having parties in neutral locations, where men are not in control. The typical party room in fraternity houses includes a place to dance but not to sit and talk. The music often is loud, making it difficult, if not impossible, to carry on conversations; however, there were more conversations at the low-risk parties, where there also was more respect shown toward women. . . .

The degree of conformity required by Greeks may be greater than that required in most social groups, with considerable pressure to adopt and maintain the image of their houses. The fraternity system intensifies the "groupthink syndrome" by solidifying the identity of the in-group and creating an us/them atmosphere. Within the fraternity culture, brothers are highly regarded and women are viewed as outsiders. For men in high-risk fraternities, women threatened their brotherhood; therefore, brothers discouraged relationships and harassed those who treated women as equals or with respect. The pressure to be one of the guys and hang out with the guys strengthens a rape culture on college campus by demeaning women and encouraging the segregation of men and women. . .

Not all men and women accepted the demeaning treatment of women, but they continued to participate in behaviors that supported aspects of a rape culture. Many women participated in the hook-up scene even after they had been humiliated and hurt because they had few other means of initiating contact with men on campus.

Men and women alike played out this scene, recognizing its injustices in many cases but being unable to change the course of their behaviors. . . .

Our findings indicate that a rape culture exists in some fraternities, especially those we identified as high-risk houses. College administrators are responding to this situation by providing counseling and educational programs that increase awareness of date rape including campaigns such as "No means no." These strategies are important in changing attitudes, values, and behaviors; however, changing individuals is not enough. The structure of campus life and the impact of that structure on gender relations on campus are highly determinative. To eliminate campus rape culture, student leaders and administrators must examine the situations in which women and men meet and restructure these settings to provide opportunities for respectful interaction. Change may not require abolishing fraternities; rather, it may require promoting settings that facilitate positive gender relations.

PART

III Social Inequality

It is impossible to have a society of equals. Despite the dreams of some to build an egalitarian society, every society will be marked by inequality. There will always be what sociologists call *social stratification*.

Each social group has a value system; that is, it values certain things above others. In a tribal group, this could be running, shooting arrows, throwing spears, or showing bravery. Some members of the tribe will have greater abilities to do the particular things that their group values—no matter what those things may be. Their abilities and accomplishments will set them apart. These people will be looked up to and likely treated differently.

By considering abilities and accomplishments, as in a tribal group, we can see why social distinctions are inevitable. Social stratification, however, is based on much more than ability and accomplishment. In fact, ability and achievement are seldom the bases of social stratification. Much more common are inherited social distinctions.

Every society stratifies its members according to whatever particular values it cherishes. That is, every human group divides its people into layers, and treats each layer differently. Once a society is stratified, birth ushers children into the various positions (statuses) that society has laid out. By virtue of where their parents are located in their society's social structure, children inherit some of the social distinctions of their parents. These can be their religion (Christian, Jew, Muslim), social class (upper, middle, lower), caste (Brahmin, Shudra), or any other distinction that their group makes.

Because their group has already set up rules about gender, children also inherit a set of wide-ranging expectations based on their sex. So it may be with their race or ethnicity. In addition, with our current geopolitics, birth also ushers children onto a world stage, where they inherit their country's position in what is known as *global stratification*. Their nation may be rich and powerful or poor and weak. Wherever it is located on the world scene, this, too, has fundamental consequences for people's lives.

In the third part of this book, we look at some of the major aspects of social inequality. We begin with a broad view of global stratification. Barbara Ehrenreich and Annette Fuentes's article makes it evident that where your nation is located in the global scheme of things makes a fundamental difference for what happens to you in life. Herbert Gans, following with a functional analysis of poverty, analyzes why society *needs* poor people. From Barrie

Thorne's observations of children in grade school, we can see how early relations between boys and girls are a prelude to inequity in adult gender roles. Karen Brodkin then turns the focus on the *social* basis of race-ethnicity, analyzing how U.S. Jews "became white." With Cynthia Loucks's report on the treatment that her mother received in a nursing home, we close this third part with a focus on the social inequality of age.

Life on the Global Assembly Line

Barbara Ehrenreich and Annette Fuentes

introduction ▪ ▪ ▪ ▪ ▪

One of the world's most significant changes is the *globalization of capitalism*. Capitalists won the Cold War and vanquished socialists (at least for the time being). Victorious, capitalists are expanding into every nook and cranny of the planet. Major targets are the Least Industrialized Nations. (In this selection, these nations are called the *Third World*, an outdated term, as it refers to nations that are neither part of the First World, the alliance led by the United States, or part of the Second World, the alliance led by the Soviet Union. Other authors use the term *undeveloped nations*, a misnomer, for "undeveloped" represents a chauvinistic, ethnocentric view of nations that are not industrialized; they all have fully developed, intricate cultures.) Eyeing the material wealth of the Most Industrialized Nations, and mindful of the West's cultural dominance, most Least Industrialized Nations long to embrace capitalism. For their part, the Most Industrialized Nations view most Least Industrialized Nations as prizes, vast sources of cheap resources and labor, as well as an expanding base of consumers.

 Downsizing, a fancy way of saying that a company s firing workers, accompanies the globalization of capitalism. In their frenetic pursuit of the bottom line, U.S. firms, followed more reluctantly by the Europeans and the Japanese, have laid off millions of workers. From the point of view of profit—which is capitalism's bottom line—this makes sense. The Least Industrialized Nations have hundreds of millions of workers who eagerly await the crumbs of the Most Industrialized Nations. This situation is a capitalist's dream: docile workers who are willing to accept peanuts for wages, and glad to get them. As Ehrenreich and Fuentes point out, the most needy of these workers—and thus the most docile and willing to work for the cheapest wages—are women.

Thinking Critically

As you read this selection, ask yourself:

1. Is the employment of young women in Western factories that have been relocated to the Least Industrialized Nations an example of exploitation by capitalists or opportunity for the workers?

2. How does work in these factories harm the workers? How does it benefit them?

3. What solutions do you see to the problems described in this selection?

In Ciudad Juárez, Mexico, Anna M. rises at 5 A.M. to feed her son before starting on the two-hour bus trip to the maquiladora (factory). He will spend the day along with four other children in a neighbor's one-room home. Anna's husband, frustrated by being unable to find work for himself, left for the United States six months ago. She wonders, as she carefully applies her new lip gloss, whether she ought to consider herself still married. It might be good to take a night course, become a secretary. But she seldom gets home before eight at night, and the factory, where she stitches brassieres that will be sold in the United States through J.C. Penney, pays only $48 a week.

In Penang, Malaysia, Julie K. is up before the three other young women with whom she shares a room, and starts heating the leftover rice from last night's supper. She looks good in the company's green-trimmed uniform, and she's proud to work in a modern, American-owned factory. Only not quite so proud as when she started working three years ago—she thinks as she squints out the door at a passing group of women. Her job involves peering all day through a microscope, bonding hair-thin gold wires to a silicon chip destined to end up inside a pocket calculator, and at twenty-one, she is afraid she can no longer see very clearly.

Every morning, between four and seven, thousands of women like Anna and Julie head out for the day shift. In Ciudad Juárez, they crowd into *ruteras* (run-down vans) for the trip from the slum neighborhoods to the industrial parks on the outskirts of the city. In Penang they squeeze, sixty or more at a time, into buses for the trip from the village to the low, modern factory buildings of the Bayan Lepas free-trade zone. In Taiwan, they walk from the dormitories—where the night shift is already asleep in the still-warm beds—through the checkpoints in the high fence surrounding the factory zone.

This is the world's new industrial proletariat: young, female, Third World. Viewed from the "first world," they are still faceless, genderless "cheap labor," signaling their existence only through a label or tiny imprint—"made in Hong Kong," or Taiwan, Korea, the Dominican Republic, Mexico, the Philippines. . . . Anyone whose image of Third World women features picturesque peasants with babies slung on their backs should be prepared to update it. Just in the last decade, Third World women have become a critical element in the global economy and a key "resource" for expanding multinational corporations.

Excerpted from "Life on the Global Assembly Line." *Ms. Magazine*, January 1981. Copyright © 1981 by Barbara Ehrenreich and Annette Fuentes. Used by permission of the authors.

It doesn't take more than second-grade arithmetic to understand what's happening. In many Third World countries, a woman will earn $3 to $5 a *day*. The logic of the situation is compelling: why pay someone in Massachusetts $5 an hour to do what someone in Manila will do for $2.50 a day? Or, as a corollary, why pay a male worker anywhere to do what a female worker will do for 40 to 60 percent less?

And so, almost everything that can be packed up is being moved out to the Third World, not heavy industry, but just about anything light enough to travel—garment manufacture, textiles, toys, footwear, pharmaceuticals, wigs, appliance parts, tape decks, computer components, plastic goods. . . . But what's going on is much more than a matter of runaway shops. Economists are talking about a "new international division of labor," in which the process of production is broken down and the fragments are dispersed to different parts of the world. In general, the low-skilled jobs are farmed out to the Third World, where labor costs are minuscule, while control over the overall process and technology remains safely at company headquarters in "first world" countries like the United States and Japan. . . .

So much any economist could tell you. What is less often noted is the *gender* breakdown of the emerging international division of labor. Eighty to ninety percent of the low-skilled assembly jobs that go to the Third World are performed by women— in a remarkable switch from earlier patterns of foreign-dominated industrialization. Until now, "development" under the aegis of foreign corporations has usually meant more jobs for men and—compared to traditional agricultural society—a diminished economic status for women. But multinational corporations and Third World governments alike consider assembly-line work—whether the product is Barbie dolls or missile parts—to be "women's work."

One reason is that women can, in many countries, still be legally paid less than men. But the sheer tedium of the jobs adds to the multinationals' preference for women workers—a preference made clear, for example, by this ad from a Mexican newspaper: *We need female workers, older than 17, younger than 30, single and without children: minimum education primary school, maximum education one year of preparatory school [high school]; available for all shifts.*

It's an article of faith with management that only women can do, or will do, the monotonous, painstaking work that American business is exporting to the Third World. Bill Mitchell, whose job is to attract United States businesses to the Bermudez Industrial Park in Ciudad Juárez, told us with a certain macho pride: "A man just won't stay in this tedious kind of work. He'd walk out in a couple of hours." The personnel manager of a light assembly plant in Taiwan told anthropologist Linda Gail Arrigo: "Young male workers are too restless and impatient to do monotonous work with no career value. If displeased, they sabotage the machines and even threaten the foreman. But girls? At most, they cry a little."

In fact, the American businessmen we talked to claimed that Third World women genuinely enjoy doing the very things that would drive a man to assault and sabotage. "You should watch these kids going into work," Bill Mitchell told us. "You don't have any sullenness here. They smile." A top-level management consultant who specializes in advising American companies on where to relocate their factories gave us this global generalization: "The [factory] girls genuinely enjoy themselves. They're away from their families. They have spending money. They can buy motorbikes, whatever. Of course, it's a regulated experience too—with dormitories to live in—so it's healthful experience."

What is the real experience of the women in the emerging Third World industrial work force? The conventional Western stereotypes leap to mind: You can't really compare, the standards are so different. . . . Everything's easier in warm countries. . . . They really don't have any alternatives. . . . Commenting on the low wages his company pays its women workers in Singapore, a Hewlett-Packard vice president said: "They live much differently here than we do. . . ." But the differences are ultimately very simple. To start with, they have less money.

The great majority of women in the new Third World work force live at or near the subsistence level for one person, whether they work for a multinational corporation or a locally owned factory. In the Philippines, for example, starting wages in U.S.-owned electronics plants are between $34 and $46 a month, compared to a cost of living of $37 a month; in Indonesia the starting wages are actually about $7 a month less than the cost of living. "Living," in these cases, should be interpreted minimally: a diet of rice, dried fish, and water—a Coke might cost a half-day's wages—and lodging in a room occupied by four or more other people. Rachael Grossman, a researcher with the Southeast Asia Resource Center, found women employees of U.S. multinational firms in Malaysia and the Philippines living four to eight in a room in boardinghouses, or squeezing into tiny extensions built onto squatter huts near the factory. Where companies do provide dormitories for their employees, they are not of the "healthful," collegiate variety implied by our corporate informant. Staff from the American Friends Service Committee report that dormitory space is likely to be crowded, with bed rotation paralleling shift rotation—while one shift works, another sleeps, as many as twenty to a room. In one case in Thailand, they found the dormitory "filthy," with workers forced to find their own place to sleep among "splintered floorboards, rusting sheets of metal, and scraps of dirty cloth.". . .

But wages on a par with what an eleven-year-old American could earn on a paper route, and living conditions resembling what Engels found in nineteenth-century Manchester are only part of the story. The rest begins at the factory gate. The work that multinational corporations export to the Third World is not only the most tedious, but often the most hazardous part of the production process. The countries they go to are, for the most part, those that will guarantee no interference from health and safety inspectors, trade unions, or even freelance reformers. As a result, most Third World factory women work under conditions that already have broken or will break their health—or their nerves—within a few years, and often before they've worked long enough to earn any more than a subsistence wage.

Consider first the electronics industry, which is generally thought to be the safest and cleanest of the exported industries. The factory buildings are low and modern, like those one might find in a suburban American industrial park. Inside, rows of young women, neatly dressed in the company uniform or T-shirt, work quietly at their stations. . . . In many plants toxic chemicals and solvents sit in open containers, filling the work area with fumes that can literally knock you out. "We have been told of cases where ten to twelve women passed out at once," an AFSC field worker in northern Mexico told us, "and the newspapers report this as 'mass hysteria.'"

In one stage of the electronics assembly process, the workers have to dip the circuits into open vats of acid. According to Irene Johnson and Carol Bragg, who toured the National Semiconductor plant in Penang, Malaysia, the women who do the dipping "wear rubber gloves and boots, but these sometimes leak, and burns are common." Occasionally, whole fingers are lost. More commonly, what electronics workers lose is the 20/20 vision they are required to have when they are hired. Most electronics workers spend seven to nine hours a day peering through microscopes, straining to meet their quota.

One study in South Korea found that most electronics assembly workers developed severe eye problems after only one year of employment; 88 percent had chronic conjunctivitis; 44 percent became near-sighted, and 19 percent developed astigmatism. A manager for Hewlett-Packard's Malaysia plant, in an interview with Rachael Grossman, denied that there were any eye problems: "These girls are used to working with 'scopes.' We've found no eye problems. But it sure makes me dizzy to look through those things."

Electronics, recall, is the "cleanest" of the exported industries. Conditions in the garment and textile industry rival those of any nineteenth-century (or twentieth—see below) sweatshops. The firms, generally local subcontractors to large American chains such as J.C. Penney and Sears, as well as smaller manufacturers, are usually even more indifferent to the health of their employees than the multinationals. Some of the worst conditions have been documented in South Korea, where the garment and textile industries have helped spark that country's "economic miracle." Workers are packed into poorly lit rooms, where summer temperatures rise above 100 degrees. Textile dust, which can cause permanent lung damage, fills the air. When there are rush orders, management may require forced overtime of as much as 48 hours at a stretch, and if that seems to go beyond the limits of human endurance, pep pills and amphetamine injections are thoughtfully provided. In her diary (originally published in a magazine now banned by the South Korean government), Min Chong Suk, thirty, a sewing-machine operator, wrote of working from 7 A.M. to 11:30 P.M. in a garment factory: "When [the apprentices] shake the waste threads from the clothes, the whole room fills with dust, and it is hard to breathe. Since we've been working in such dusty air, there have been increasing numbers of people getting tuberculosis, bronchitis, and eye diseases. Since we are women, it makes us so sad when we have pale, unhealthy, wrinkled faces like dried-up spinach. . . . It seems to me that no one knows our blood dissolves into the threads and seams, with sighs and sorrow."

In all the exported industries, the most invidious, inescapable health hazard is stress. On their home ground United States corporations are not likely to sacrifice human comfort for productivity. On someone else's home ground, however, anything goes. Lunch breaks may be barely long enough for a woman to stand in line at the canteen or hawkers' stalls. Visits to the bathroom are treated as a privilege; in some cases, workers must raise their hands for permission to use the toilet, and waits up to a half hour are common. Rotating shifts—the day shift one week, the night shift the next—wreak havoc with sleep patterns. Because inaccuracies or failure to meet production quotas can mean substantial pay losses, the pressures are quickly internalized; stomach ailments and nervous problems are not unusual in the multinationals' Third World female work force. . . .

As if poor health and the stress of factory life weren't enough to drive women into early retirement, management actually encourages a high turnover in many industries. "As you know, when seniority rises, wages rise," the management consultant in U.S. multinationals told us. He explained that it's cheaper to train a fresh supply of teenagers than to pay experienced women higher wages. "Older" women, aged twenty-three or twenty-four, are likely to be laid off and not rehired.

We estimate, based on fragmentary data from several sources, that the multinational corporations may already have used up (cast off) as many as 6 million Third World workers—women who are too ill, too old (thirty is over the hill in most industries), or too exhausted to be useful any more. Few "retire" with any transferable skills or savings. The lucky ones find husbands.

The unlucky ones find themselves at the margins of society—as bar girls, "hostesses," or prostitutes.

> At 21, Julie's greatest fear is that she will never be able to find a husband. She knows that just being a "factory girl" is enough to give anyone a bad reputation. When she first started working at the electronics company, her father refused to speak to her for three months. Now every time she leaves Penang to go back to visit her home village she has to put up with a lecture on morality from her older brother—not to mention a barrage of lewd remarks from men outside her family. If they knew that she had actually gone out on a few dates, that she had been to a discotheque, that she had once kissed a young man who said he was a student. . . . Julie's stomach tightens as she imagines her family's reaction. She tries to concentrate on the kind of man she would like to marry: an engineer or technician of some sort, someone who had been to California, where the company headquarters are located and where even the grandmothers wear tight pants and lipstick—someone who had a good attitude about women. But if she ends up having to wear glasses, like her cousin who worked three years at the "scopes," she might as well forget about finding anyone to marry her.

One of the most serious occupational hazards that Julie and millions of women like her may face is the lifelong stigma of having been a "factory girl." Most of the cultures favored by multinational corporations in their search for cheap labor are patriarchal in the grand old style: any young woman who is not under the wing of a father, husband, or older brother must be "loose." High levels of unemployment among men, as in Mexico, contribute to male resentment of working women. Add to all this the fact that certain companies—American electronics firms are in the lead—actively promote Western-style sexual objectification as a means of ensuring employee loyalty: there are company-sponsored cosmetics classes, "guess whose legs these are" contests, and swimsuit-style beauty contests where the prize might be a free night *for two* in a fancy hotel. Corporate-promoted Westernization only heightens the hostility many men feel toward any independent working women—having a job is bad enough, wearing jeans and mascara to work is going too far.

Anthropologist Patricia Fernandez, who has worked in a *maquiladora* herself, believes that the stigmatization of working women serves, indirectly, to keep them in line. "You have to think of the kind of socialization that girls experience in a very Catholic—or, for that matter, Muslim—society. The fear of having a 'reputation' is enough to make a lot of women bend over backward to be 'respectable' and ladylike, which is just what management wants." She points out that in northern Mexico, the tabloids delight in playing up stories of alleged vice in the *maquiladoras*—indiscriminate sex on the job, epidemics of venereal disease, fetuses found in factory rest rooms. "I worry about this because there are those who treat you differently as soon as they know you have a job at the *maquiladora*," one woman told Fernandez. "Maybe they think that if you have to work, there is a chance you're a whore."

And there is always the chance you'll wind up as one. Probably only a small minority of Third World factory workers turn to prostitution when their working days come to an end. But it is, as for women everywhere, the employment of last resort, the only thing to do when the factories don't need you and traditional society won't—or, for economic reasons, can't—take you back. In the Philippines, the brothel business is expanding as fast as the factory system. If they can't use you one way, they can use you another.

There has been no international protest about the exploitation of Third World women by multinational corporations—no thundering denunciations from the floor of the United Nations General Assembly, no angry resolutions from the Conference of the Non-Aligned Countries. Sociologist Robert Snow, who has been tracing the multinationals on their way south and eastward for years, explained why: "The Third World governments *want* the multinationals to move in. There's cutthroat competition to attract the corporations."

The governments themselves gain little revenue from this kind of investment, though—especially since most offer tax holidays and freedom from export duties in order to attract the multinationals in the first place. Nor do the people as a whole benefit, according to a highly placed Third World woman within the UN. "The multinationals like to say they're contributing to development," she told us, "but they come into our countries for one thing—cheap labor. If the labor stops being so cheap, they can move on. So how can you call that development? It depends on the people being poor and staying poor." But there are important groups that do stand to gain when the multinationals set up shop in their countries: local entrepreneurs who subcontract to the multinationals; Harvard- or Berkeley-educated "technocrats" who become local management; and government officials who specialize in cutting red tape for an "agent's fee" or an outright bribe.

In the competition for multinational investment, local governments advertise their women shamelessly, and an investment brochure issued by the Malaysian government informs multinational executives that: "The manual dexterity of the Oriental female is famous the world over. Her hands are small, and she works fast with extreme care. Who, therefore, could be better qualified by nature and inheritance, to contribute to the efficiency of a bench-assembly production line than the Oriental girl?"

The Royal Thai Embassy sends American businesses a brochure guaranteeing that in Thailand, "the relationship between the employer and the employee is like that of a guardian and ward. It is easy to win and maintain the loyalty of workers as long as they are treated with kindness and courtesy." The facing page offers a highly selective photo-study of Thai womanhood: giggling shyly, bowing submissively, and working cheerfully on an assembly line. . . .

The governments advertise their women, sell them, and keep them in line for the multinational "johns." But there are other parties to the growing international traffic in women—such as the United Nations Industrial Development Organization (UNIDO), the World Bank, and the United States government itself.

UNIDO, for example, has been a major promoter of "free trade zones." These are enclaves within nations that offer multinational corporations a range of creature comforts, including: freedom from paying taxes and export duties; low-cost water, power, and buildings; exemption from whatever labor laws may apply in the country as a whole; and, in some cases, such security features as barbed wire, guarded check-points, and government-paid police.

Then there is the World Bank, which over the past decade has lent several billion dollars to finance the roads, airports, power plants, and even the first-class hotels that multinational corporations need in order to set up business in Third World countries. The Sri Lankan garment industry, which like other Third World garment industries survives by subcontracting to major Western firms, was set up on the advice of the World Bank and with a $20 million World Bank loan. This particular experiment in "development" offers young women jobs at a global low of $5 for a six-day week. Gloria Scott, the head of the World Bank's Women and Development Program, sounded distinctly uncomfortable when we asked her about the bank's role in promoting the exploitation of Third World women. "Our job is to help eliminate poverty. It is not our responsibility if the multinationals come in and offer such low wages. It's the responsibility of the governments.". . .

But the most powerful promoter of exploitative conditions for Third World women is the United States government itself. For example, the notoriously repressive Korean textile industry was developed with the help of $400 million in aid from the U.S. State Department. Malaysia became a low-wage haven for the electronics industry, thanks to technical assistance financed by AID, and to U.S. money (funneled through the Asian Development Bank) to help set up free trade zones. Taiwan's status as a "showcase for the free world" and a comfortable berth for multinationals is the result of three decades of financial transfusions from the United States. . . .

But the most obvious form of United States involvement, according to Lenny Siegel, the director of the Pacific Studies Center, is through "our consistent record of military aid to Third World governments that are capitalist, politically repressive, and are not striving for economic independence." Ironically, says Siegel, there are "cases where the United States made a big investment to make sure that any unions that formed would be pretty tame. Then we put in even more money to support some dictator who doesn't allow unions at all.". . .

What does our government have to say for itself? It's hard to get a straight answer—the few parts of the bureaucracy that deal with women and development seem to have little connection with those that are concerned with larger foreign policy issues. A spokesman for the Department of State told us that if multinationals offer poor working conditions (which he questioned), this was not their fault: "There are just different standards in different countries." Offering further evidence of a sheltered life, he told us that "corporations today are generally more socially responsible than even ten years ago. . . . We can expect them to treat their employees in the best way they can." But he conceded in response to a barrage of unpleasant examples, "Of course, you're going to have problems wherever you have human beings doing things." Our next stop was the Women's Division within AID. Staffer Emmy Simmons was aware of the criticisms of the quality of employment multinationals offer, but cautioned that "we can get hung up in the idea that it's exploitation without really looking at the alternatives for women." AID's concern, she said, was with the fact that population is outgrowing the agricultural capacity of many Third World countries, dislocating millions of people. From her point of view, multinationals at least provide some sort of alternative: "These people have to go somewhere."

The Uses of Poverty: The Poor Pay All

Herbert J. Gans

introduction ▪ ▪ ▪ ▪ ▪

Of the several social classes in the United States, sociologists have concentrated their studies on the poor. The super-rich and, for the most part, the ordinarily wealthy are beyond the reach of researchers. Sociologists are not members of the wealthy classes or of the power elite, and members of these groups have the means to insulate themselves from the prying eyes (and questionnaires and tape recorders) of sociologists. When it comes to the middle classes, sociologists are likely to take their members for granted. The middle classes are part of their everyday life, and, like others, sociologists often overlook the things closest to them. The characteristics and situations of the poor, however, are different enough to strike the eye of sociologists. And the poor are accessible. People in poverty are generally willing to be interviewed. They are even a bit flattered that sociologists, for the most part members of the upper middle class, will take the time to talk to them. Hardly anyone else takes them seriously.

A couple of thousand years ago, Jesus said, "The poor you'll always have with you." In this selection, as Herbert Gans places the sociological lens yet again on people in poverty, he uses a functionalist perspective to explain why we always will have people in poverty. Simply put, from a functionalist perspective, we *need* poor people.

Thinking Critically

As you read this selection, ask yourself:

1. What functions (or uses) of poverty does Gans identify?

2. Of the functions of poverty that Gans identifies, which two do you think are the most important? Which two the least important? Why?

3. Do you think that Gans has gone overboard with his analysis? That he has stretched the functionalist perspective beyond reason? Or do you agree with him? Why or why not?

Some years ago Robert K. Merton applied the notion of functional analysis to explain the continuing though maligned existence of the urban political machine: If it continued to exist, perhaps it fulfilled latent—unintended or unrecognized—positive functions. Clearly it did. Merton pointed out how the political machine provided central authority to get things done when a decentralized local government could not act, humanized the services of the impersonal bureaucracy for fearful citizens, offered concrete help (rather than abstract law or justice) to the poor, and otherwise performed services needed or demanded by many people but considered unconventional or even illegal by formal public agencies.

Today, poverty is more maligned than the political machine ever was; yet it, too, is a persistent social phenomenon. Consequently, there may be some merit in applying functional analysis to poverty, in asking whether it also has positive functions that explain its persistence.

Merton defined functions as "those observed consequences [of a phenomenon] which make for the adaptation or adjustment of a given [social] system." I shall use a slightly different definition; instead of identifying functions for an entire social system, I shall identify them for the interest groups, socioeconomic classes, and other population aggregates with shared values that "inhabit" a social system. I suspect that in a modern heterogeneous society, few phenomena are functional or dysfunctional for the society as a whole, and that most result in benefits to some groups and costs to others. Nor are any phenomena indispensable; in most instances, one can suggest what Merton calls "functional alternatives" or equivalents for them, i.e., other social patterns or policies that achieve the same positive functions but avoid the dysfunction. (In the following discussion, positive functions will be abbreviated as functions and negative functions as dysfunctions. Functions and dysfunctions, in the planner's terminology, will be described as benefits and costs.)

Associating poverty with positive functions seems at first glance to be unimaginable. Of course, the slumlord and the loan shark are commonly known to profit from the existence of poverty, but they are viewed as evil men, so their activities are classified among the dysfunctions of poverty. However, what is less often recognized, at least by the conventional wisdom, is that poverty also makes possible the existence or expansion of respectable professions and occupations, for example, penology, criminology, social work, and public health. More recently, the poor have provided jobs for professional and para-professional "poverty warriors," and for journalists and social scientists, this author included, who have supplied the information demanded by the revival of public interest in poverty.

Clearly, then, poverty and the poor may well satisfy a number of positive functions for many nonpoor groups in American society. I shall describe 13 such functions—economic, social and political—that seem to me most significant.

■ ■ ■ THE FUNCTIONS OF POVERTY

First, the existence of poverty ensures that society's "dirty work" will be done. Every society has such work: physically dirty or dangerous, temporary, dead-end and underpaid, undignified, and menial jobs. Society can fill these jobs by paying higher wages than for "clean" work, or it can force people who have no other choice to do the dirty work—and at low wages. In America, poverty functions to provide a low-wage labor pool that is willing—or rather, unable to be *un*willing—to perform dirty work at low cost. Indeed, this function of the poor is so important that in some Southern states, welfare payments have been cut off during the summer months when the poor are needed to work in the fields. Moreover, much of the debate about the Negative Income Tax and the Family Assistance Plan [welfare programs] has concerned their impact on the work incentive, by which is actually meant the incentive of the poor to do the needed dirty work if the wages therefrom are no larger than the income grant. Many economic activities that involve dirty work depend on the poor for their existence: restaurants, hospitals, parts of the garment industry, and "truck farming," among others, could not persist in their present form without the poor.

Second, because the poor are required to work at low wages, they subsidize a variety of economic activities that benefit the affluent. For example, domestics subsidize the upper-middle and upper classes, making life easier for their employers and freeing affluent women for a variety of professional, cultural, civic, and partying activities. Similarly, because the poor pay a higher proportion of their income in property and sales taxes, among others, they subsidize many state and local governmental services that benefit more affluent groups. In addition, the poor support innovation in medical practice as patients in teaching and research hospitals and as guinea pigs in medical experiments.

Third, poverty creates jobs for a number of occupations and professions that serve or "service" the poor, or protect the rest of society from them. As already noted, penology would be minuscule without the poor, as would the police. Other activities and groups that flourish because of the existence of poverty are the numbers game, the sale of heroin and cheap wines and liquors, Pentecostal ministers, faith healers, prostitutes, pawn shops, and the peacetime army, which recruits its enlisted men mainly from among the poor.

Fourth, the poor buy goods others do not want and thus prolong the economic usefulness of such goods—day-old bread, fruit and vegetables that otherwise would have to be thrown out, secondhand clothes, and deteriorating automobiles and buildings. They also provide incomes for doctors, lawyers, teachers, and others who are too old, poorly trained or incompetent to attract more affluent clients.

In addition to economic functions, the poor perform a number of social functions.

Fifth, the poor can be identified and punished as alleged or real deviants in order to uphold the legitimacy of conventional norms. To justify the desirability of hard work, thrift, honesty, and monogamy, for example, the defenders of these norms must be able to find people who can be accused of being lazy, spendthrift, dishonest, and promiscuous. Although there is some evidence that the poor are about as moral and law-abiding as anyone else, they are more likely than middle-class transgressors to be caught and punished when they participate in deviant acts. Moreover, they lack the political and cultural power to correct the stereotypes that other people hold of them and thus continue to be thought of as lazy, spendthrift, etc., by those who need living proof that moral deviance does not pay.

Sixth, and conversely, the poor offer vicarious participation to the rest of the population in the uninhibited sexual, alcoholic, and narcotic behavior in which they are alleged to participate and which, being freed from the constraints of affluence, they are often thought to enjoy more than the middle classes. Thus many people, some social scientists included, believe that the poor not only are more given to uninhibited behavior (which may be true, although it is often motivated by despair more than by lack of inhibition) but derive more pleasure from it than affluent people (which research by Lee Rainwater, Walter Miller and others shows to be patently untrue). However, whether the poor actually have more sex and enjoy it more is irrelevant; so long as middle-class people believe this to be true, they can participate in it vicariously when instances are reported in factual or fictional form.

Seventh, the poor also serve a direct cultural function when culture created by or for them is adopted by the more affluent. The rich often collect artifacts from extinct folk cultures of poor people; and almost all Americans listen to the blues, Negro spirituals, and country music, which originated among the Southern poor. Recently they have enjoyed the rock styles that were born, like the Beatles, in the slums, and in the last year, poetry written by ghetto children has become popular in literary circles. The poor also serve as culture heroes, particularly, of course, to the left; but the hobo, the cowboy, the hipster, and the mythical prostitute with a heart of gold have performed this function for a variety of groups.

Eighth, poverty helps to guarantee the status of those who are not poor. In every hierarchical society, someone has to be at the bottom; but in American society, in which social mobility is an important goal for many and people need to know where they stand, the poor function as a reliable and relatively permanent measuring rod for status comparisons. This is particularly true for the working class, whose politics is influenced by the need to maintain status distinctions between themselves and the poor, much as the aristocracy must find ways of distinguishing itself from the *nouveaux riches.*

Ninth, the poor also aid the upward mobility of groups just above them in the class hierarchy. Thus a goodly number of Americans have entered the middle class through the profits earned from the provision of goods and services in the slums, including illegal or nonrespectable ones that upper-class and upper-middle-class businessmen shun because of their low prestige. As a result, members of almost every immigrant group have financed their upward mobility by providing slum housing, entertainment, gambling, narcotics, etc., to later arrivals—most recently to blacks and Puerto Ricans.

Tenth, the poor help to keep the aristocracy busy, thus justifying its continued existence. "Society" uses the poor as clients of settlement houses and beneficiaries of charity affairs; indeed, the aristocracy must have the poor to demonstrate its superiority over other elites who devote themselves to earning money.

Eleventh, the poor, being powerless, can be made to absorb the costs of change and growth in American society. During the nineteenth century, they did the back-breaking work that built the cities; today, they are pushed out of their neighborhoods to make room for "progress." Urban renewal projects to hold middle-class taxpayers in the city and expressways to enable suburbanites to commute downtown have typically been located in poor neighborhoods, since no other group will allow itself to be displaced. For the same reason, universities, hospitals, and civic centers also expand into land occupied by the poor. The major costs of the industrialization of agriculture have been borne by the poor, who are pushed off the land without recompense; and they have paid a large share of the human cost of the growth of American power overseas, for they have provided many of the foot soldiers for Vietnam and other wars.

Twelfth, the poor facilitate and stabilize the American political process. Because they vote and participate in politics less than other groups, the political system is often free to ignore them. Moreover, since they can rarely support Republicans, they often provide the Democrats with a captive constituency that has no other place to go. As a result, the Democrats can count on their votes, and be more responsive to voters—for example, the white working class—who might otherwise switch to the Republicans.

Thirteenth, the role of the poor in upholding conventional norms (see the *fifth* point, above) also has a significant political function. An economy based on the ideology of laissez-faire requires a deprived population that is allegedly unwilling to work or that can be considered inferior because it must accept charity or welfare in order to survive. Not only does the alleged moral deviancy of the poor reduce the moral pressure on the present political economy to eliminate poverty but socialist alternatives can be made to look quite unattractive if those who will benefit most from them can be described as lazy, spendthrift, dishonest and promiscuous.

■ ■ ■ ■ THE ALTERNATIVES

I have described 13 of the more important functions poverty and the poor satisfy in American society, enough to support the functionalist thesis that poverty, like any other social phenomenon, survives in part because it is useful to society or some of its parts. This analysis is not intended to suggest that because it is often functional, poverty *should* exist, or that it *must* exist. For one thing, poverty has many more dysfunctions than functions; for another, it is possible to suggest functional alternatives.

For example, society's dirty work could be done without poverty, either by automation or by paying "dirty workers" decent wages. Nor is it necessary for the poor to subsidize the many activities they support through their low-wage jobs. This would, however, drive up the costs of these activities, which would result in higher prices to their customers and clients. Similarly, many of the professionals who flourish because of the poor could be given other roles. Social workers could provide counseling to the affluent, as they prefer to do anyway; and the police could devote themselves to traffic and organized crime. Other roles would have to be found for badly trained or incompetent professionals now relegated to serving the poor, and someone else would have to pay their salaries. Fewer penologists would be employable, however. And Pentecostal religion could probably not survive without the poor—nor would parts of the second- and third-hand-goods market. And in many cities, "used" housing that no one else wants would then have to be torn down at public expense.

Alternatives for the cultural functions of the poor could be found more easily and cheaply. Indeed, entertainers and adolescents are already serving as the deviants needed to uphold traditional morality and as devotees of orgies to "staff" the fantasies of vicarious participation.

The status functions of the poor are another matter. In a hierarchical society, some people must be defined as inferior to everyone else with respect to a variety of attributes, but they need not be poor in the absolute sense. One could conceive of a society in which the "lower class," though last in the pecking order, received 75 percent of the median income, rather than 15–40 percent, as is now the case. Needless to say, this would require considerable income redistribution.

The contribution the poor make to the upward mobility of the groups that provide them with goods and services could also be maintained without the poor's having such low incomes. However, it is true that if the poor were more affluent, they would have access to enough capital to take over the provider role, thus competing with, and perhaps rejecting, the "outsiders.". . . Similarly, if the poor were more affluent, they would make less willing clients for upper-class philanthropy, although some would still use settlement houses to achieve upward mobility, as they do now. Thus "Society" could continue to run its philanthropic activities.

The political functions of the poor would be more difficult to replace. With increased affluence the poor would probably obtain more political power and be more active politically. With higher incomes and more political power, the poor would be likely to resist paying the costs of growth and change. Of course, it is possible to imagine urban renewal and highway projects that properly reimbursed the displaced people, but such projects would then become considerably more expensive, and many might never be built. This, in turn, would reduce the comfort and convenience of those who now benefit from urban renewal and expressways.

In sum, then, many of the functions served by the poor could be replaced if poverty were eliminated, but almost always at higher costs to others, particularly more affluent others. Consequently, a functional analysis must conclude that poverty persists not only because it fulfills a number of positive functions but also because many of the functional alternatives to poverty would be quite dysfunctional for the affluent members of society. A functional analysis thus ultimately arrives at much the same conclusion as radical sociology, except that radical thinkers treat as manifest what I describe as latent: that social phenomena that are functional for affluent or powerful groups and dysfunctional for poor or powerless ones persist; that when the elimination of such phenomena through functional alternatives would generate dysfunctions for the affluent or powerful, they will continue to persist; and that phenomena like poverty can be eliminated only when they become dysfunctional for the affluent or powerful, or when the powerless can obtain enough power to change society.

■ ■ ■ POSTSCRIPT*

Over the years, this article has been interpreted as either a direct attack on functionalism or a tongue-in-cheek satirical comment on it. Neither interpretation is true. I wrote the article for two reasons. First and foremost, I wanted to point out that there are, unfortunately, positive functions of poverty which have to be dealt with by antipoverty policy. Second, I was trying to show that functionalism is not the inherently conservative approach for which it has often been criticized, but that it can be employed in liberal and radical analyses.

*A note from the author to the editor.

Girls and Boys Together ... But Mostly Apart

Barrie Thorne

introduction ▪ ▪ ▪ ▪ ▪

Many experiences from grade school remain firmly embedded in our minds—friendships, embarrassments, and perhaps times of pride and triumph. We all remember some of our teachers, the good and the bad. We all saw bullies at work. Some of us were even their victims. We all had crushes—on teachers, perhaps, and on classmates. We all found ourselves unprepared for some interaction, experiencing clumsiness, awkwardness, shyness. All of us were socialized by our grade schools into the dominant expectations of our society, with teachers doing their best to weed out our tendencies toward deviance.

One of the main lessons we learned in grade school had nothing to do with the school's curriculum. It was what we learned about *gender,* the expectations that others held of us because we were a boy or a girl. We learned, to a limited extent from our teachers, but primarily from our classmates, what others expected of us—and to what extent we were living up to those gender expectations. These lessons were ongoing, a part of our everyday lives, and they weren't always subtle. Pity the poor kids who didn't meet the expectations of our classmates, those who violated the fiercely delimited social boundaries that marked female from male.

As you will see in this selection, children's play is much more than mere play. Thorne, who observed how grade school children separate their friendships and activities on the basis of sex, concludes that the gender boundaries that the children guard so fiercely are a prelude to their adult roles. In short, as grade school boys and girls help to socialize one another into gender roles, they are helping to write the "scripts" that they will follow as adults.

Thinking Critically

As you read this selection, ask yourself:

1. How do your experiences in grade school compare with those reported in this selection? Did you play similar games? Did you have any games of "contamination" or "pollution?"

2. What did you learn about gender from grade school? How have those lessons become a part of your current life?

3. Why do attempts by adults to make children unisexual (making both boys and girls similar) fail? Why do children so vigorously enforce divisions between the sexes?

Throughout the years of elementary school, children's friendships and casual encounters are strongly separated by sex. . . . When children choose seats in classrooms or the cafeteria, or get into line, they frequently arrange themselves in same-sex clusters. At lunchtime, they talk matter-of-factly about "girls' tables" and "boys' tables." Playgrounds have gendered turfs, with some areas and activities, such as large playing fields and basketball courts, controlled mainly by boys, and others—smaller enclaves like jungle-gym areas and concrete spaces for hopscotch or jumprope—more often controlled by girls. Sex segregation is so common in elementary schools that it is meaningful to speak of separate girls' and boys' worlds.

Studies of gender and children's social relations have mostly followed this "two worlds" model, separately describing and comparing the subcultures of girls and of boys. In brief summary: Boys tend to interact in larger, more age-heterogeneous groups. They engage in more rough and tumble play and physical fighting. Organized sports are both a central activity and a major metaphor in boys' subcultures; they use the language of "teams" even when not engaged in sports, and they often construct interaction in the form of contests. The shifting hierarchies of boys' groups are evident in their more frequent use of direct commands, insults, and challenges.

Fewer studies have been done of girls' groups, and—perhaps because categories for description and analysis have come more from male than female experience—researchers have had difficulty seeing and analyzing girls' social relations. Recent work has begun to correct this skew. In middle childhood, girls' worlds are less public than those of boys; girls more often interact in private places and in smaller groups or friendship pairs. Their play is more cooperative and turn-taking. Girls have more intense and exclusive friendships, which take shape around keeping and telling secrets, shifting alliances, and indirect ways of expressing disagreement. Instead of direct commands, girls more often use directives which merge speaker and hearer, such as, "let's" or "we gotta.". . .

Sex segregation is far from total, and is a more complex and dynamic process than the portrayal of separate worlds reveals. Erving Goffman (1977) has observed that sex segregation has a "with-then-apart" structure; the sexes segregate periodically, with separate spaces, rituals, groups, but they also come together and are, in crucial ways, part of the same world. This is certainly true in the social environment of elementary schools. Although girls and boys do interact as bound-aried collectivities—an image suggested by the separate worlds approach—there are other occasions when they work or play in relaxed and integrated ways. Gender is less central to the organization and meaning of some situations than others. In short, sex segregation is not static, but is a variable and complicated process.

To gain an understanding of gender which can encompass both the "with" and the "apart" of sex segregation, analysis should start not with the individual, nor with a search for sex differences, but with social relationships. Gender should be concep-tualized as a system of relationships rather than as an immutable and dichotomous given. . . .

■ ■ ■ METHODS AND SOURCES OF DATA

This study is based on two periods of participant observation. . . . I observed for 8 months in a largely working-class elementary school in California, a school with 8% Black and 12% Chicana/o students. . . . I did fieldwork for 3 months in a Michi-gan elementary school of similar size (around 400 students), social class, and racial composition. I observed in several classrooms—a kindergarten, a second grade, and a combined fourth–fifth grade—and in school hallways, cafeterias, and playgrounds. I set out to follow the round of the school day as children experience it, recording their interactions with one another, and with adults, in varied settings. . . .

■ ■ ■ DAILY PROCESSES OF SEX SEGREGATION

In the school settings I observed, much segregation happened with no mention of gen-der. Gender was implicit in the contours of friendship, shared interest, and perceived risk which came into play when children chose companions—in their prior planning, invitations, seeking-of-access; saving-of-places, denials of entry, and allowing or pro-testing of "cuts" by those who violated the rules for lining up. Sometimes children formed mixed-sex groups for play, eating, talking, working on a classroom project, or moving through space. When adults or children explicitly invoked gender—and this was nearly always in ways which separated girls and boys—boundaries were heightened and mixed-sex interaction became an explicit arena of risk.

In the schools I studied, the physical space and curricula were not formally divided by sex, as they have been in the history of elementary schooling (a his-tory evident in separate entrances to old school buildings, where the words "Boys" and "Girls" are permanently etched in concrete). Nevertheless, gender was a visible marker in the adult-organized school day. In both schools, when the public address system sounded, the principal inevitably opened with: "Boys and girls . . . ," and in addressing clusters of children, teachers and aides regularly used gender terms ("Heads down, girls"; "The girls are ready and the boys aren't"). These forms of address made gender visible and salient, conveying an assumption that the sexes are separate social groups.

Teachers and aides sometimes drew upon gender as a basis for sorting children and organizing activities. Gender is an embodied and visual social category which roughly divides the population in half, and the separation of girls and boys permeates the history and lore of schools and playgrounds. In both schools—although through awareness of Title IX, many teachers had changed this practice—one could see separate girls' and boys' lines moving, like caterpillars, through the school halls. In the 4th–5th grade classroom the teacher frequently pitted girls against boys for spelling and math contests. On the playground in the Michigan school, aides regarded the space close to the building as girls' territory, and the playing fields "out there" as boys' territory. They sometimes shooed children of the other sex away from those spaces, especially boys who ventured near the girls' area and seemed to have teasing in mind.

In organizing their activities, both within and apart from the surveillance of adults, children also explicitly invoked gender. During my fieldwork in the Michigan school, I kept daily records of who sat where in the lunchroom. The amount of sex segregation varied: It was least at the first-grade tables and almost total among sixth graders. There was also variation from classroom to classroom within a given age, and from day to day. Actions like the following heightened the gender divide:

> In the lunchroom, when the two second-grade tables were filling, a high-status boy walked by the inside table, which had a scattering of both boys and girls, and said loudly, "Oooo, too many girls," as he headed for a seat at the far table. The boys at the inside table picked up their trays and moved, and no other boys sat at the inside table, which the pronouncement had effectively made taboo.

In the end, that day (which was not the case every day), girls and boys ate at separate tables.

Eating and walking are not sex-typed activities, yet in forming groups in lunchrooms and hallways children often separated by sex. Sex segregation assumed added dimensions on the playground, where spaces, equipment, and activities were infused with gender meanings. My inventories of activities and groupings on the playground showed similar patterns in both schools: Boys controlled the large fixed spaces designated for team sports (baseball diamonds, grassy fields used for football or soccer); girls more often played closer to the building, doing tricks on the monkey bars (which, for sixth graders, became an area for sitting and talking) and using cement areas for jumprope, hopscotch, and group games like four-square. Girls and boys most often played together in kickball, and in group (rather than team) games like four-square, dodgeball, and handball. When children used gender to exclude others from play, they often drew upon beliefs connecting boys to some activities and girls to others:

> A first-grade boy avidly watched an all-female game of jump rope. When the girls began to shift positions, he recognized a means of access to the play and he offered, "I'll swing it." A girl responded, "No way, you don't know how to do it, to swing it. You gotta be a girl." He left without protest.

Although children sometimes ignored pronouncements about what each sex could or could not do, I never heard them directly challenge such claims.

When children had explicitly defined an activity or a group as gendered, those who crossed the boundary—especially boys who moved into female-marked space—risked being teased. ("Look! Mike's in the girls' line!"; "'That's a girl over there,' a girl said loudly, pointing to a boy sitting at an otherwise all-female table in the lunchroom.") Children, and occasionally adults, used teasing—especially the tease of "liking" someone of the other sex, or of "being" that sex by virtue of being in their midst—to police gender boundaries. Much of the teasing drew upon heterosexual romantic definitions, making cross-sex interaction risky, and increasing social distance between boys and girls.

■ ■ ■ RELATIONSHIPS BETWEEN THE SEXES

Because I have emphasized the "apart" and ignored the occasions of "with," this analysis of sex segregation falsely implies that there is little contact between girls and boys in daily school life. In fact, relationships between girls and boys—which should be studied as fully as, and in connection with, same-sex relationships—are of several kinds:

1. "Borderwork," or forms of cross-sex interaction which are based upon and reaffirm boundaries and asymmetries between girls' and boys' groups;
2. Interactions which are infused with heterosexual meanings;
3. Occasions where individuals cross gender boundaries to participate in the world of the other sex; and
4. Situations where gender is muted in salience, with girls and boys interacting in more relaxed ways.

Borderwork

In elementary school settings boys' and girls' groups are sometimes spatially set apart. Same-sex groups sometimes claim fixed territories such as the basketball court, the bars, or specific lunchroom tables. However, in the crowded, multifocused, and adult-controlled environment of the school, groups form and disperse at a rapid rate and can never stay totally apart. Contact between girls and boys sometimes lessens sex segregation, but gender-defined groups also come together in ways which emphasize their boundaries.

"Borderwork" refers to interaction across, yet based upon and even strengthening gender boundaries. . . . In elementary schools there are several types of borderwork: contests or games where gender-defined teams compete; cross-sex rituals of chasing and pollution; and group invasions. These interactions are asymmetrical, challenging the separate-but-parallel model of "two worlds."

Contests.   Boys and girls are sometimes pitted against each other in classroom competitions and playground games. The 4th–5th grade classroom had a boys' side and a girls' side, an arrangement that re-emerged each time the teacher asked children to choose their own desks. Although there was some within-sex shuffling, the result was always a spatial moiety [divided in half] system—boys on the left, girls on the right—with the exception of one girl (the "tomboy" whom I'll describe later), who twice chose a desk with the boys and once with the girls. Drawing upon and reinforcing the children's self-segregation, the teacher often pitted the boys against the girls in spelling and math competitions, events marked by cross-sex antagonism and within-sex solidarity:

> The teacher introduced a math game; she would write addition and subtraction problems on the board, and a member of each team would race to be the first to write the correct answer. She wrote two score-keeping columns on the board: 'Beastly Boys'... 'Gossipy Girls.' The boys yelled out, as several girls laughed, 'Noisy girls! Gruesome girls!' The girls sat in a row on top of their desks; sometimes they moved collectively, pushing their hips or whispering 'pass it on.' The boys stood along the wall, some reclining against desks. When members of either group came back victorious from the front of the room, they would do the 'giving five' hand-slapping ritual with their team members.

On the playground a team of girls occasionally played against a team of boys, usually in kickball or team two-square. Some times these games proceeded matter-of-factly, but if gender became the explicit basis of team solidarity, the interaction changed, becoming more antagonistic and unstable:

> Two fifth-grade girls played against two fifth-grade boys in a team game of two-square. The game proceeded at an even pace until an argument ensued about whether the ball was out or on the line. Karen, who had hit the ball, became annoyed, flashed her middle finger at the other team, and called to a passing girl to join their side. The boys then called out to other boys, and cheered as several arrived to play. 'We got five and you got three!' Jack yelled. The game continued, with the girls yelling, 'Bratty boys! Sissy boys!' and the boys making noises—'weee haw' 'ha-ha-ha'—as they played.

Chasing.   Cross-sex chasing dramatically affirms boundaries between girls and boys. The basic elements of chase and elude, capture and rescue are found in various kinds of tag with formal rules, and in informal episodes of chasing which punctuate life on playgrounds. These episodes begin with a provocation (taunts like "You can't get me!" or "Slobber monster!"; bodily pokes or the grabbing of possessions). A provocation may be ignored, or responded to by chasing. Chaser and chased may then alternate roles. . . . Boys frequently chase one another, an activity which often ends in wrestling and mock fights. When girls chase girls, they are usually less physically aggressive; they less often, for example, wrestle one another to the ground.

Cross-sex chasing is set apart by special names—"girls chase the boys"; "boys chase the girls"; "the chase"; "chasers"; "chase and kiss"; "kiss chase"; "kissers and chasers"; "kiss or kill"—and by children's animated talk about the activity. The names vary by region and school, but contain both gender and sexual meanings.

In "boys chase the girls" and "girls chase the boys" (the names most frequently used in both the California and Michigan schools) boys and girls become, by definition, separate teams. Gender terms override individual identities, especially for the other team ("Help, a girl's chasin' me!"; "C'mon Sarah, let's get that boy"; "Tony, help save me from the girls"). Individuals may call for help from, or offer help to, others of their sex. They may also grab someone of their sex and turn them over to the opposing team: "Ryan grabbed Billy from behind, wrestling him to the ground. 'Hey girls, get 'im,' Ryan called."

Boys more often mix episodes of cross-sex with same-sex chasing. Girls more often have safety zones, places like the girls' restroom or an area by the school wall, where they retreat to rest and talk (sometimes in animated postmortems) before new episodes of cross-sex chasing begin.

Early in the fall in the Michigan school, where chasing was especially prevalent, I watched a second-grade boy teach a kindergarten girl how to chase. He slowly ran backwards, beckoning her to pursue him, as he called, "Help, a girl's after me." In the early grades chasing mixes with fantasy play, for example, a first-grade boy who played "sea monster," his arms outflung and his voice growling, as he chased a group of girls. By third grade, stylized gestures—exaggerated stalking motions, screams (which only girls do), and karate kicks—accompany scenes of chasing.

Names like "chase and kiss" mark the sexual meanings of cross-sex chasing. . . . The threat of kissing—most often girls threatening to kiss boys—is a ritualized form of provocation. Cross-sex chasing among sixth graders involves elaborate patterns of touch and touch avoidance, which adults see as sexual. The principal told the sixth graders in the Michigan school that they were not to play "pom-pom," a complicated chasing game, because it entailed "inappropriate touch."

Rituals of Pollution.   Cross-sex chasing is sometimes entwined with rituals of pollution, as in "cooties," where specific individuals or groups are treated as contaminating or carrying "germs." Children have rituals for transferring cooties (usually touching someone else and shouting "You've got cooties!"), for immunization (e.g., writing "CV" for "cootie vaccination" on their arms), and for eliminating cooties (e.g., saying "no gives" or using "cootie catchers" made of folded paper). While girls may give cooties to girls, boys do not generally give cooties to one another.

In cross-sex play, either girls or boys may be defined as having cooties, which they transfer through chasing and touching. Girls give cooties to boys more often than vice versa. In Michigan, one version of cooties is called "girl stain." "Cootie queens," or "cootie girls" (there are no "kings" or "boys") are female pariahs, the ultimate school untouchables, seen as contaminating not only by virtue of gender, but also through some added stigma such as being overweight or poor. That girls are seen as more polluting than boys is a significant asymmetry, which echoes cross-cultural patterns, although in other cultures female pollution is generally connected to menstruation, and not applied to prepubertal girls.

Invasions.   Playground invasions are another asymmetric form of borderwork. On a few occasions I saw girls invade and disrupt an all-male game, most memorably a group of tall sixth-grade girls who ran onto the playing field and grabbed a football which was in play. The boys were surprised and frustrated, and, unusual for boys this old, finally tattled to the aide. But in the majority of cases, boys disrupt girls' activities rather than vice versa. Boys grab the ball from girls playing four-square, stick feet into a jumprope and stop an ongoing game, and dash through the area of the bars, where girls are taking turns performing, sending the rings flying. Sometimes boys ask to join a girls' game and then, after a short period of seemingly earnest play, disrupt the game:

> Two second-grade boys begged to "twirl" the jumprope for a group of second-grade girls who had been jumping for some time. The girls agreed, and the boys began to twirl. Soon, without announcement, the boys changed from "seashells, cockle bells" to "hot peppers" (spinning the rope very fast), and tangled the jumper in the rope. The boys ran away laughing.

Boys disrupt girls' play so often that girls have developed almost ritualized responses: They guard their ongoing play, chase boys away, and tattle to the aides. In a playground cycle which enhances sex segregation, aides who try to spot potential trouble before it occurs sometimes shoo boys away from areas where girls are playing. Aides do not anticipate trouble from girls who seek to join groups of boys, with the exception of girls intent on provoking a chase sequence. And indeed, if they seek access to a boys' game, girls usually play with boys in earnest rather than breaking up the game. . . .

A close look at the organization of border work—or boundaried interactions between the sexes—shows that the worlds of boys and girls may be separate, but they are not parallel, nor are they equal. The worlds of girls and boys articulate in several asymmetric ways:

1. On the playground, boys control as much as ten times more space than girls, when one adds up the area of large playing fields and compares it with the much smaller areas where girls predominate. Girls, who play closer to the building, are more often watched over and protected by the adult aides.

2. Boys invade all-female games and scenes of play much more than girls invade boys. This, and boys' greater control of space, correspond with other findings about the organization of gender, and inequality, in our society: Compared with men and boys, women and girls take up less space, and their space, and talk, are more often violated and interrupted.

3. Although individual boys are occasionally treated as contaminating (e.g., a third-grade boy who both boys and girls said was "stinky" and "smelled like pee"), girls are more often defined as polluting. . . . It is more taboo for a boy to play with (as opposed to invade) girls, and girls are more sexually defined than boys.

A look at the boundaries between the separated worlds of girls and boys illuminates within-sex hierarchies of status and control. For example, in the sex-divided seating in the 4th–5th grade classroom, several boys recurrently sat near "female space": Their desks were at the gender divide in the classroom, and they were more likely than other boys to sit at a predominantly female table in the lunchroom. These boys—two nonbilingual Chicanos and an overweight "loner" boy who was afraid of sports—were at the bottom of the male hierarchy. Gender is sometimes used as a metaphor for male hierarchies; the inferior status of boys at the bottom is conveyed by calling them "girls":

> Seven boys and one girl were playing basketball. Two younger boys came over and asked to play. While the girl silently stood, fully accepted in the company of players, one of the older boys disparagingly said to the younger boys, 'You girls can't play.'

In contrast, the girls who more often travel in the boys' world, sitting with groups of boys in the lunchroom or playing basketball, soccer, and baseball with them, are not stigmatized. Some have fairly high status with other girls. The worlds of girls and boys are asymmetrically arranged, and spatial patterns map out interacting forms of inequality.

Heterosexual Meanings

. . . Children are less heterosexually defined than adults, and we have nonsexual imagery for relations between girls and boys. However, both children and adults sometimes use heterosexual language—"crushes," "like," "goin' with," "girlfriends," and "boyfriends"—to define cross-sex relationships. This language increases through the years of elementary school; the shift to adolescence consolidates a gender system organized around the institution of heterosexuality.

In everyday life in the schools, heterosexual and romantic meanings infuse some ritualized forms of interaction between groups of boys and girls (e.g., "chase and kiss") and help maintain sex segregation. "Jimmy likes Beth" or "Beth likes Jimmy" is a major form of teasing, which a child risks in choosing to sit by or walk with someone of the other sex. The structure of teasing, and children's sparse vocabulary for relationships between girls and boys, are evident in the following conversation which I had with a group of third-grade girls in the lunchroom:

> Susan asked me what I was doing, and I said I was observing the things children do and play. Nicole volunteered, 'I like running, boys chase all the girls. See Tim over there? Judy chases him all around the school. She likes him.' Judy, sitting across the table, quickly responded, 'I hate him. I like him for a friend.' 'Tim loves Judy,' Nicole said in a loud, sing-song voice.

In the younger grades, the culture and lore of girls contains more heterosexual romantic themes than that of boys. In Michigan, the first-grade girls often jumped rope to a rhyme which began: "Down in the valley where the green grass grows, there sat Cindy (name of jumper), as sweet as a rose. She sat, she sat, she sat so sweet. Along came Jason, and kissed her on the cheek . . . first comes love, then comes marriage, then along comes Cindy with a baby carriage. . . ." Before a girl took her turn at jumping, the chanters asked her "Who do you want to be your boyfriend?" The jumper always proffered a name, which was accepted matter-of-factly. In chasing, a girl's kiss carried greater threat than a boy's kiss; "girl touch," when defined as contaminating, had sexual connotations. In short, starting at an early age, girls are more sexually defined than boys.

Through the years of elementary school, and increasing with age, the idiom of heterosexuality helps maintain the gender divide. Cross-sex interactions, especially when children initiate them, are fraught with the risk of being teased about "liking" someone of the other sex. I learned of several close cross-sex friendships, formed and maintained in neighborhoods and church, which went underground during the school day.

By the fifth grade a few children began to affirm, rather than avoid, the charge of having a girlfriend or a boyfriend; they introduced the heterosexual courtship rituals of adolescence:

> In the lunchroom in the Michigan school, as the tables were forming, a high-status fifth-grade boy called out from his seat at the table: 'I want Trish to sit by me.' Trish came over, and almost like a king and queen, they sat at the gender divide—a row of girls down the table on her side, a row of boys on his.

In this situation, which inverted earlier forms, it was not a loss, but a gain in status to publically choose a companion of the other sex. By affirming his choice, the boy became unteasable (note the familiar asymmetry of heterosexual courtship rituals: the male initiated). This incident signals a temporal shift in arrangements of sex and gender.

Traveling in the World of the Other Sex

Contests, invasions, chasing, and heterosexually defined encounters are based upon and reaffirm boundaries between girls and boys. In another type of cross-sex interaction, individuals (or sometimes pairs) cross gender boundaries, seeking acceptance in a group of the other sex. Nearly all the cases I saw of this were tomboys—girls who played organized sports and frequently sat with boys in the cafeteria or classroom. If these girls were skilled at activities central in the boys' world, especially games like soccer, baseball, and basketball, they were pretty much accepted as participants.

Being a tomboy is a matter of degree. Some girls seek access to boys' groups but are excluded; other girls limit their "crossing" to specific sports. Only a few—such as the tomboy I mentioned earlier, who chose a seat with the boys in the sex-divided 4th–5th grade—participate fully in the boys' world. That particular girl was skilled at the various organized sports which boys played in different seasons of the year. She was also adept at physical fighting and at using the forms of arguing, insult, teasing, naming, and sports-talk of the boys' subculture. She was the only Black child in her classroom, in a school with only 8% Black students; overall that token status, along with unusual athletic and verbal skills, may have contributed to her ability to move back and forth across the gender divide. Her unique position in the children's world was widely recognized in the school. Several times, the teacher said to me, "She thinks she's a boy."

I observed only one boy in the upper grades (a fourth grader) who regularly played with all-female groups, as opposed to "playing at" girls' games and seeking to disrupt them. He frequently played jumprope and took turns with girls doing tricks on the bars, using the small gestures—for example, a helpful push on the heel of a girl who needed momentum to turn her body around the bar—which mark skillful and earnest participation. Although I never saw him play in other than an earnest spirit, the girls often chased him away from their games, and both girls and boys teased him. The fact that girls seek, and have more access to boys' worlds than vice versa, and the fact that girls who travel with the other sex are less stigmatized for it, are obvious asymmetries, tied to the asymmetries previously discussed.

Relaxed Cross-Sex Interactions

Relationships between boys and girls are not always marked by strong boundaries, heterosexual definitions, or by interacting on the terms and turfs of the other sex. . . . Occasions where boys and girls interact without strain, where gender wanes, rather than waxes in importance, frequently have one or more of the following characteristics:

1. The situations are organized around an absorbing task, such as a group art project or creating a radio show, which encourages cooperation and lessens attention to gender. This pattern accords with other studies finding that cooperative activities reduce group antagonism (e.g., Sherif & Sherif, 1933, who studied divisions between boys in a summer camp; and Aronson et al., 1978, who used cooperative activities to lessen racial divisions in a classroom).

2. Gender is less prominent when children are not responsible for the formation of the group. Mixed-sex play is less frequent in games like football, which require the choosing of teams, and more frequent in games like handball or dodgeball which individuals can join simply by getting into a line or a circle. When adults organize mixed-sex encounters—which they frequently do in the classroom and in physical education periods on the playground—they legitimize cross-sex contact. This removes the risk of being teased for choosing to be with the other sex.

3. There is more extensive and relaxed cross-sex interaction when principles of grouping other than gender are explicitly invoked—for example, counting off to form teams for spelling or kickball, dividing lines by hot lunch or cold lunch, or organizing a work group on the basis of interests or reading ability.

4. Girls and boys may interact more readily in less-public and crowded settings. Neighborhood play, depending on demography, is more often sex- and age-integrated than play at school, partly because with fewer numbers, one may have to resort to an array of social categories to find play partners or to constitute a game. And in less-crowded environments there are fewer potential witnesses to "make something of it" if girls and boys play together.

Relaxed interactions between girls and boys often depend on adults to set up and legitimize the contact. Perhaps because of this contingency—and the other, distancing patterns which permeate relations between girls and boys—the easeful moments of interaction rarely build to close friendship.

■ ■ ■ ■ IMPLICATIONS FOR DEVELOPMENT

. . . Sex and gender are differently organized and defined across situations, even within the same institution. This situational variation (e.g., in the extent to which an encounter heightens or lessens gender boundaries, or is infused with sexual meanings) shapes and constrains individual behavior. Features which a developmental perspective might attribute to individuals, and understand as relatively internal attributes unfolding over time, may, in fact, be highly dependent on context. For example, children's avoidance of cross-sex friendship may be attributed to individual gender development in middle-childhood. But attention to varied situations may show that this avoidance is contingent on group size, activity, adult behavior, collective meanings, and the risk of being teased. . . .

A situated analysis of arrangements of sex and gender among those of different ages may point to crucial disjunctions in the life course. In the fourth and fifth grades, culturally defined heterosexual rituals ("goin' with") begin to suppress the presence and visibility of other types of interaction between girls and boys, such as nonsexualized and comfortable interaction, and traveling in the world of the other sex. As "boyfriend/girlfriend" definitions spread, the fifth-grade tomboy I described had to work to sustain "buddy" relationships with boys. Adult women who were tomboys often speak of early adolescence as a painful time when they were pushed away from participation in boys' activities. . . .

As heterosexual encounters assume more importance, they may alter relations in same-sex groups. For example, Schofield (1981) reports that for sixth- and seventh-grade children in a middle school, the popularity of girls with other girls was affected by their popularity with boys, while boys' status with other boys did not depend on their relations with girls. This is an asymmetry familiar from the adult world; men's relationships with one another are defined through varied activities (occupations, sports), while relationships among women—and their public status—are more influenced by their connections to individual men.

A full understanding of gender and social relations should encompass cross-sex as well as within-sex interactions. "Borderwork" helps maintain separate, gender-linked subcultures, which, as those interested in development have begun to suggest, may result in different milieux for learning. Daniel Maltz and Ruth Borker (1983) for example, argue that because of different interactions within girls' and boys' groups, the sexes learn different rules for creating and interpreting friendly conversation, rules which carry into adulthood and help account for miscommunication between men and women. . . .

This separate worlds approach, as I have illustrated, also has limitations. The occasions when the sexes are together should also be studied, and understood as contexts for experience and learning. For example, asymmetries in cross-sex relationships convey a series of messages: that boys are more entitled to space and to the non-reciprocal right of interrupting or invading the activities of the other sex; that girls are more in need of adult protection, and are lower in status, more defined by sexuality, and may even be polluting. Different types of cross-sex interaction—relaxed, boundaried, sexualized, or taking place on the terms of the other sex—provide different contexts for development. . . .

REFERENCES

Aronson, E. et al. (1978). *The jigsaw classroom.* Beverly Hills, CA: Sage.

Goffman, E. (1977). The arrangement between the sexes. *Theory and Society, 4,* 301–336.

Maltz, D. N., & Borker, R. A. (1983). A cultural approach to male–female miscommunication. In J. J. Gumperz (Ed.), *Language and social identity* (pp. 195–216). New York: Cambridge University Press.

Schofield, J. W. (1981). Complementary and conflicting identities: Images and interaction in an interracial school. In S. R. Asher & J. M. Gottman (Eds.), *The development of children's friendships* (pp. 53–90). New York: Cambridge University Press.

Sherif, M., & Sherif, C. (1953). *Groups in harmony and tension.* New York: Harper.

How the Jews Became White Folks

Karen Brodkin

introduction ▪ ▪ ■ ▪ ■

One of the main points made at the beginning of Chapter 12 of *Sociology* is that race is a *social* category. Although most people think of race purely as biological (you "are" or "are not," depending on the biological characteristics you receive at conception and show at birth), race is actually a matter of definition. Examples in the chapter include the familiar U.S. classification of a child born to "white" and "black" parents and the fascinating example of how a plane ride can change someone's race. I suppose that many students, firmly planted in their ideas, shrug off such examples as irrelevant to the "real" world. To think that a plane ride can change someone's race certainly sounds far-fetched.

How do we break through our idea that race is biological, since this view is fixed so firmly in our minds? An example that might help is this: In the 1800s and even into the early 1900s, U.S. immigrants from southern Europe (Greeks, Italians, Sicilians, Czechs, Poles, Hungarians, and so on) were not classified as whites. Neither were the Irish. Immigrants from these backgrounds were considered some variant of "non-white," and they were discriminated against by the Anglos who had preceded them and who ran the U.S. social institutions. Gradually, with the passage of time and their assimilation into mainstream culture, people from these backgrounds "became white." That is, they were accorded (assigned) membership in the "white race."

As you will read in this article, the same thing happened with Jews. As Brodkin analyzes how this transformation occurred, the *social* basis of race-ethnicity should become more apparent.

Thinking Critically

As you read this selection, ask yourself:

1. How can "race" actually be a social category, when everyone knows that race is biological?

2. How did U.S. Jews "become white"? What was the relationship between social class and changing racial-ethnic identity?

3. How would you explain the concept of race as social to a non-sociology student?

This article is about the ways our racial-ethnic backgrounds—American Jewishness in particular—contribute to the making of social identity in the United States. We fashion identities in the context of a wider conversation about American nationhood—to whom it belongs and what belonging means. Race and ethnicity, class, gender, and sexuality have been staple ingredients of this conversation. They are salient aspects of social being from which economic practices, political policies, and popular discourses create "Americans." Because all these facets of social being have such significant meanings on a national scale, they also have significant consequences for the life chances of individuals and groups, which is why they are such important parts of our social and political identities.

I focus on American Jews partly for personal reasons and partly because the history of Jews in the United States is a history of racial change that provides useful insights on race in America. Prevailing classifications at a particular time have sometimes assigned us to the white race, and at other times have created an off-white race for Jews to inhabit. Those changes in our racial assignment have shaped the ways in which American Jews who grew up in different eras have constructed their ethnoracial identities. Those changes give us a kind of double vision that comes from racial middleness: of an experience of marginality vis-à-vis whiteness, and an experience of whiteness and belonging vis-à-vis blackness.

Historical changes in Jews' racial assignment make for different constructions of Jewish political selves within the same family. Consequently, we may experience our racial selves in multiple ways, even within our own families. One of my teenage pranks showed me the differences between my parents' racial experience and mine. As a child, I spent summer vacations at a lake in Vermont in a bungalow colony of Jewish families whose adult members were mostly New York City public school teachers. Late one summer night, a group of us tied up all the rowboats that belonged to our group of families out in the middle of the lake. We looked forward to parental surprise when they woke up, but we weren't prepared for their genuine alarm: This could only be an anti-Semitic act by angry Yankees. What did it portend for our group? We were surprised on two counts: that the adults didn't assume we had done it, since we were always playing practical jokes, and that they thought our Jewishness mattered to Vermont Yankees. . . .

In relation to Vermonters and other mainstream white folks, my parents and grandparents lived in a time when Jews were not white. They expected that particular racial assignment to shape their relationship with such people. This was the larger context within which they formed their sense of Jewish ethnoracial identity.

It is important to make a conceptual distinction between ethnoracial assignment and ethnoracial identity. Assignment is about popularly held classifications and their deployment by those with national power to make them matter economically, politically, and socially to the individuals classified. We construct ethnoracial identities ourselves, but we do it within the context of ethnoracial assignment.

However, even though ethnoracial assignment and ethnoracial identity are conceptually distinct, they are also deeply interrelated. The Jewish world of my childhood was a product of the community that anti-Semitism produced, and my Jewish identity has its roots there. However, because my racial assignment differed from that of my parents, so too did the ethnoracial content of my Jewish identity. Different generations in my family have different ethnoracial identities. My sons, who did not grow up in a Jewish milieu, tell me they don't really think of themselves as Jewish but rather as generic whites. When I asked my parents, Sylvia and Jack Brodkin, what they thought of that, they both gave me a funny look. "We're Jewish," was my father's answer, to which my mother added that, yes, she supposed that was white, but Jewish was how she saw herself. I see myself as both—white and Jewish. . . .

Although my parents' Jewishness was formed in a community context organized to cope with times when Jews weren't white, most of my childhood coincided with America's philo-Semitic 1950s, where Jews were a wonderful kind of white folks. We lived where Jews had not been allowed to live a few generations earlier, and we interacted easily with people whose families had been white for a very long time. So, while my parents taught me their Jewishness-as-not-quite-white, they also wanted our family to adjust to Jews' new postwar, racially white place.

This meant we all had to learn the ways of whiteness. Shortly after we moved to Valley Stream, perhaps to help me figure it out, my parents bought me a storybook, *The Happy Family,* where life began in the kitchen and stopped at the borders of the lawn, where Mom, Dad, the kids, and the dog were relentlessly cheerful, and where no one ever raised their voices except to laugh. It was my favorite, and I desperately wanted my family to look like the one in the book. When I became an adolescent, my goal in life became to have a pageboy hairstyle and to own a camel-hair coat, like the pictures in *Seventeen* magazine. I thought of storybook and magazine people as "the blond people," a species for whom life naturally came easily, who inherited happiness as a birthright, and I wanted my family to be like that, to be "normal." Maybe then I'd be normal too. My childhood divide was between everyone I knew and the blond people, between most of the real people I knew, whether in the suburbs or in the city, and the mythical, "normal" America of the then-primitive but still quite effective mass media—radio, magazines, and the new TV.

Still, to be Jewish, to have Jewishness as a central part of my political identity, meant being a little different. At the very least it meant being part of a Jewish social and work world that I shared with my parents. True, this community differed from the Jewish community of my parents' youth, but it also differed from my suburban community of school and neighborhood, not to mention from that of the mythical blond people. Trying to be "normal," that is, white, and Jewish presented a double bind. Neither was satisfactory by itself, and it seemed to me that each commented negatively on the other: to be "normal" meant to reject the Jewishness of my family and our circle, as well as a more congenial kind of girlhood; to be Jewish meant to be a voluntary outsider at school. I wanted to embrace my family *and* to be an insider. At the time, it seemed that I had a choice and that I had to choose; one couldn't be both at the same time and in the same place.

■ ■ ■ EURORACES

*The late nineteenth century and early decades of the twentieth saw a steady
stream of warnings by scientists, policymakers, and the popular press that "mon-
grelization" of the Nordic or Anglo-Saxon race—the real Americans—by inferior
European races (as well as by inferior non-European ones) was destroying the
fabric of the nation.*

—Kenneth Roberts,
"Why Europe Leaves Home"

I continue to be surprised when I read books that indicate that America once
regarded its immigrant European workers as something other than white, as biologi-
cally different. My parents are not surprised; they expect anti-Semitism to be part of
the fabric of daily life, much as I expect racism to be part of it. They came of age in
the Jewish world of the 1920s and 1930s, at the peak of anti-Semitism in America.
They are rightly proud of their upward mobility and think of themselves as pulling
themselves up by their own bootstraps. I grew up during the 1950s in the Euro-
ethnic New York suburb of Valley Stream, where Jews were simply one kind of white
folks and where ethnicity meant little more to my generation than food and family
heritage. Part of my ethnic heritage was the belief that Jews were smart and that our
success was due to our own efforts and abilities, reinforced by a culture that valued
sticking together, hard work, education, and deferred gratification. . . .

It is certainly true that the United States has a history of anti-Semitism and of
beliefs that Jews are members of an inferior race. But Jews were hardly alone. American anti-Semitism was part of a broader pattern of late-nineteenth-century racism
against all southern and eastern European immigrants, as well as against Asian immigrants, not to mention African Americans, Native Americans, and Mexicans. These
views justified all sorts of discriminatory treatment, including closing the doors, between 1882 and 1927, to immigration from Europe and Asia. This picture changed
radically after World War II. Suddenly, the same folks who had promoted nativism
and xenophobia were eager to believe that the Euro-origin people whom they had
deported, reviled as members of inferior races, and prevented from immigrating only
a few years earlier, were now model middle-class white suburban citizens.

It was not an educational epiphany that made those in power change their
hearts, their minds, and our race. Instead, it was the biggest and best affirmative
action program in the history of our nation, and it was for Euromales. That is not
how it was billed, but it is the way it worked out in practice. I tell this story to show
the institutional nature of racism and the centrality of state policies to creating and
changing races. Here, those policies reconfigured the category of whiteness to include
European immigrants. There are similarities and differences in the ways each of the
European immigrant groups became "whitened." I tell the story in a way that links
anti-Semitism to other varieties of anti-European racism because this highlights what
Jews shared with other Euro-immigrants.

The U.S. "discovery" that Europe was divided into inferior and superior races
began with the racialization of the Irish in the mid-nineteenth century and flowered
in response to the great waves of immigration from southern and eastern Europe

that began in the late nineteenth century. Before that time, European immigrants—including Jews—had been largely assimilated into the white population. However, the 23 million European immigrants who came to work in U.S. cities in the waves of migration after 1880 were too many and too concentrated to absorb. Since immigrants and their children made up more than 70 percent of the population of most of the country's largest cities, by the 1890s urban American had taken on a distinctly southern and eastern European immigrant flavor. Like the Irish in Boston and New York, their urban concentrations in dilapidated neighborhoods put them cheek by jowl next to the rising elites and the middle class with whom they shared public space and to whom their working-class ethnic communities were particularly visible.

The Red Scare of 1919 clearly linked anti-immigrant with anti-working-class sentiment—to the extent that the Seattle general strike by largely native-born workers was blamed on foreign agitators. The Red Scare was fueled by an economic depression, a massive postwar wave of strikes, the Russian Revolution, and another influx of postwar immigration. Strikers in the steel and garment industries in New York and New England were mainly new immigrants. "As part of a fierce counteroffensive, employers inflamed the historic identification of class conflict with immigrant radicalism." Anticommunism and anti-immigrant sentiment came together in the Palmer raids and deportation of immigrant working-class activists. There was real fear of revolution. One of President Wilson's aides feared it was "the first appearance of the soviet in this country."

Not surprisingly, the belief in European races took root most deeply among the wealthy, U.S.-born Protestant elite, who feared a hostile and seemingly inassimilable working class. By the end of the nineteenth century, Senator Henry Cabot Lodge pressed Congress to cut off immigration to the United States; Theodore Roosevelt raised the alarm of "race suicide" and took Anglo-Saxon women to task for allowing "native" stock to be outbred by inferior immigrants. In the early twentieth century, these fears gained a great deal of social legitimacy thanks to the efforts of an influential network of aristocrats and scientists who developed theories of eugenics—breeding for a "better" humanity—and scientific racism. . . .

By the 1920s, scientific racism sanctified the notion that real Americans were white and that real whites came from northwest Europe. Racism by white workers in the West fueled laws excluding and expelling the Chinese in 1882. Widespread racism led to closing the immigration door to virtually all Asians and most Europeans between 1924 and 1927, and to deportation of Mexicans during the Great Depression.

Racism in general, and anti-Semitism in particular, flourished in higher education. Jews were the first of the Euro-immigrant groups to enter college in significant numbers, so it was not surprising that they faced the brunt of discrimination there. The Protestant elite complained that Jews were unwashed, uncouth, unrefined, loud, and pushy. Harvard University President A. Lawrence Lowell, who was also a vice president of the Immigration Restriction League, was open about his opposition to Jews at Harvard. The Seven Sister schools had a reputation for "flagrant discrimination." M. Carey Thomas, Bryn Mawr president, may have been some kind of feminist, but she was also an admirer of scientific racism and an advocate of immigration restriction. She "blocked both the admission of black students and the promotion of Jewish instructors."

Jews are justifiably proud of the academic skills that gained them access to the most elite schools of the nation despite the prejudices of their gatekeepers. However, it is well to remember that they had no serious competition from their Protestant classmates. This is because college was not about academic pursuits. It was about social connection—through its clubs, sports and other activities, as well as in the friendships one was expected to forge with other children of elites. From this, the real purpose of the college experience, Jews remained largely excluded. . . .

■ ■ ■ WHITENING EURO-ETHNICS

By the time I was an adolescent, Jews were just as white as the next white person. Until I was eight, I was a Jew in a world of Jews. Everyone on Avenue Z in Sheepshead Bay was Jewish. I spent my days playing and going to school on three blocks of Avenue Z, and visiting my grandparents in the nearby Jewish neighborhoods of Brighton Beach and Coney Island. There were plenty of Italians in my neighborhood, but they lived around the corner. They were a kind of Jew, but on the margins of my social horizons. Portuguese were even more distant, at the end of the bus ride, at Sheepshead Bay. The *shul,* or temple, was on Avenue Z, and I begged my father to take me like all the other fathers took their kids, but religion wasn't part of my family's Judaism. Just how Jewish my neighborhood was hit me in first grade, when I was one of two kids to go to school on Rosh Hashanah. My teacher was shocked— she was Jewish too—and I was embarrassed to tears when she sent me home. I was never again sent to school on Jewish holidays. We left that world in 1949 when we moved to Valley Stream, Long Island, which was Protestant and Republican and even had farms until Irish, Italian, and Jewish ex-urbanites like us gave it a more suburban and Democratic flavor.

Neither religion nor ethnicity separated us at school or in the neighborhood. Except temporarily. During my elementary school years, I remember a fair number of dirt-bomb (a good suburban weapon) wars on the block. Periodically, one of the Catholic boys would accuse me or my brother of killing his god, to which we'd reply, "Did not," and start lobbing dirt bombs. Sometimes he'd get his friends from Catholic school and I'd get mine from public school kids on the block, some of whom were Catholic. Hostilities didn't last for more than a couple of hours and punctuated an otherwise friendly relationship. They ended by our junior high years, when other things became more important. Jews, Catholics and Protestants, Italians, Irish, Poles, "English" (I don't remember hearing WASP as a kid), were mixed up on the block and in school. We thought of ourselves as middle class and very enlightened because our ethnic backgrounds seemed so irrelevant to high school culture. We didn't see race (we thought), and racism was not part of our peer consciousness. Nor were the immigrant or working-class histories of our families.

As with most chicken-and-egg problems, it is hard to know which came first. Did Jews and other Euro-ethnics become white because they became middle-class? That is, did money whiten? Or did being incorporated into an expanded version of whiteness open up the economic doors to middle-class status? Clearly, both tendencies were at work.

Some of the changes set in motion during the war against fascism led to a more inclusive version of whiteness. Anti-Semitism and anti-European racism lost respectability. The 1940 Census no longer distinguished native whites of native parentage from those, like my parents, of immigrant parentage, so Euro-immigrants and their children were more securely white by submersion in an expanded notion of whiteness.

Theories of nurture and culture replaced theories of nature and biology. Instead of dirty and dangerous races that would destroy American democracy, immigrants became ethnic groups whose children had successfully assimilated into the mainstream and risen to the middle class. In this new myth, Euro-ethnic suburbs like mine became the measure of American democracy's victory over racism. Jewish mobility became a new Horatio Alger story. In time and with hard work, every ethnic group would get a piece of the pie, and the United States would be a nation with equal opportunity for all its people to become part of a prosperous middle-class majority. And it seemed that Euro-ethnic immigrants and their children were delighted to join middle America. . . .

Although changing views on who was white made it easier for Euro-ethnics to become middle class, economic prosperity also played a very powerful role in the whitening process. The economic mobility of Jews and other Euro-ethnics derived ultimately from America's postwar economic prosperity and its enormously expanded need for professional, technical, and managerial labor, as well as on government assistance in providing it.

The United States emerged from the war with the strongest economy in the world. Real wages rose between 1946 and 1960, increasing buying power a hefty 22 percent and giving most Americans some discretionary income. American manufacturing, banking, and business services were increasingly dominated by large corporations, and these grew into multinational corporations. Their organizational centers lay in big, new urban headquarters that demanded growing numbers of clerical, technical, and managerial workers. The postwar period was a historic moment for real class mobility and for the affluence we have erroneously come to believe was the American norm. It was a time when the old white and the newly white masses became middle class. . . .

■ ■ ■ **EDUCATION AND OCCUPATION**

It is important to remember that, prior to the war, a college degree was still very much a "mark of the upper class," that colleges were largely finishing schools for Protestant elites. Before the postwar boom, schools could not begin to accommodate the American masses. Even in New York City before the 1930s, neither the public schools nor City College had room for more than a tiny fraction of potential immigrant students.

Not so after the war. The almost 8 million GIs who took advantage of their educational benefits under the GI Bill caused "the greatest wave of college building in American history." White male GIs were able to take advantage of their educational benefits for college and technical training, so they were particularly well positioned to seize the opportunities provided by the new demands for professional, managerial, and technical labor. . . .

Postwar expansion made college accessible to Euromales in general and to Jews in particular. My generation's "Think what you could have been!" answer to our parents became our reality as quotas and old occupational barriers fell and new fields opened up to Jews. The most striking result was a sharp decline in Jewish small businesses and a skyrocketing increase in Jewish professionals. For example, as quotas in medical schools fell, the numbers of Jewish M.D.'s shot up. If Boston is any indication, just over 1 percent of all Jewish men before the war were doctors, but 16 percent of the postwar generation became M.D.'s. A similar Jewish mass movement took place into college and university faculties, especially in "new and expanding fields in the social and natural sciences."

Although these Jewish college professors tended to be sons of businessmen and professionals, the postwar boom saw the first large-scale class mobility among Jewish men. Sons of working-class Jews now went to college and became professionals themselves. . . .

Even more significantly, the postwar boom transformed America's class structure—or at least its status structure—so that the middle class expanded to encompass most of the population. Before the war, most Jews, like most other Americans, were part of the working class, defined in terms of occupation, education, and income. Already upwardly mobile before the war relative to other immigrants, Jews floated high on this rising economic tide, and most of them entered the middle class. The children of other immigrants did too. Still, even the high tide missed some Jews. As late as 1973, some 15 percent of New York's Jews were poor or near poor, and in the 1960s, almost 25 percent of employed Jewish men remained manual workers.

The reason I refer to educational and occupational GI benefits as affirmative action programs for white males is because they were decidedly not extended to African Americans or to women of any race. Theoretically they were available to all veterans; in practice women and black veterans did not get anywhere near their share. Women's Army and Air Force units were initially organized as auxiliaries, hence not part of the military. When that status was changed, in July 1943, only those who re-enlisted in the armed forces were eligible for veterans' benefits. Many women thought they were simply being demobilized and returned home. The majority remained and were ultimately eligible for veterans' benefits. But there was little counseling, and a social climate that discouraged women's careers and independence cut down on women's knowledge and sense of entitlement. The Veterans Administration kept no statistics on the number of women who used their GI benefits.

The barriers that almost completely shut African American GIs out of their benefits were even more formidable. Black GIs anticipated starting new lives, just like their white counterparts. Over 43 percent hoped to return to school, and most expected to relocate, to find better jobs in new lines of work. The exodus from the South toward the North and West was particularly large. So it was not a question of any lack of ambition on the part of African American GIs. White male privilege was shaped against the backdrop of wartime racism and postwar sexism.

During and after the war, there was an upsurge in white racist violence against black servicemen, in public schools, and by the Ku Klux Klan. It spread to California and New York. The number of lynchings rose during the war, and in 1943 there were antiblack race riots in several large northern cities. Although there was a wartime labor shortage, black people were discriminated against when it came to well-paid defense industry jobs and housing. In 1946, white riots against African Americans occurred across the South and in Chicago and Philadelphia. . . .

Black GIs faced discrimination in the educational system as well. Despite the end of restrictions on Jews and other Euro-ethnics, African Americans were not welcome in white colleges. Black colleges were overcrowded, but the combination of segregation and prejudice made for few alternatives. About 20,000 black veterans attended college by 1947, most in black colleges, but almost as many, 15,000, could not gain entry. Predictably, the disproportionately few African Americans who did gain access to their educational benefits were able, like their white counterparts, to become doctors and engineers, and to enter the black middle class.

■ ■ ■ ■ SUBURBANIZATION

In 1949, ensconced in Valley Stream, I watched potato farms turn into Levittown and Idlewild (later Kennedy) airport. This was the major spectator sport in our first years on Long Island. A typical weekend would bring various aunts, uncles, and cousins out from the city. After a huge meal, we'd pile into the car—itself a novelty—to look at the bulldozed acres and comment on the matchbox construction. During the week, my mother and I would look at the houses going up within walking distance.

Bill Levitt built a basic, 900–1,000 square foot, somewhat expandable house for a lower-middle-class and working-class market on Long Island, and later in Pennsylvania and New Jersey. Levittown started out as 2,000 units of rental housing at $60 a month, designed to meet the low-income housing needs of returning war vets, many of whom, like my Aunt Evie and Uncle Julie, were living in Quonset huts. By May 1947, Levitt and Sons had acquired enough land in Hempstead Township on Long Island to build 4,000 houses, and by the next February, he had built 6,000 units and named the development after himself. After 1948, federal financing for the construction of rental housing tightened, and Levitt switched to building houses for sale. By 1951, Levittown was a development of some 15,000 families.

At the beginning of World War II, about one-third of all American families owned their houses. That percentage doubled in twenty years. Most Levittowners looked just like my family. They came from New York City or Long Island; about 17 percent were military, from nearby Mitchell Field; Levittown was their first house, and almost everyone was married. Three-quarters of the 1947 inhabitants were white collar, but by 1950 more blue-collar families had moved in, so that by 1951, "barely half" of the new residents were white collar, and by 1960 their occupational profile was somewhat more working class than for Nassau County as a whole. By this time too, almost one-third of Levittown's people were either foreign-born or, like my parents, first-generation U.S.-born.

The Federal Housing Administration (FHA) was key to buyers and builders alike. Thanks to the FHA, suburbia was open to more than GIs. People like us would never have been in the market for houses without FHA and Veterans Administration (VA) low-down-payment, low-interest, long-term loans to young buyers. Most suburbs were built by "merchant builders," large-scale entrepreneurs like Levitt, who obtained their own direct FHA and VA loans. . . .

In residential life, as in jobs and education, federal programs and GI benefits were crucial for mass entry into a middle-class, home-owning suburban lifestyle. Together they raised the American standard of living to a middle-class one.

It was in housing policy that the federal government's racism reached its high point. . . . The FHA believed in racial segregation. Throughout its history, it publicly and actively promoted restrictive covenants. Before the war, these forbade sales to Jews and Catholics as well as to African Americans. The deed to my house in Detroit had such a covenant, which theoretically prevented it from being sold to Jews or African Americans. Even after the Supreme Court outlawed restrictive covenants in 1948, the FHA continued to encourage builders to write them in against African Americans. FHA underwriting manuals openly insisted on racially homogenous neighborhoods, and their loans were made only in white neighborhoods. . . .

With the federal government behind them, virtually all developers refused to sell to African Americans. Palo Alto and Levittown, like most suburbs as late as 1960, were virtually all white. Out of 15,741 houses and 65,276 people, averaging 4.2 people per house, only 220 Levittowners, or 52 households, were "nonwhite." In 1958, Levitt announced publicly, at a press conference held to open his New Jersey development, that he would not sell to black buyers. This caused a furor because the state of New Jersey (but not the U.S. government) prohibited discrimination in federally subsidized housing. Levitt was sued and fought it. There had been a white riot in his Pennsylvania development when a black family moved in a few years earlier. In New Jersey, he was ultimately persuaded by township ministers to integrate. West Coast builder Joe Eichler had a policy of selling to any African American who could afford to buy. But his son pointed out that his father's clientele in more affluent Palo Alto was less likely to feel threatened. They liked to think of themselves as liberal, which was relatively easy to do because there were relatively few African Americans in the Bay area, and fewer still could afford homes in Palo Alto.

The result of these policies was that African Americans were totally shut out of the suburban boom. . . .

Urban renewal was the other side of the process by which Jewish and other working-class Euro-immigrants became middle class. It was the push to suburbia's seductive pull. The fortunate white survivors of urban renewal headed disproportionately for suburbia, where they could partake of prosperity and the good life. There was a reason for its attraction. It was often cheaper to buy in the suburbs than to rent in the city. Even Euro-ethnics and families who would be considered working class, based on their occupations, were able to buy into the emerging white suburban lifestyle. And as Levittown indicates, they did so in increasing numbers, so that by 1966 half of all workers and 75 percent of those under forty nationwide lived in suburbs. They too were considered middle-class. . . .

■ ■ ■ ■ **CONCLUSION**

The myth that Jews pulled themselves up by their own bootstraps ignores the fact that it took federal programs to create the conditions whereby the abilities of Jews and other European immigrants could be recognized and rewarded rather than denigrated and denied. The GI Bill and FHA and VA mortgages, even though they were advertised as open to all, functioned as a set of racial privileges. They were privileges because they were extended to white GIs but not to black GIs. Such privileges were forms of affirmative action that allowed Jews and other Euro-American men to become suburban homeowners and to get the training that allowed them—but much less so women vets or war workers—to become professionals, technicians, salesmen, and managers in a growing economy. Jews and other white ethnics' upward mobility was due to programs that allowed us to float on a rising economic tide. . . .

Those racially skewed gains have been passed across the generations, so that racial inequality seems to maintain itself "naturally," even after legal segregation ended. Today, I own a house in Venice, California, like the one in which I grew up in Valley Stream, and my brother until recently owned a house in Palo Alto much like an Eichler house. Both of us are where we are thanks largely to the postwar benefits our parents received and passed on to us, and to the educational benefits we received in the 1960s as a result of affluence. . . .

Conventional wisdom has it that the United States has always been an affluent land of opportunity. But the truth is that affluence has been the exception and that real upward mobility has required massive affirmative action programs. The myth of affluence persists today long after the industrial boom, and the public policies that supported good union contracts and real employment opportunities for (almost) all are gone. It is increasingly clear that the affluent period between 1940 and 1970 or 1975 was an aberrant one for America's white working class. The Jewish ethnic wisdom I grew up with, that we pulled ourselves up by our own bootstraps, by sticking together, by being damned smart, leaves out an important part of the truth: that not all Jews made it, and that those who did had a great deal of help from the federal government.

"But This Is My Mother!" The Plight of Elders in Nursing Homes

Cynthia Loucks

introduction

As discussed in *Sociology*, the globe is graying. Not only is the number of elderly increasing around the world, but also the elderly are becoming a larger proportion of the population of most countries. A generation ago, people age sixty-five and over made up 10 percent of the population in the United States. Today, about 13 percent of Americans are elderly. In another generation, just before the year 2050, the proportion of the elderly is expected to reach 20 percent. At that time, on average, every fifth person you see will be age sixty-five or older. (Of course, by that time, you too will be elderly, so with your network of elderly friends, almost everyone you see will be old.)

As also discussed in *Sociology*, being elderly is not itself a problem. As you read in Chapter 13, the "facts" of old age differ from one culture to another. There is, for example, no cross-cultural agreement about the age at which people become old. And when a group does apply the label of *old* to someone, there is no cross-cultural consensus about what being old means. A global problem of old age, however, is the dependency that sometimes accompanies it. In our society, the growing number of elderly means that we need more medical care and changing medical specialties. Although the average elderly American is independent and healthy, some of the elderly are poor, and even larger numbers are in poor health.

The frail elderly present special problems. When people grow old and no longer are able to take care of themselves, what should be done? Every society has to find ways of taking care of their frail elderly, but, as you read in Chapter 13 with the example of the Tiwi, sometimes those solutions are detrimental to the elderly. So it often is with our own particular solution—nursing homes, the topic of this selection by Cynthia Loucks.

Thinking Critically

As you read this selection, ask yourself:

1. What problems of nursing homes does the author describe? This is just the plight of one person in a single nursing home; why should we pay attention to it?

2. Inadequate care in nursing homes and the harm this does to the elderly have been well documented as a national problem. Why does this situation continue?

3. How are you going to ensure that you will receive adequate health care when you are elderly? How will you avoid being exploited?

*W*hether elders have bed sores is a good indicator of the quality of care that is being provided. Elders who can no longer move themselves must be repositioned regularly so that their body weight is not resting in any one place for too long. A head nurse on my mother's ward told me that nursing home regulations require that immobile residents be turned every two hours while in bed in order to shift their weight distribution and to vary the pressure on their body parts. If necessary, pillows can be used to position residents on their sides. But when there is a shortage of pillows, the efforts of conscientious aides who try to keep up with the necessary regimen are hampered.

In the course of a person's physical disintegration, bed sores become more difficult to prevent. When someone is very near death, subjecting them to the disturbance of repositioning can be unduly inconsiderate. However, until that point, nursing home staff need to follow the guidelines for preventing bed sores. The reality remains that in many facilities, including the one my mother was in, dependent elders are moved as little as once during an eight hour shift. Even then, most of the movements that occur are merely back and forth between bed and chair, which may not provide any relief if the weight of the body remains on the same spot. In addition, many nursing home residents are in effect lying down even when they are in their chairs, since the recliners are cranked back in order to use gravity to keep flaccid bodies from sliding onto the floor.

Other methods of preventing bed sores, such as gentle massage to stimulate circulation, are seldom employed by overworked staff in nursing homes. Although various devices can be used in chairs and beds to relieve sacral pressure—doughnut-shaped pillows, "egg crate" foam cushions and mattresses, gel-filled mattresses and pillows—these items are often in short supply in many nursing homes. A resident's personal cushion also can lie unnoticed in a closet where one staff person may have stored it and the next staff person does not rediscover it.

It distressed me a great deal to know that Mama couldn't turn herself over in bed or shift her weight in her chair without assistance. She easily could be left in an uncomfortable position for hours, unable to do anything about it. According to her last doctor, the one with geriatric training, part of the nature of Mama's condition was that she no longer felt the uncomfortable pressure or nerve stimuli that prompt the rest of us to shift our positions frequently. I hoped he was right and that Mama never felt too uncomfortable.

When immobile residents aren't being repositioned regularly, it often means they aren't being checked on frequently, either. As a result, nursing home residents have been found stuck in some very bizarre and even potentially life-threatening positions. Sometimes I would find Mama in an incredibly uncomfortable-looking posture. She would be so still, just staring, waiting, as though resigned to something she knew she was helpless to alter. On at least two occasions I know of, Mama somehow rolled to the side of her bed and wound up with her head stuck between the bed rails for who knows how long before someone found her. At the time, I was unaware of how terribly dangerous this phenomenon can actually be. I learned later that many nursing home residents have lost their lives from getting trapped in their bed rails and not being discovered in time to be rescued.

Mama also often slipped down in her chair, another typical side effect of paralysis and other conditions that impede the ability to resist gravity. It was part of the conundrum of having to be left fully upright after meals with no wherewithal to maintain the position herself. I feared that hours might go by before anyone noticed she had slumped. She could even slip all the way out of the chair and wind up injured on the floor before anyone might come to reposition her. I vividly remember one instance when I walked into Mama's room and found that she had slid so far out of her slippery vinyl recliner that only her sacrum and the back of her neck were in contact with the chair. Her chin was pressed to her chest and her legs were sticking out straight in front of her, well beyond the support of the chair's leg rest. She was staring straight ahead, her blank expression revealing little of the soul trapped in that poor old vessel.

I often wondered what Mama was thinking at those times, unsure whether she just checked out or maybe even went into some sort of trance induced by her extreme helplessness. I would notice a particularly blank expression on her face on such occasions, as well as sometimes when the aides were cleaning her, another undoubtedly unpleasant event. This common psychological response of distancing oneself in some way when under such circumstances is called dissociation. When something in life is too disagreeable, people employ defense mechanisms in order to handle the stress. What happens to the people who have to do this every day, several times a day, in order to deal with their circumstances? It is a question that needs to be addressed on behalf of all nursing home residents.

Another highly disconcerting and recurring event in Mama's life took place whenever she had to be transferred. In medical settings, to "transfer" someone is to move an immobilized person from one conveyance to another—from bed to geri-chair or wheelchair, from chair to toilet, etc., and back again. This particular aspect of caring for disabled elders is probably the most strenuous for all concerned. Those elders who cannot bear any weight on their feet are the most difficult to transfer. Even with a small person like Mama, who weighed less than one hundred pounds by the time she was admitted to the nursing home, the bulk and stiffness of the person render the process awkward.

Mama often screamed when she was being transferred, a habit that rattled many of her aides. I think she was frightened to be picked up, afraid she would be dropped or otherwise injured, which is not an unrealistic fear for someone in such impotent circumstances. To ease fears about being transferred and to limit the possibility of injury, there is an approved procedure for moving dependent residents. Two aides or nurses lift the resident along four points—the two armpits and the backs of the two knees—so that the person's weight is evenly distributed. In Mama's case, she was often transferred, whether by one aide or two, by lifting her up by her armpits only. Not only was that a very uncomfortable way to be lifted, but it also risked injury to her unsupported lower torso and limbs. Throughout Mama's stay in the nursing home I tried constantly to get the aides to use their other hand to support Mama beneath her knees. Trying to motivate them, I pointed out that Mama surely wouldn't cry out so much if they used this method. But with each subsequent visit I would see that the aides had reverted to their armpit-only transfer. Considering that Mama was probably transferred between bed and chair an average of 6 times per day, 365 days a year, it was quite an ordeal for her to endure.

There are other chronic physical care issues, albeit non-life-threatening, that are frequently left unattended to in nursing homes. For example, Mama's feet were often cold, so I bought her several pairs of socks and focused on trying to get the aides to remember to put them on her when she needed them. I shouldn't have been surprised when I realized they were putting socks on her all the time, even if her feet weren't cold. At times I would find Mama so hot that she was perspiring. It seemed like such a small thing to pay attention to—a person's skin temperature and then dressing her accordingly. Yet, such consideration was almost totally outside the bounds of the care that Mama received.

The paralysis that followed Mama's stroke and the subsequent lack of movement that ensued resulted in the contraction of her left arm and hand. During the first few months after Mama's arrival at the nursing home, a young woman came in from time to time to perform range-of-motion movements with Mama's limbs, a means for both reducing contraction and improving circulation. When the therapy was discontinued, for whatever reason I do not know, I didn't protest. The young woman had seemed so inexperienced, and Mama clearly didn't enjoy having her arms and legs tugged this way and that. I couldn't bring myself to insist on more.

Mama spent a lot of time either in bed or in her chair with her legs outstretched. Before long, her ankles became rotated such that her feet were always turned in toward one another. Knowing she would never walk again, I didn't think it made a difference how her ankles were positioned so long as there were no indications of discomfort. The color and the condition of her skin looked all right. One of the nurses told me that people's ankles naturally rotated inward once they can no longer walk. I believed her and assumed that she had probably seen it happen many times before. But when I later learned how easily this condition could have been prevented by using pillows to hold her ankles in a neutral position, I felt remorse for having left it at that. I was not aware of the stress that this rotated position placed on all of Mama's connecting joints, and probably on the bones themselves, all the way up to her hips. (To see what this is like, lie down on your back when you are in bed tonight, with your legs outstretched, and slowly rotate your ankles inward as far as they will go. Notice the sensations that occur immediately, even as far up as the small of your back. Ouch!)

Mama's skin had gotten as thin as an old shirt that's been worn and washed so many times it has become transparent and easily torn. Yet, the aides would take a terry washcloth, coarse from heavy bleaching, and scrub her as though she had been digging ditches all day. Although stimulating the skin is beneficial, their methods looked excessive. When I suggested that Mama didn't need such vigorous bathing, they humored me and washed her more gently; but I had no doubt that as soon as I wasn't available to monitor them, they returned to doing it their way.

It wasn't long before Mama developed a skin rash. Considered a redhead (though her hair was more a deep auburn), Mama always had sensitive skin, so it was not surprising that it protested the treatment it received in the nursing home. The doctors and nurses discussed prescribing medication for her, both cortisone-based pills and lotions. As usual, the medical approach was to suppress the symptom without attempting to alleviate its cause.

Aides give bed baths by bringing a plastic tub of warm, soapy water to the bed of a resident, who then gets washed down with a washcloth. To my dismay, I discovered that after washing Mama, some of the aides simply dried her off without first rinsing her skin. Others would bring fresh water for rinsing her but would still use the same sudsy washcloth. The source of Mama's rash seemed obvious to me. When I pointed out the detrimental shortcuts, the aides countered that it was difficult to rinse her properly without getting the bed unduly wet. I suggested that they might try rinsing out the washcloth first with clean water and that if they used less soap when they filled up the plastic tub—it was usually frothing with suds—the rinsing might go more easily. They grudgingly agreed to try it, and Mama's rash soon subsided.

I also had to lobby to add moisturizing lotion to Mama's required skin-care regimen. I scrawled Mama's name in big black letters on her lotion dispenser in the hope that it would actually remain in her room. Since care supplies are seldom adequately stocked in nursing homes, staff freely "borrow" from one resident to give to another—the best solution they can find when needing something otherwise unavailable. Thanks partly to the ongoing vigilance of Aunt Margaret and the steady supply the family provided, lotion was always available. How often it was used on Mama, however, was less reliable. I bought facial moisturizer for Mama, too, but I could tell by how much remained in the jar that it was seldom applied by anyone else but me. I enjoyed rubbing the lotion onto her face. It was a chance to express the gentleness and tenderness that I felt for her, to nurture her in some small way.

It was also apparent that duties such as providing oral care were getting checked off on Mama's chart when they were not actually being performed. Her dentures had disappeared within a few weeks of her arrival at the nursing home. A nurse speculated that they were probably thrown out with her soiled laundry. Their loss, of course, did not preclude her need for oral care. One method of providing this care involves using a little sponge that is attached to the end of a stick. When dipped in water, the sponge emits a mouthwash-like substance. The sponge is then used to massage and freshen a person's mouth and gums without the need for rinsing. But like most medical supplies, these implements are ridiculously expensive and are invariably in short supply at nursing homes.

The physical care of nursing home residents is further complicated by the maladies that are endemic in today's long term care facilities, and Mama certainly wasn't immune to any of these problems. Urinary tract infections, diarrhea, congestion, dehydration, rashes, and bed sores—these ailments never seem to surprise the doctors, who attribute them to residents' advanced ages and poor physical conditions. While elders do tend to have diminished immune systems and increased susceptibility to sickness, especially when they are inactive, this knowledge should be a warning for increased preventive care rather than an excuse for the various skin, digestive, and bacterial problems that occur. These afflictions could be greatly reduced with good, consistent attention to residents' hygiene as well as to their prescribed care regimens. There should be no excuse for failing to avert the preventable.

When nursing home residents are no longer able to control the flow of their urine, they develop rashes from the prolonged exposure of their skin to the urine in their bedding and diapers. In typical fashion, nursing homes respond to the frequency of these rashes by inserting catheters into aged urethras. While reducing the need for frequent cleanup, catheters provide ideal conditions for the proliferation of infection-causing bacteria. Improperly used and monitored, as they often are in nursing homes, they can present other hazards as well. I once found that my mother had been placed in her bed lying on the tubing, which of course blocked the flow.

In addition, many elderly recipients of these contraptions, no longer constrained by subservience to authority, yank them out, causing subsequent irritation to tender tissue. After Mama suffered through several urinary tract infections, I decided that she, too, had had enough. I told the staff that I did not want any more foreign objects inserted anywhere into my mother and vetoed the further use of a catheter on her. While the doctors never seemed to question writing an order for a catheter and following it with the almost inevitable antibiotic prescription a week or two later, the nursing staff, who saw the human result of that cycle in increased bowel difficulties due to the loss of healthy intestinal flora, were more willing to break the cycle and acquiesce to my request, even though they had requested the catheter in the first place. One nurse admitted to me that she knew I was right, although overall, the staff was miffed that I expected them to keep Mama clean and dry enough to avoid further rashes.

Such medical aspects of Mama's care were never ending. I had to function as a conduit of information among the ever-changing nursing home staff, the doctor, and hospital staff whenever Mama was hospitalized for conditions such as internal bleeding episodes. It was especially important to provide the hospital staff with information because they never seemed to be notified of the particulars of Mama's health care. Once I was just in time to prevent a hospital nurse from attempting to feed Mama solid food, an act that would almost certainly have choked her.

I also had to keep trying to get Mama a diet that took into consideration her pre-existing condition of chronic colitis (inflammation of the colon). I needed to be on the lookout for cuts, sores, infections, and problems with her G-tube, so that these problems were attended to promptly, regularly, and effectively. I tried to be sure that she was not given treatments that would precipitate yet another condition requiring treatment. I checked that she was given sufficient fluids to avoid dehydration, which became a problem due to her inability to consume sufficient quantities at meal times and the unavailability of staff to provide the fluids she needed between meals.

It was very frustrating to review Mama's treatment and consider that she was in a reputable nursing home. At best, her care was tolerable, with rare instances of very good. Frequently, it was heedless, insensitive, rough, and even dangerous. Yet, I was determined to keep fighting for Mama, to keep taking yet another grievance to the head nurse, the doctor, the social worker, whomever I thought might be able to help us. There was never any question of giving up, even though overseeing Mama's care in that nursing home was truly the most demanding, frustrating, and disheartening job I have ever had.

It galled me again and again to witness the indifference with which so many of the nursing home staff treated my mother. They seemed unwilling to look at what they were doing and apparently regarded my efforts to intervene as just so much nagging. Even those who responded positively to my suggestions would either soon revert to their usual methods or not be taking care of my mother any more. Between staff rotations and people quitting, Mama never had the same caregivers for long, which deprived her of the comfort and reassurance that familiarity and continuity could have provided.

The unkindness that some of the aides displayed toward Mama—and that they would behave that way right in front of me—was not only distressing but downright baffling. Throughout her stay at the nursing home, when she wasn't too ill or too sleepy to respond, Mama always had an enthusiastically friendly greeting for one and all. To me it was a reflection of the wonderful graciousness that she managed to retain throughout so much of her ordeal.

One day a young male aide came into Mama's room to attend to her. True to form, Mama called out a cheery "Hi!" when the young man approached her bed. Silence. Seconds passed. Undaunted, Mama said "Hi!" again, with no less warmth or cheer. Her voice and what she said were clear and unmistakable. Still silence. Despite my pounding heart and the fury rising in my throat, I remained calm so as not to make a scene in front of Mama. I said to the young man, "She said 'hi' to you." As though coming out of a trance, he finally uttered a dull, flat "Hello." And without another word, he proceeded to perform his duties in an efficient but perfunctory manner. Mama fell silent.

When I later saw the aide in the corridor, I questioned him about his thoughtless behavior. Vaguely apologetic, he informed me that he had a lot on his mind. I was less than sympathetic and complained about the incident to the head nurse. She shared my dismay at the aide's behavior, agreeing that professional caregivers should leave their personal problems at the door when they come to work. It was good to have her agreement, but it didn't change anything.

I winced whenever I watched aides and nurses tend to Mama without speaking to her or speak to her without looking at her. I desperately wanted them to act in a manner that was kind, civil, and respectful. I knew what a difference it would make for Mama if they took a moment to explain what they were going to do and if they made an effort to listen to her, responding as much as possible to what she indicated.

All nursing home residents have psychological, emotional, and social needs regardless of their conditions. They need eye contact and whatever else seems appropriate to foster a feeling of connection and respect for their basic humanity. The lack of such behavior constitutes an assault on the human spirit and is, in many ways, the most painful offense for people to bear. It wounds more deeply than the discomfort and indignity of poor physical care.

PART

IV Social Institutions

In the previous parts, you have seen many of the social forces that influence your life, those that twist and turn you in one direction or another. You have read about culture and socialization, social control and deviance, and various forms of social stratification. In this part, we turn our focus onto *social institutions,* the standard ways that society sets up to meet its basic needs.

To exist, every society must solve certain problems. Babies must be nourished and children socialized into adult roles. The sex drive must be held within bounds. To help accomplish these things, every society has set up some form of marriage and family, the first social institution we meet on the stage of life. Social order—keeping people from robbing and killing one another—also has to be established. To accomplish this, each social group sets up some form of what we call *politics.* Goods and services also have to be produced and distributed. This leads to what is called the *economy.* The new generation also has to be taught how to view the world in the "correct" way, as well as to learn the skills to participate in the economy. For this, we have some form of education. Then there are views of the spiritual world, of God and morality, perhaps of an afterlife. For this, we have religion.

We are immersed in social institutions, and we never escape from them. We are born into one (the family), we attend school in another (education), and we make our living in still another (economy). Even if we don't vote, the political institution surrounds us with the demands of its laws. Even if we don't worship at a church, synagogue, or mosque, we can't avoid religion, for practices such as closing most offices, schools, and factories on Sunday are based on religion.

Social institutions, then, are another way that society nudges us to fit in. Like a curb or median is to an automobile, so social institutions are to our lives. They set boundaries around us, directing us to think, act, and feel along certain avenues, pushing us to turn one way instead of another.

Social institutions are so significant that sociologists specialize in them. Some focus on marriage and family, others study politics or the economy, whereas still others do research on religion or education. After this introductory course—which is a survey of sociology—students usually can take courses on specific social institutions. Often, for example, departments of sociology teach a course on marriage and family. In large departments, there may be a course on each social institution, one on the sociology of religion, another on the sociology of education, and so on. In very large departments, the social institutions may be broken down into smaller components, and there may be several courses on the sociology of family, politics, education, and so on.

To focus on social institutions, we open this part with an article by George Ritzer, who examines how changes in the economy are affecting our lives, how society is being McDonaldized. The selection that follows has become a classic in sociology, C. Wright Mills's analysis of the ruling elite of the United States. What Mills calls the *power elite* is the group that makes the major decisions that affect our lives. Arlie Hochschild then analyzes a major change that is taking place in some work and family settings, where work becomes more enjoyable than family life. In the selection on education, Peter and Patricia Adler, husband and wife sociologists, report on their study of college basketball players, analyzing why so few of them graduate from college. As you read this article, you will understand the dynamics of organizations and subcultures that defeat what should be the purpose of education. To examine religion, Marvin Harris then explains why letting cows wander about India's streets is functional for that society. We conclude this part with a look at the medical institution, a participant observation study by Daniel Chambliss that takes us behind the scenes of the hospital.

The McDonaldization of Society

George Ritzer

introduction ▪ ▪ ▪ ▪ ▪

A key term in sociology is *rationalization*. This term refers to choosing the most efficient means to accomplish tasks. As Max Weber, the sociologist to first analyze rationalization, noted, the traditional ways of doing things—which may be inefficient but provides personal satisfactions and a sense of belonging—are passing. Weber didn't know how far-reaching and accurate his analysis would prove. In most cases, traditional ways have passed into history and now are mere memories. Rationalization has led to the dominance of the bottom line, to calculating costs in order to produce the most gain. In the place of traditional ways we have bureaucracies, where cold analyses are applied to every act of workers with little concern for the people who make up the work setting. Profit has become king, while people, evaluated according to what they bring to the bottom line, become expendable.

As the rationalization of society continues, it threatens to ensnare us all, locking us in what Weber called an iron cage of rationality. College administrators, for example, want to evaluate instructors not by how they challenge students to think, by how creatively they present core concepts, or by how they open minds to new perceptions, but, rather, by the sheer numbers of students they turn out each semester. Even the routine, everyday aspects of family life are not immune to this process of rationality, as becomes evident in Ritzer's analysis in this selection.

Thinking Critically

As you read this selection, ask yourself:

1. What areas of your life are still marked by a traditional orientation? Are any of those areas now giving way to rationality?

2. If rationality continues, little will be left of our lives that has not been rationalized. Can you identify areas of life that cannot be rationalized?

3. What do you think about the McDonaldization of society? In what ways do you see it as good and bad?

McDonald's has sought to construct highly efficient systems, and *McDonaldization* implies the search for maximum efficiency in increasingly numerous and diverse social settings. *Efficiency* means the choice of the optimum means to a given end, but this definition requires some clarification. Although we use the term *optimum*, it is rare that the truly optimum means to an end is ever found. Rather, there is a search for a . . . far better means to an end than would be employed under ordinary circumstances. . . .

■ ■ ■ WIRELESS KEYBOARDS AND SELF–SERVICE SLURPEES

The emphasis of McDonaldization on efficiency implies that contrasting, nonrational systems are less efficient, or even inefficient. The fast-food restaurant grew as a result of its greater efficiency in comparison to alternative methods of obtaining a meal. In the early 1950s, at the dawning of the era of the fast-food restaurant, the major alternative was the home-cooked meal made largely from ingredients previously purchased at various markets. . . .

But the home-cooked meal was, and still is, a relatively inefficient way of obtaining a meal. The restaurant has long been a more efficient alternative. But restaurants can be inefficient in that it may take several hours to go to the restaurant, consume a meal, and then return home. The desire for more efficient restaurants led to the rise of some of the ancestors of the fast-food restaurant—diners, cafeterias, and early drive-through or drive-in restaurants. The modern fast-food restaurant can be seen as being built on the latter models and as a further step in the direction of more efficient food consumption. . . .

Above all else, it was the efficiency of the McDonald brothers' operation that impressed Ray Kroc [the individual behind the franchising of McDonald's], as well as the enormous profit potential of such a system if it were applied in a large number of sites. Here is how Kroc described his initial reactions to the McDonald's system:

> I was fascinated by the simplicity and effectiveness of the system. . . . Each step in producing the limited menu was stripped down to its essence and accomplished with a minimum of effort. They sold hamburgers and cheeseburgers only. The burgers were . . . all fried the same way.

Kroc and his associates looked at each component of the hamburger in order to increase the efficiency with which it could be produced and served. For example, they started with only partially sliced buns that were attached to one another. However, it was found that buns could be used more efficiently if they were sliced all the way through and separated from one another. At first, the buns arrived in cardboard boxes and the griddle workers had to spend time opening the boxes, separating the buns, slicing them, and discarding the leftover paper and cardboard. In addition to separating and preslicing them, buns were made efficient to use by having them shipped in reusable boxes. Similar attention was devoted to the meat patty. For example, the paper between the patties had to have just the right amount of wax so that the patties would readily slide off the paper and onto the grill.

Kroc makes it clear that the goal of these kinds of refinements was greater efficiency:

> The purpose of all these refinements, and we never lost sight of it, was to make our griddle man's job easier to do quickly and well. And the other considerations of cost cutting, inventory control, and so forth were important to be sure, but they were secondary to the critical detail of what happened there at the smoking griddle. This was the vital passage of our *assembly-line*, and the product had to flow through it smoothly or the whole plant would falter. (Italics added)

. . . Once diners enter the fast-food restaurant, the process continues to appear to be efficient. Parking lots are adjacent to the restaurant and parking spots are readily available. It's a short walk to the counter, and although there is sometimes a line, food is usually quickly ordered, obtained, and paid for. The highly limited menu makes the choice of a meal's components quite easy. This contrasts to the many choices available in many of the alternatives to the fast-food restaurant. With the food obtained, it is but a few steps to a table and the beginning of the "dining experience." The fare almost always involves an array of finger foods (for example, Chicken McNuggets and french fries) that can be popped into the diner's mouth with the result that the entire meal is ordinarily consumed in a few minutes. Because there is little inducement to linger, the diners generally gather the leftover paper, Styrofoam, and plastic, discard them in a nearby trash receptacle, and are back in their car and on their way to the next (often McDonaldized) activity.

Not too many years ago, those in charge of fast-food restaurants discovered that there was a way—the drive-through window—to make this whole process far more efficient for both themselves and the consumer. Instead of the "laborious" and "inefficient" process of parking the car, walking to the counter, waiting in line, ordering, paying, carrying the food to the table, eating, and disposing of the remnants, the drive-through window offered diners the choice of driving to the window (perhaps waiting in a line of cars), ordering, paying, and driving off with the meal. It was even possible to engage in the highly efficient act of eating while driving, thereby eliminating the need to devote a separate time period to dining. The drive-through window is also efficient from the perspective of the fast-food restaurant. As more and more people use the drive-through window, fewer parking spaces, tables, and employees are needed. Further, consumers take their debris with them as they drive away, thereby eliminating the need for additional trash receptacles and employees to periodically empty those receptacles. . . .

■ ■ ■ "HOME-MADE" FAST FOOD AND THE STAIRMASTER

Given the efficiency of the fast-food restaurant, the home kitchen has had to grow more efficient or it might have faced total extinction. Had the kitchen not grown more efficient, a comedian could have envisioned a time when the kitchen would have been replaced by a large, comfortable telephone lounge used for calling Domino's for pizza delivery. The key to the salvation of the kitchen was the development and widespread adoption of the microwave oven. The microwave is simply a far more efficient means than its major alternative, the convection oven, for preparing a meal. It is usually faster than the old oven and one can prepare a wider array of foods in it than the old-fashioned oven. Perhaps most importantly from the point of view of this chapter, it spawned the development of a number of microwavable foods (including soup, pizza, hamburgers, fried chicken, french fries, and popcorn) that permit the efficient preparation of the fare one usually finds in the fast-food restaurants. For example, one of the first microwavable foods produced by Hormel was an array of biscuit-based breakfast sandwiches "popularized in recent years by many of the fast-food chains," most notably McDonald's and its Egg McMuffin. Banquet rushed to market with microwavable chicken breast nuggets. In fact, many food companies now employ people who continually scout fast-food restaurants for new ideas for foods that can be marketed for the home. As one executive put it, "Instead of having a breakfast sandwich at McDonald's, you can pick one up from the freezer of your grocery store." As a result, one can now, in effect, enjoy fast food at home without venturing out to the fast-food restaurant. . . .

Another factor in the continued success of the fast-food restaurant is that it has many advantages over the "home-cooked" microwave dinner. For example, a trip to the fast-food restaurant offers people a dinner out rather than just another meal at home. For another, as Stan Luxenberg has pointed out in *Roadside Empires,* McDonald's offers more than an efficient meal, it offers fun—brightly lit, colorful, and attractive settings, garish packaging, special inducements to children, giveaways, contests—in short, it offers a kind of carnival-like atmosphere in which to buy and consume fast food. Thus, faced with the choice of an efficient meal at home or one in a fast-food restaurant, many people are still likely to choose the fast-food restaurant because it not only offers efficiency but a range of other rewards.

The microwave oven (as well as the range of products it spawned) is but one of many contributors to the increasing efficiency of home cooking. Among other obvious technological advances are the replacement of the hand beater by the electric beater; slicers, dicers, and even knives by the Cuisinart; and the presence of either stand-alone freezers or those that are an integral part of the refrigerator.

The large freezer has permitted a range of efficiencies, such as a few trips to the market for enormous purchases rather than many trips for small purchases. It has permitted the storage of a wide range of ingredients that can be readily extracted when needed for food preparation. It has allowed for the cooking of large portions which can then be divided up, frozen, and defrosted periodically for dinner. The widespread availability of the home freezer led to the expansion of the production of frozen foods of all types. The most notable frozen food from the point of view of efficiency is the "TV dinner." People can stock their freezers with an array of such dinners (for example, Chinese, Italian, and Mexican dinners as well as a wide variety of "American" cooking) and quite readily bring them out and pop them into the oven, sometimes even the microwave. . . .

The McDonaldization of food preparation and consumption has been extended to the booming diet industry. Diet books promising all sorts of efficient shortcuts to weight loss are often at the top of the best-seller lists. Losing weight is normally difficult and time-consuming, hence the lure of various diet books that promise to make weight loss easier and quicker, that is, more efficient.

For those on a diet, and many people are on more or less perpetual diets, the preparation of low-calorie food has been made more efficient. Instead of needing to cook diet foods from scratch, they may now purchase an array of prepared foods in frozen and/or microwavable form. For those who do not wish to go through the inefficient process of eating those diet meals, there are the diet shakes, like Slim•Fast, that can be mixed and consumed in a matter of seconds.

A fairly recent development is the growth of diet centers like Nutri/System and Jenny Craig. Nutri/System sells dieters, at substantial cost, prepackaged freeze-dried food. All the dieter need do is add water when it is time for the next meal. Freeze-dried foods are not only efficient for the dieter but also for Nutri/System, because they can be efficiently packaged, transported, and stored. Furthermore, the dieter's periodic visit to a Nutri/System center is efficiently organized. A counselor is allotted ten minutes with each client. During that brief time the counselor takes the client's weight, blood pressure, and measurements, asks routine questions, fills out a chart, and devotes some time to "problem-solving." If the session extends beyond the allotted ten minutes and other clients are waiting, the receptionist will buzz the counselor's room. Counselors learn their techniques at Nutri/System University where, after a week of training (no inefficient years of matriculation here), they earn certification and an NSU diploma.

There is a strong emphasis on efficiency in modern health clubs, including such chains as Holiday Spas. These clubs often offer, under one roof, virtually everything needed to lose weight and stay in shape, including a wide array of exercise machines, as well as a running track and a swimming pool. The exercise machines are highly specialized so that one may efficiently increase fitness in specific areas of the body. Thus, working out on running machines and the StairMaster—one kind of exercise machine—increases cardiovascular fitness, whereas using various weightlifting machines increases strength and muscularity in targeted areas of the body. Another efficiency associated with many of these machines is that one can do other things while exercising. Thus, many clubs have television sets throughout the gym allowing people to both watch television and exercise. The exerciser can also read, listen to music, or even listen to a book-on-tape while working out. The exercise machines also offer a high degree of calculability, with many of them registering miles run, level of difficulty, and calories burned. All of this in the kind of clean, sterile environment we have come to associate with McDonaldization.

■ ■ ■ ■ "SELLING MACHINES" AND L. L. BEAN

Shopping has also grown more efficient. The department store obviously is a more efficient place in which to shop than a series of specialty shops dispersed throughout the city or suburbs. The shopping mall increases efficiency by bringing a wide range of department stores and specialty shops under one roof. Kowinsky describes the mall as "an extremely efficient and effective selling machine." It is cost-efficient for retailers because it is the collection of shops and department stores ("mall synergy") that brings in throngs of people. And it is efficient for consumers because in one stop they can visit numerous shops, have lunch at a "food court" (likely populated by many fast-food chains), see a movie, have a drink, and go to an exercise or diet center.

The drive for shopping efficiency did not end with the malls. In recent years, there has been a great increase in catalogue sales (via L. L. Bean, Lands' End, and other mail-order companies), which enables people to shop while never leaving the comfort of their homes. Still more efficient, although it may require many hours in front of the tube, is home television shopping. A range of products is paraded in front of viewers who may simply phone each time a product catches their eye and conveniently charge their purchase to their credit card accounts. The latest advance in home shopping is the "scanfone," an at-home phone machine that includes "a pen-sized bar-code scanner, a credit card magnetic-strip reader, and a key pad." The customer merely "scans items from a bar-coded catalogue and also scans delivery dates and payment methods. The orders are then electronically relayed to the various stores, businesses, and banks involved." Some mall operators fear that they will ultimately be put out of business because of the greater efficiency of shopping at home.

■ ■ ■ ■ VIDEO RENTALS AND PACKAGE TOURS

With the advent of videotapes and video rental stores, many people no longer deem it efficient to drive to their local theater to see a movie. Movies can now be viewed, often more than one at a sitting, in one's own den. For those who wish even greater efficiency, viewers can buy one of the new televisions sets that enable viewers to see a movie while also watching a favorite television program on an inset on the television screen.

The largest video rental franchise in the United States is Blockbuster, which, predictably, "considers itself the McDonald's of the video business." Blockbuster has more than 2,000 outlets. . . . However, there may already be signs that Blockbuster is in danger of being replaced by even more efficient alternatives. One is pay-per-view movies offered by many cable companies. Instead of trekking to the video store, all one need do is turn to the proper channel and phone the cable company. Another experimental alternative is an effort by GTE to deliver movies to one's home through fiber-optic cables. Just as the video store replaced many movie theaters, video stores themselves may soon be displaced by even more efficient alternatives.

. . . [T]ravel to exotic . . . locales has also grown more efficient. The best example of this is the package tour. Let us take, for example, a thirty-day tour of Europe. To make these efficient, only the major locales in Europe are visited. Within each of these locales, the tourist is directed toward the major sights. (In Paris, the tour would definitely stop at the Louvre, but perhaps not at the Rodin Museum.) Because the goal is to see as many of the major sights as possible in a short period of time, the emphasis is on the efficient transportation of people to, through, and from each of them. Buses hurtle to and through the city, allowing the tourist to glimpse the maximum number of sights in the time allowed. At particularly interesting or important sights, the bus may slow down or even stop to permit some picture-taking. At the most important locales, a brief stopover is planned; there the visitor can hurry through the site, take a few pictures, buy a souvenir, and then hop back on the bus to head to the next attraction.

There is no question that this is a highly efficient way of seeing the major tourist attractions of Europe. Indeed, the package tour can be seen as a vast people-moving mechanism that permits the efficient transport of people from one locale to another. If tourists attempted to see the major sights of Europe on their own, it would take more time to see the same things and the expense would be greater. There are, of course, costs associated with the package tour (for example, does the tourist ever really have time to experience Europe?), as there are with every other highly rational system, but we will reserve a discussion of them for later. . . .

CUSTOMIZED TEXTBOOKS, BOOKS-ON-TAPE, "NEWS MCNUGGETS," AND DRIVE-IN CHURCHES

Turning to the educational system, specifically the university, one manifestation of the pressure for greater efficiency is the machine-graded, multiple-choice examination. In a much earlier era, students were examined on a one-to-one basis by their professors. This may have been a very good way of finding out what students know, but it was (and is) highly labor intensive and inefficient. Later, the essay examination became very popular. While grading a set of essays was more efficient from the professor's perspective than giving individual oral examinations, it was still relatively inefficient and time-consuming. Enter the multiple-choice examination, the grading of which was a snap in comparison to giving oral tests or reading essays. In fact, the grading could be passed on to graduate assistants, an act that was very efficient for the professor. Now we have computer-graded examinations that maximize efficiency for both professors and graduate students.

The multiple-choice examinations still left the professor saddled with the in-efficient task of composing the necessary sets of questions. Furthermore, at least some of the questions had to be changed each semester because new students were likely to gain possession of old exams. The solution: Textbook companies provided professors with books (free of charge) full of multiple-choice questions to go along with the textbooks required for use in large classes. Professors no longer had to make up their own questions; they could use those previously provided by the publisher. However, the professor still had to retype the questions or to have them retyped by the office staff. Recently, however, publishers have been kind enough to provide their sets of questions on computer disks. Now all the professor needs to do is select the desired questions and let the printer do the rest. . . .

Publishers have provided other services to make teaching more efficient for those professors who adopt their textbooks. With the adoption of a textbook, a professor may receive many materials with which to fill class hours—lecture outlines, computer simulations, discussion questions, videotapes, movies, even ideas for guest lecturers and student projects. With luck, professors can use all of these devices and do little or nothing on their own for their classes. Needless to say, this is a highly efficient means of teaching from a professor's perspective, and it frees up valuable time for the much more valued activities (by professors, but not students) of writing and research. . . .

Another example of efficiency in publishing is the advent of books-on-tape. There is a number of companies that now rent or sell books recorded on audiotape. The availability of such tapes permits greater efficiency in "reading" books. Instead of doing nothing but reading, one can now engage in other activities (driving, walking, jogging, watching TV with the sound off) while listening to a book. Greater efficiency is also provided by many of these books-on-tape being available in abridged form so that they can be devoured far more quickly. Gone are the "wasted" hours listening to "insignificant" parts of novels. With liberal cutting, a book such as *War and Peace* can now be listened to in a sitting.

Most "serious," nontabloid newspapers (for example, *The New York Times* and *The Washington Post*) are relatively inefficient to read. This is especially true of stories that begin on page one and then carry over to one or more additional pages. Stories that carry over to additional pages are said to have "jumped," and many readers are resistant to "jumping" with the stories. *USA Today* eliminated this inefficient way of presenting and reading stories by starting and finishing most of them on the same page, in other words, by offering "News McNuggets." This was accomplished by ruthlessly editing stories so that narrative was dramatically reduced (and no words wasted), leaving a series of relatively bare facts. . . .

In the realm of religion, McDonaldization is manifest, among other places, in drive-in churches. Another is the widespread development of televised religious programs whereby people can get their religion in the comfort of their living rooms. A particularly noteworthy example of such religious rationalization occurred in 1985 when the Vatican announced that Catholics could receive indulgences through the Pope's annual Christmas benediction on TV or radio. ("Indulgences are a release by way of devotional practices from certain forms of punishment resulting from sin.") Before this development Catholics had to engage in the far less efficient activity of going to Rome for the Christmas benediction, and manifesting the "proper intention and attitude" in order to receive their indulgences in person. . . .

■ ■ ■ [DESTROYING RELATIONSHIPS]

The fast-food restaurant offers its employees a dehumanizing setting within which to work. Few skills are required on the job. Said Burger King workers, "A moron could learn this job, it's so easy" and "Any trained monkey could do this job." Thus workers are asked to use only a minute proportion of all their skills and abilities. Employees are not only not using all of their skills, but they are also not being allowed to think and to be creative on the job. This leads to a high level of resentment, job dissatisfaction, alienation, absenteeism, and turnover among those who work in fast-food restaurants. In fact, the fast-food industry has the highest turnover rate—approximately 100 percent a year—of any industry in the United States. That means that the average worker lasts only about four months at a fast-food restaurant; the entire workforce of the fast-food industry turns over three times a year. . . .

The fast-food restaurant is also dehumanizing as far as the customer is concerned. Instead of a human dining experience, what is offered is eating on a sort of moving conveyor belt or assembly line. The diner is reduced to a kind of overwound automaton who is made to rush through the meal. Little gratification is derived from the dining experience or from the food itself. The best that can usually be said is that it is efficient and it is over quickly.

Some customers might even feel as if they are being fed like livestock in a highly rationalized manner. This point was made a number of years ago on television in a *Saturday Night Live* skit entitled "Trough and Brew," a take-off on a small fast-food chain called Burger and Brew. In the skit, some young executives learn that a new fast-food restaurant called Trough and Brew has opened and they decide to try it for lunch. They are next seen entering the restaurant and having bibs tied around their necks. After that, they discover a long trough, resembling a pig trough. The trough is filled with chili and is periodically refilled by a waiter scooping new supplies from a bucket. The customers bend over, stick their heads into the trough, and begin lapping up the chili as they move along the length of the trough making high-level business decisions. Every so often they come up for air and lap some beer from the communal "brew basin." After they have finished their "meal," they pay their bills, "by the head." Since their faces are smeared with chili, they are literally "hosed off" before they leave the restaurant. The young executives are last seen being herded out of the restaurant, which is being closed for a half-hour so that it can be "hosed down." *Saturday Night Live* was clearly pointing out, and ridiculing, the fact that fast-food restaurants tend to treat their customers like lower animals.

■ ■ ■ ■ "GET LOST" AND *WHEEL OF FORTUNE*

Another dehumanizing aspect of fast-food restaurants is that they minimize contact among human beings. Let us take, for example, the issue of how customers and employees relate. The nature of the fast-food restaurant turns these into fleeting relationships. Because the average employee stays only a few months, and even then only works on a part-time basis, the customer, even the regular customer, is rarely able to develop a long-term personal relationship with a counterperson. Gone are the days when one got to know well a waitress at a diner or the short-order cook at a local greasy spoon. Gone are the days when an employee knows who you are and knows what you are likely to order.

Not only are the relationships with a McDonald's employee fleeting (because the worker remains on the job only a short period of time), but each contact between worker and customer is of a very short duration. It takes little time at the counter to order, receive one's food, and pay for it. Both employees and customers are likely to feel rushed and to want to move on, customers to their dinner and employees to the next order. There is virtually no time for customer and counterperson to interact in such a context. This is even more true of the drive-through window, where thanks to the speedy service and the physical barriers, the server is but a dim and distant image.

The highly impersonal and anonymous relationship between customer and counterperson is heightened by the employees having been trained to interact in a staged and limited manner with customers. Thus, the customers may feel that they are dealing with automatons who have been taught to utter a few phrases rather than with fellow human beings. For their part, the customers are supposed to be, and often are, in a hurry, so they have little to say to the McDonald's employee. Indeed, it could be argued that one of the reasons for the success of fast-food restaurants is that they are in tune with our fast-paced and impersonal society. People in the modern world want to get on with their business without unnecessary personal relationships. The fast-food restaurant gives them precisely what they want.

Not only are the relationships between employee and customer limited greatly, but also other potential relationships. Because employees remain on the job for only a few months, satisfying personal relationships among employees are unlikely to develop. . . .

Relationships among customers are largely curtailed as well. Although some McDonald's ads would have us believe otherwise, gone are the days when people met in the diner or cafeteria for coffee, breakfast, lunch, or dinner and lingered to socialize with one another. Fast-food restaurants are clearly not conducive to such socializing. If nothing else, the chairs are designed to make people uncomfortable and interested in moving on to something else. The drive-through windows are a further step toward McDonaldization, by completely eliminating the possibility of interacting with other customers. . . .

Fast-food restaurants also tend to have negative effects on other human relationships. There is, for example, the effect on the so-called "family meal." The fast-food restaurant is not conducive to a long, leisurely, conversation-filled dinnertime. The family is unlikely to linger long over a meal at McDonald's. Furthermore, as the children grow into their teens, the nature of fast-food restaurants leads to separate meals as the teens go at one time with their friends, and the parents go at another time. Of course, the drive-through window only serves to reduce the possibility of a family meal. The family that gobbles its food while driving on to its next stop can hardly be seen as having what is called these days "quality time" with each other. Here is the way one journalist describes what is happening to the family meal:

> Do families who eat their suppers at the Colonel's, swinging on plastic seats, or however the restaurant is arranged, say grace before picking up a crispy brown chicken leg? Does dad ask junior what he did today as he remembers he forgot the piccalilli

and trots through the crowds over to the counter to get some? Does mom find the atmosphere conducive to asking little Mildred about the problems she was having with third-conjugation French verbs, or would it matter since otherwise the family might have been at home chomping down precooked frozen food, warmed in the microwave oven, and watching *Hollywood Squares?*

There is much talk these days about the disintegration of the family, and the fast-food restaurants may well be a crucial contributor to that disintegration.

In fact, as implied above, dinners at home may now not be much different from meals at the fast-food restaurant. Families tended to stop having lunch together by the 1940s and breakfast altogether by the 1950s. Today, the family dinner is following the same route. Even when they eat dinner at home, the meal will probably not be what it once was. Following the fast-food model, people are growing more likely to "graze," "refuel," nibble on this, or snack on that, than they are to sit down to a formal meal. Also, because it is now deemed inefficient to do nothing but just eat, families are likely to watch television while they are eating, thereby efficiently combining two activities. However, the din, to say nothing of the lure, of dinnertime TV programs such as *Wheel of Fortune* is likely to make it difficult for family members to interact with one another.

A key technology in the destruction of the family meal is the microwave oven and the vast array of microwavable foods it helped generate. It is striking to learn that more than 70 percent of American households have a microwave oven. A recent *Wall Street Journal* poll indicated that Americans consider the microwave their favorite household product. In fact, the microwave in a McDonaldizing society is seen as an advance over the fast-food restaurant. Said one consumer researcher, "It has made even fast-food restaurants not seem fast because at home you don't have to wait in line." As a general rule, consumers are demanding meals that take no more than ten minutes to microwave, whereas in the past people were more often willing to spend about a half hour or even an hour cooking dinner. This emphasis on speed has, of course, brought with it poorer taste and lower quality, but people do not seem to mind this loss: "We're just not as critical of food as we used to be.". . .

■ ■ ■ FAST FOOD [AND HOMOGENIZATION]

Another dehumanizing effect of the fast-food restaurant is that it has contributed to homogenization around the country and, increasingly, throughout the world. Diversity, which many people crave, is being reduced or eliminated by the fast-food restaurant. This decline in diversity is manifest in the extension of the fast-food model to all sorts of ethnic foods. The settings are all modeled after McDonald's in one way or another and the food has been rationalized and compromised so that it is acceptable to the tastes of virtually all diners. One cannot find an authentically different meal in any of these ethnic fast-food chains.

The expansion of these franchises across the landscape of America means that one finds little difference among regions and among cities throughout the country.

Tourists find more familiarity and predictability and less diversity as they travel around the nation, and this is increasingly true on a global scale. Apparently exotic settings are likely to be overrun with both American fast-food chains as well as indigenous varieties. The new and world's largest McDonald's and Kentucky Fried Chicken in Beijing are but two examples of this. . . . The spread of American and indigenous fast food throughout much of the world means that there is less and less diversity from one setting to another. The human craving for new and diverse experiences is being limited, if not progressively destroyed, by the national and international spread of fast-food restaurants. The craving for diversity is being supplanted by the desire for uniformity and predictability. . . .

■ ■ ■ CONCLUSION

Although I have emphasized the irresistibility of McDonaldization, my fondest hope is that I am wrong. Indeed, a major motivation is to alert readers to the dangers of McDonaldization and to motivate them to act to stem its tide. I hope that we are able to resist McDonaldization and can create instead a more reasonable, more human world.

McDonald's was recently sued by the famous French chef, Paul Bocuse, for using his picture on a poster without his permission. Enraged, Bocuse said: "How can I be seen promoting this tasteless, boneless food in which everything is soft." Nevertheless, Bocuse seemed to acknowledge the inevitability of McDonaldization: "There's a need for this kind of thing . . . and trying to get rid of it seems to me to be as futile as trying to get rid of the prostitutes in the Bois de Boulogne." Lo and behold, two weeks later, it was announced that the Paris police had cracked down on prostitution in the Bois de Boulogne. Said a police spokesman, "There are none left." Thus, just as chef Bocuse was wrong about the prostitutes, perhaps I was wrong about the irresistibility of McDonaldization. Yet, before we grow overly optimistic, it should be noted that "everyone knows that the prostitutes will be back as soon as the operation is over. In the spring, police predict, there will be even more than before." Similarly, it remains likely that no matter how intense the opposition, the future will bring with it more rather than less McDonaldization. . . . [F]aced with Max Weber's iron cage imagery of a future dominated by the polar night of icy darkness and hardness, the least the reader can do is to follow the words of the poet Dylan Thomas: "Do not go gentle into that good night. . . . Rage, rage against the dying of the light."

The Power Elite

C. Wright Mills

introduction

A theme that has run through many of the preceding selections is how groups influence us—how they guide direct, and even control our behavior. Our membership in some of these groups (as with gender in Reading 11) comes with birth and is involuntary. Other groups, we join because we desire the membership. All groups—whether our membership is voluntary or involuntary—influence our thinking and behavior. The broad, overarching groups, which lay the general boundaries for our actions and even our thinking and feelings, are called *social institutions*. We are born and we die within social institutions. And between birth and death, we live within them—from family and school to politics and religion.

A central question that sociologists ask concerns power: Who has it, and how is it exercised? In this selection, C. Wright Mills says that power in U.S. society has become concentrated in our economic, political, and military institutions. Not only have these three grown larger, but also they have become more centralized and interconnected. As a result, their power has outstripped that of our other social institutions. In this "triangle of power," the interests of the top business, political, and military leaders have coalesced, says Mills, and in his term, they now form a *power elite*. This elite makes the major decisions that so vitally affect our welfare—and increasingly, with the dominance of the United States in global affairs, the welfare of the world.

Thinking Critically

As you read this selection, ask yourself:

1. If the members of the power elite don't meet together, how can they be considered the primary source of power in the United States today?

2. Not everyone agrees with Mills. Compare what Mills says in this selection with the *pluralist* view of power summarized in Chapter 15 of *Sociology*.

3. Mills identifies the top leaders of the top corporations as the pinnacle of U.S. power. Why doesn't he identify the top military or political leaders as this pinnacle?

The powers of ordinary men* are circumscribed by the everyday worlds in which they live, yet even in these rounds of job, family, and neighborhood they often seem driven by forces they can neither understand nor govern. "Great changes" are beyond their control, but affect their conduct and outlook nonetheless. The very framework of modern society confines them to projects not their own, but from every side, such changes now press upon the men and women of the mass society, who accordingly feel that they are without purpose in an epoch in which they are without power.

But not all men are in this sense ordinary. As the means of information and of power are centralized, some men come to occupy positions in American society from which they can look down upon, so to speak, and by their decisions mightily affect, the everyday worlds of ordinary men and women. They are not made by their jobs; they set up and break down jobs for thousands of others; they are not confined by simple family responsibilities; they can escape. They may live in many hotels and houses, but they are bound by no one community. They need not merely "meet the demands of the day and hour"; in some part, they create these demands, and cause others to meet them. Whether or not they profess their power, their technical and political experience of it far transcends that of the underlying population. What Jacob Burckhardt said of "great men," most Americans might well say of their elite: "They are all that we are not."

The power elite is composed of men whose positions enable them to transcend the ordinary environments of ordinary men and women; they are in positions to make decisions having major consequences. Whether they do or do not make such decisions is less important than the fact that they do occupy such pivotal positions: Their failure to act, their failure to make decisions, is itself an act that is often of greater consequence than the decisions they do make. For they are in command of the major hierarchies and organizations of modern society. They rule the big corporations. They run the machinery of the state and claim its prerogatives. They direct the military establishment. They occupy the strategic command posts of the social structure, in which are now centered the effective means of the power and the wealth and the celebrity which they enjoy.

The power elite are not solitary rulers. Advisers and consultants, spokesmen and opinion-makers are often the captains of their higher thought and decision. Immediately below the elite are the professional politicians of the middle levels of power, in the Congress and in the pressure groups, as well as among the new and old upper classes of town and city and region. Mingling with them, in curious ways which we shall explore, are those professional celebrities who live by being continually displayed but are never, so long as they remain celebrities, displayed enough. If such celebrities are not at the head of any dominating hierarchy, they do often have the power to distract the attention of the public or afford sensations to the masses, or,

---

*As with the first article in this anthology, when Mills wrote, the literary custom was to use "men" to refer to both men and women and "his" to both hers and his. Although the writing style has changed, the sociological ideas are as significant as ever

more directly, to gain the ear of those who do occupy positions of direct power. More or less unattached, as critics of morality and technicians of power, as spokesmen of God and creators of mass sensibility, such celebrities and consultants are part of the immediate scene in which the drama of the elite is enacted. But that drama itself is centered in the command posts of the major institutional hierarchies.

The truth about the nature and the power of the elite is not some secret which men of affairs know but will not tell. Such men hold quite various theories about their own roles in the sequence of event and decision. Often they are uncertain about their roles, and even more often they allow their fears and their hopes to affect their assessment of their own power. No matter how great their actual power, they tend to be less acutely aware of it than of the resistances of others to its use. Moreover, most American men of affairs have learned well the rhetoric of public relations, in some cases even to the point of using it when they are alone, and thus coming to believe it. The personal awareness of the actors is only one of the several sources one must examine in order to understand the higher circles. Yet many who believe that there is no elite, or at any rate none of any consequence, rest their argument upon what men of affairs believe about themselves, or at least assert in public.

There is, however, another view: those who feel, even if vaguely, that a compact and powerful elite of great importance does now prevail in America often base that feeling upon the historical trend of our time. They have felt, for example, the domination of the military event, and from this they infer that generals and admirals, as well as other men of decision influenced by them, must be enormously powerful. They hear that the Congress has again abdicated to a handful of men decisions clearly related to the issue of war or peace. They know that the bomb was dropped over Japan in the name of the United States of America, although they were at no time consulted about the matter. They feel that they live in a time of big decisions; they know that they are not making any. Accordingly, as they consider the present as history, they infer that at its center, making decisions or failing to make them, there must be an elite of power.

On the one hand, those who share this feeling about big historical events assume that there is an elite and that its power is great. On the other hand, those who listen carefully to the reports of men apparently involved in the great decisions often do not believe that there is an elite whose powers are of decisive consequence.

Both views must be taken into account, but neither is adequate. The way to understand the power of the American elite lies neither solely in recognizing the historic scale of events nor in accepting the personal awareness reported by men of apparent decision. Behind such men and behind the events of history, linking the two, are the major institutions of modern society. *These hierarchies of state [politics] and corporation [business] and army [military] constitute the means of power* [italics added]; as such they are now of a consequence not before equaled in human history—and at their summits, there are now those command posts of modern society which offer us the sociological key to an understanding of the role of the higher circles in America.

Within American society, major national power now resides in the economic, the political, and the military domains. Other institutions seem off to the side of modern history, and, on occasion, duly subordinated to these. No family is as directly powerful in national affairs as any major corporation; no church is as directly powerful in the external biographies of young men in America today as the military establishment; no college is as powerful in the shaping of momentous events as the National Security Council. Religious, educational, and family institutions are not autonomous centers of national power; on the contrary, these decentralized areas are increasingly shaped by the big three, in which developments of decisive and immediate consequence now occur.

Families and churches and schools adapt to modern life; governments and armies and corporations shape it; and, as they do so, they turn these lesser institutions into means for their ends. Religious institutions provide chaplains to the armed forces where they are used as a means of increasing the effectiveness of its morale to kill. Schools select and train men for their jobs in corporations and their specialized tasks in the armed forces. The extended family has, of course, long been broken up by the industrial revolution, and now the son and the father are removed from the family, by compulsion if need be, whenever the army of the state sends out the call. And the symbols of all these lesser institutions are used to legitimate the power and the decisions of the big three.

The life-fate of the modern individual depends not only upon the family into which he was born or which he enters by marriage, but increasingly upon the corporation in which he spends the most alert hours of his best years; not only upon the school where he is educated as a child and adolescent, but also upon the state which touches him throughout his life; not only upon the church in which on occasion he hears the word of God, but also upon the army in which he is disciplined.

If the centralized state could not rely upon the inculcation of nationalist loyalties in public and private schools, its leaders would promptly seek to modify the decentralized educational system. If the bankruptcy rate among the top five hundred corporations were as high as the general divorce rate among the [57] million married couples, there would be economic catastrophe on an international scale. If members of armies gave to them no more of their lives than do believers to the churches to which they belong, there would be a military crisis.

Within each of the big three, the typical institutional unit has become enlarged, has become administrative, and, in the power of its decisions, has become centralized. Behind these developments there is a fabulous technology, for as institutions, they have incorporated this technology and guide it, even as it shapes and paces their developments.

The economy—once a great scatter of small productive units in autonomous balance—has become dominated by two or three hundred giant corporations, administratively and politically interrelated, which together hold the keys to economic decisions.

The political order, once a decentralized set of several dozen states with a weak spinal cord, has become a centralized, executive establishment which has taken up into itself many powers previously scattered, and now enters into each and every crany of the social structure.

The military order, once a slim establishment in a context of distrust fed by state militia, has become the largest and most expensive feature of government, and, although well versed in smiling public relations, now has all the grim and clumsy efficiency of a sprawling bureaucratic domain.

In each of these institutional areas, the means of power at the disposal of decision makers have increased enormously; their central executive powers have been enhanced; within each of them modern administrative routines have been elaborated and tightened up.

As each of these domains becomes enlarged and centralized, the consequences of its activities become greater, and its traffic with the others increases. The decisions of a handful of corporations bear upon military and political as well as upon economic developments around the world. The decisions of the military establishment rest upon and grievously affect political life as well as the very level of economic activity. The decisions made within the political domain determine economic activities and military programs. There is no longer, on the one hand, an economy, and, on the other hand, a political order containing a military establishment unimportant to politics and to money-making. There is a political economy linked, in a thousand ways, with military institutions and decisions. On each side of the world-split running through central Europe and around the Asiatic rimlands, there is an ever-increasing inter-locking of economic, military, and political structures. If there is government intervention in the corporate economy, so is there corporate intervention in the governmental process. In the structural sense, this triangle of power is the source of the interlocking directorate that is most important for the historical structure of the present.

The fact of the interlocking is clearly revealed at each of the points of crisis of modern capitalist society—slump, war, and boom. In each, men of decision are led to an awareness of the interdependence of the major institutional orders. In the nineteenth century, when the scale of all institutions was smaller, their liberal integration was achieved in the automatic economy, by an autonomous play of market forces, and in the automatic political domain, by the bargain and the vote. It was then assumed that out of the imbalance and friction that followed the limited decisions then possible a new equilibrium would in due course emerge. That can no longer be assumed, and it is not assumed by the men at the top of each of the three dominant hierarchies.

For given the scope of their consequences, decisions—and indecisions—any one of these ramify into the others, and hence top decisions tend either to become coordinated or to lead to a commanding indecision. It has not always been like this. When numerous small entrepreneurs made up the economy, for example, many of them could fail and the consequences still remain local; political and military authorities did not intervene. But now, given political expectations and military commitments, can they afford to allow key units of the private corporate economy to break down in slump? Increasingly, they do intervene in economic affairs, and as they do so, the controlling decisions in each order are inspected by agents of the other two, and economic, military, and political structures are interlocked.

At the pinnacle of each of the three enlarged and centralized domains, there have arisen those higher circles which make up the economic, the political, and the military elites. At the top of the economy, among the corporate rich, there are the chief executives; at the top of the political order, the members of the political directorate; at the top of the military establishment, the elite of soldier-statesmen clustered in and around the Joint Chiefs of Staff and the upper echelon. As each of these domains has coincided with the others, as decisions tend to become total in their consequence, the leading men in each of the three domains of power—the warlords, the corporation chieftains, the political directorate—tend to come together, to form the power elite of America.

The higher circles in and around these command posts are often thought of in terms of what their members possess: They have a greater share than other people of the things and experiences that are most highly valued. From this point of view, the elite are simply those who have the most of what there is to have, which is generally held to include money, power, and prestige—as well as all the ways of life to which these lead. But the elite are not simply those who have the most, for they could not "have the most" were it not for their positions in the great institutions. For such institutions are the necessary bases of power, of wealth, and of prestige, and at the same time, the chief means of exercising power, of acquiring and retaining wealth, and of cashing in the higher claims for prestige.

By the powerful we mean, of course, those who are able to realize their will, even if others resist it. No one, accordingly, can be truly powerful unless he has access to the command of major institutions, for it is over these institutional means of power that the truly powerful are, in the first instance, powerful. Higher politicians and key officials of government command such institutional power; so do admirals and generals, and so do the major owners and executives of the larger corporations. Not all power, it is true, is anchored in and exercised by means of such institutions, but only within and through them can power be more or less continuous and important.

Wealth also is acquired and held in and through institutions. The pyramid of wealth cannot be understood merely in terms of the very rich; for the great inheriting families, as we shall see, are now supplemented by the corporate institutions of modern society: Every one of the very rich families has been and is closely connected—always legally and frequently managerially as well—with one of the multimillion-dollar corporations.

The modern corporation is the prime source of wealth, but, in latter-day capitalism, the political apparatus also opens and closes many avenues to wealth. The amount as well as the source of income, the power over consumers' goods as well as over productive capital, are determined by position within the political economy. If our interest in the very rich goes beyond their lavish or their miserly consumption, we must examine their relations to modern forms of corporate property as well as to the state; for such relations now determine the chances of men to secure big property and to receive high income.

Great prestige increasingly follows the major institutional units of the social structure. It is obvious that prestige depends, often quite decisively, upon access to the publicity machines that are now a central and normal feature of all the big institutions of modern America. Moreover, one feature of these hierarchies of corporation, state, and military establishment is that their top positions are increasingly interchangeable. One result of this is the accumulative nature of prestige. Claims for prestige, for example, may be initially based on military roles, then expressed in and augmented by an educational institution run by corporate executives; and cashed in, finally, in the political order, where, for [top military leaders who become president, such as] General Eisenhower and those [they represent], power and prestige finally meet at the very peak. Like wealth and power, prestige tends to be cumulative: The more of it you have, the more you can get. These values also tend to be translatable into one another: The wealthy find it easier than the poor to gain power; those with status find it easier than those without it to control opportunities for wealth.

If we took the one hundred most powerful men in America, the one hundred wealthiest, and the one hundred most celebrated away from the institutional positions they now occupy, away from their resources of men and women and money, away from the media of mass communication that are now focused upon them—then they would be powerless and poor and uncelebrated. For power is not of a man. Wealth does not center in the person of the wealthy. Celebrity is not inherent in any personality. To be celebrated, to be wealthy, to have power requires access to major institutions, for the institutional positions men occupy determine in large part their chances to have and to hold these valued experiences.

The people of the higher circles may also be conceived as members of a top social stratum, as a set of groups whose members know one another, see one another socially and at business, and so, in making decisions, take one another into account. The elite, according to this conception, feel themselves to be, and are felt by others to be, the inner circle of "the upper social classes." They form a more or less compact social and psychological entity; they have become self-conscious members of a social class. People are either accepted into this class or they are not, and there is a qualitative split, rather than merely a numerical scale, separating them from those who are not elite. They are more or less aware of themselves as a social class and they behave toward one another differently from the way they do toward members of other classes. They accept one another, understand one another, marry one another, tend to work and to think if not together at least alike.

Now, we do not want by our definition to prejudge whether the elite of the command posts are conscious members of such a socially recognized class, or whether considerable proportions of the elite derive from such a clear and distinct class. These are matters to be investigated. Yet in order to be able to recognize what we intend to investigate, we must note something that all biographies and memoirs of the wealthy and the powerful and the eminent make clear: No matter what else they may be, the people of these higher circles are involved in a set of overlapping "crowds" and intricately connected "cliques." There is a kind of mutual attraction among those who "sit on the same terrace"—although this often becomes clear to them, as well as to others, only at the point at which they feel the need to draw the line; only when, in their common defense, they come to understand what they have in common, and so close their ranks against outsiders.

The idea of such ruling stratum implies that most of its members have similar social origins, that throughout their lives they maintain a network of internal connections, and that to some degree there is an interchangeability of position between the various hierarchies of money and power and celebrity. We must, of course, note at once that if such an elite stratum does exist, its social visibility and its form, for very solid historical reasons, are quite different from those of the noble cousinhoods that once ruled various European nations.

That American society has never passed through a feudal epoch is of decisive importance to the nature of the American elite, as well as to American society as a historic whole. For it means that no nobility or aristocracy, established before the capitalist era, has stood in tense opposition to the higher bourgeoisie. It means that this bourgeoisie has monopolized not only wealth but prestige and power as well. It means that no set of noble families has commanded the top positions and monopolized the values that are generally held in high esteem; and certainly that no set has done so explicitly by inherited right. It means that no high church dignitaries or court nobilities, no entrenched landlords with honorific accouterments, no monopolists of high army posts have opposed the enriched bourgeoisie and in the name of birth and prerogative successfully resisted its self-making.

But this does *not* mean that there are no upper strata in the United States. That they emerged from a "middle class" that had no recognized aristocratic superiors does not mean they remained middle class when enormous increases in wealth made their own superiority possible. Their origins and their newness may have made the upper strata less visible in America than elsewhere. But in America today there are in fact tiers and ranges of wealth and power of which people in the middle and lower ranks know very little and may not even dream. There are families who, in their well-being, are quite insulated from the economic jolts and lurches felt by the merely prosperous and those farther down the scale. There are also men of power who in quite small groups make decisions of enormous consequence for the underlying population. . . .

When Work Becomes Home and Home Becomes Work

Arlie Russell Hochschild

introduction ▪ ▪ ▪ ▪ ▪

The social institution that introduces us to society is the family. Because it is within the family that we learn our basic orientations to social life, the family is considered to be the basic building block of society. Within this great socializer, we learn our language, basic norms of behavior and etiquette, even highly refined norms that are difficult to put into words, such as how much self-centeredness we are allowed to display in our interactions. Our family also introduces us to its ways of viewing gender, race, social class, religion, people with disabilities, the elderly—even our own body. With such far-reaching implications for what we become in life, it is difficult to overstate the influence of the family.

Like our other social institutions, U.S. families are changing. They have become smaller, they have more disposable income, parental authority has decreased, people are marrying later, wives have more power, and divorce has made families fragile. (Some sociologists point out that because parents used to die at a much earlier age, today's children have about the same chance as children of two hundred years ago of living through childhood with both their biological parents. Either way, marriage *is* fragile.) Sociologists have uncovered another change that is affecting family life, one that has just begun to appear. As factory work has declined in importance in our society and vast numbers of women have become white-collar workers, more emphasis is being placed on social relationships at work. This has made work more pleasant and satisfying. At the same time, children seem to be placing greater demands on parents. One result, as Hochschild found in her study of a company she calls Amerco, is a reversal of conditions: Many parents are finding work to be a refuge from home, rather than their family being a refuge from work.

Thinking Critically

As you read this selection, ask yourself:

1. Do you think you will prefer work to family life? Why or why not?

2. Hochschild says that there are two sides of the same family: the rushed family that they actually are, and the relaxed family that they imagine they might be if only they had time. How does this apply to your own family life?

3. What does Hochschild mean when she says that the corporate world is creating a sense of "neighborhood" and a "feminine culture"? How does this development pertain to family life?

It's 7:40 A.M. when Cassie Bell, 4, arrives at the Spotted Deer Child-Care Center, her hair half-combed, a blanket in one hand, a fudge bar in the other. "I'm late," her mother, Gwen, a sturdy young woman whose short-cropped hair frames a pleasant face, explains to the child-care worker in charge. "Cassie wanted the fudge bar so bad, I gave it to her," she adds apologetically.

"*Please,* can't you take me with you?" Cassie pleads.

"You know I can't take you to work," Gwen replies in a tone that suggests that she has been expecting this request. Cassie's shoulders droop. But she has struck a hard bargain—the morning fudge bar—aware of her mother's anxiety about the long day that lies ahead at the center. As Gwen explains later, she continually feels that she owes Cassie more time than she gives her—she has a "time debt."

Arriving at her office just before 8, Gwen finds on her desk a cup of coffee in her personal mug, milk no sugar (exactly as she likes it), prepared by a co-worker who managed to get in ahead of her. As the assistant to the head of public relations at a company I will call Amerco, Gwen has to handle responses to any reports that may appear about the company in the press—a challenging job, but one that gives her satisfaction. As she prepares for her first meeting of the day, she misses her daughter, but she also feels relief; there's a lot to get done at Amerco.

Gwen used to work a straight eight-hour day. But over the last three years, her workday has gradually stretched to eight and a half or nine hours, not counting the e-mail messages and faxes she answers from home. She complains about her hours to her co-workers and listens to their complaints—but she loves her job. Gwen picks up Cassie at 5:45 and gives her a long, affectionate hug.

At home, Gwen's husband, John, a computer programmer, plays with their daughter while Gwen prepares dinner. To protect the dinner "hour"—8:00–8:30—Gwen checks that the phone machine is on, hears the phone ring during dinner but resists the urge to answer. After Cassie's bath, Gwen and Cassie have "quality time," or "Q.T.," as John affectionately calls it. Half an hour later, at 9:30, Gwen tucks Cassie into bed.

There are, in a sense, two Bell households: the rushed family they actually are and the relaxed family they imagine they might be if only they had time. Gwen and John complain that they are in a time bind. What they say they want seems so modest—time to throw a ball, to read to Cassie, to witness the small dramas of her development, not to speak of having a little fun and romance themselves. Yet even these modest wishes seem strangely out of reach. Before going to bed, Gwen has to e-mail messages to her colleagues in preparation for the next day's meeting; John goes to bed early, exhausted—he's out the door by 7 every morning.

Nationwide, many working parents are in the same boat. More mothers of small children than ever now work outside the home. American men average 48.8 hours of work a week, and women 41.7 hours, including overtime and commuting. All in all, more women are on the economic train, and for many—men and women alike—that train is going faster.

But Amerco has "family-friendly" policies. If your division head and supervisor agree, you can work part time, share a job with another worker, work some hours at home, take parental leave or use "flex time." But hardly anyone uses these policies. In seven years, only two Amerco fathers have taken formal parental leave. Fewer than 1 percent have taken advantage of the opportunity to work part time. Of all such policies, only flex time—which rearranges but does not shorten work time—has had a significant number of takers (perhaps a third of working parents at Amerco).

Forgoing family-friendly policies is not exclusive to Amerco workers. A study of 188 companies conducted by the Families and Work Institute found that while a majority offered part-time shifts, fewer than 5 percent of employees made use of them. Thirty-five percent offered "flex place"—work from home—and fewer than 3 percent of their employees took advantage of it. And a Bureau of Labor Statistics survey asked workers whether they preferred a shorter workweek, a longer one or their present schedule. About 62 percent preferred their present schedule; 28 percent would have preferred longer hours. Fewer than 10 percent said they wanted a cut in hours.

Still, I found it hard to believe that people didn't protest their long hours at work. So I contacted Bright Horizons, a company that runs 136 company-based child-care centers associated with corporations, hospitals and Federal agencies in 25 states. Bright Horizons allowed me to add questions to a questionnaire they sent out to 3,000 parents whose children attended the centers. The respondents, mainly middle-class parents in their early 30s, largely confirmed the picture I'd found at Amerco. A third of fathers and a fifth of mothers described themselves as "workaholic," and 1 out of 3 said their partners were.

To be sure, some parents have tried to shorten their hours. Twenty-one percent of the nation's women voluntarily work part time, as do 7 percent of men. A number of others make under-the-table arrangements that don't show up on surveys. But while working parents say they need more time at home, the main story of their lives does not center on a struggle to get it. Why? Given the hours parents are working these days, why aren't they taking advantage of an opportunity to reduce their time at work?

The most widely held explanation is that working parents cannot afford to work shorter hours. Certainly this is true for many. But if money is the whole explanation, why would it be that at places like Amerco, the best-paid employees—upper-level managers and professionals—were the least interested in part-time work or job sharing, while clerical workers who earned less were more interested?

Similarly, if money were the answer, we would expect poorer new mothers to return to work more quickly after giving birth than rich mothers. But among working women nationwide, well-to-do new mothers are not much more likely to stay home after 13 weeks with a new baby than low-income new mothers. When asked what they look for in a job, only a third of respondents in a recent study said salary came first. Money is important, but by itself, money does not explain why many people don't want to cut back hours at work.

Were workers uninformed about the company's family-friendly policies? No. Some even mentioned that they were proud to work for a company that offered such enlightened policies. Were rigid middle managers standing in the way of workers using these policies? Sometimes. But when I compared Amerco employees who worked for flexible managers with those who worked for rigid managers, I found that the flexible managers reported only a few more applicants than the rigid ones. The evidence, however counterintuitive, pointed to a paradox: workers at the company I studied weren't protesting the time bind. They were accommodating to it.

Why? I did not anticipate the conclusion I found myself coming to: namely, that work has become a form of "home" and home has become "work." The worlds of home and work have not begun to blur, as the conventional wisdom goes, but to reverse places. We are used to thinking that home is where most people feel the most appreciated, the most truly "themselves," the most secure, the most relaxed. We are used to thinking that work is where most people feel like "just a number" or "a cog in a machine." It is where they have to be "on," have to "act," where they are least secure and most harried.

But new management techniques so pervasive in corporate life have helped transform the workplace into a more appreciative, personal sort of social world. Meanwhile, at home the divorce rate has risen, and the emotional demands have become more baffling and complex. In addition to teething, tantrums and the normal developments of growing children, the needs of elderly parents are creating more tasks for the modern family—as are the blending, unblending, reblending of new stepparents, stepchildren, exes and former in-laws.

This idea began to dawn on me during one of my first interviews with an Amerco worker. Linda Avery, a friendly, 38-year-old mother, is a shift supervisor at an Amerco plant. When I meet her in the factory's coffee-break room over a couple of Cokes, she is wearing blue jeans and a pink jersey, her hair pulled back in a long, blond ponytail. Linda's husband, Bill, is a technician in the same plant. By working different shifts, they manage to share the care of their 2-year-old son and Linda's 16-year-old daughter from a previous marriage. "Bill works the 7 A.M. to 3 P.M. shift while I watch the baby," she explains. "Then I work the 3 P.M. to 11 P.M. shift and he watches the baby. My daughter works at Walgreen's after school."

Linda is working overtime, and so I begin by asking whether Amerco required the overtime or whether she volunteered for it. "Oh, I put in for it," she replies. I ask her whether, if finances and company policy permitted, she'd be interested in cutting back on the overtime. She takes off her safety glasses, rubs her face and, without answering my question, explains: "I get home, and the minute I turn the key, my daughter is right there. Granted, she needs somebody to talk to about her day. . . . The baby is still up. He should have been in bed two hours ago, and that upsets me. The dishes are piled in the sink. My daughter comes right up to the door and complains about anything her stepfather said or did, and she wants to talk about her job. My husband is in the other room hollering to my daughter, 'Tracy, I don't ever get any time to talk to your mother, because you're always monopolizing her time before I even get a chance!' They all come at me at once."

Linda's description of the urgency of demands and the unarbitrated quarrels that await her homecoming contrast with her account of arriving at her job as a shift supervisor: "I usually come to work early, just to get away from the house. When I arrive, people are there waiting. We sit, we talk, we joke. I let them know what's going on, who has to be where, what changes I've made for the shift that day. We sit and chitchat for 5 or 10 minutes. There's laughing, joking, fun."

For Linda, home has come to feel like work and work has come to feel a bit like home. Indeed, she feels she can get relief from the "work" of being at home only by going to the "home" of work. Why has her life at home come to seem like this? Linda explains it this way: "My husband's a great help watching our baby. But as far as doing housework or even taking the baby when I'm at home, no. He figures he works five days a week; he's not going to come home and clean. But he doesn't stop to think that I work seven days a week. Why should I have to come home and do the housework without help from anybody else? My husband and I have been through this over and over again. Even if he would just pick up from the kitchen table and stack the dishes for me, that would make a big difference. He does nothing. On his weekends off, he goes fishing. If I want any time off, I have to get a sitter. He'll help out if I'm not here, but the minute I am, all the work at home is mine."

With a light laugh, she continues: "So I take a lot of overtime. The more I get out of the house, the better I am. It's a terrible thing to say, but that's the way I feel."

When Bill feels the need for time off, to relax, to have fun, to feel free, he climbs in his truck and takes his free time without his family. Largely in response, Linda grabs what she also calls "free time"—at work. Neither Linda nor Bill Avery wants more time together at home, not as things are arranged now.

How do Linda and Bill Avery fit into the broader picture of American family and work life? Current research suggests that however hectic their lives, women who do paid work feel less depressed, think better of themselves and are more satisfied than women who stay at home. One study reported that women who work outside the home feel more valued at home than housewives do. Meanwhile, work is where many women feel like "good mothers." As Linda reflects: "I'm a good mom at home, but I'm a better mom at work. At home, I get into fights with Tracy. I want her to apply to a junior college, but she's not interested. At work, I think I'm better at seeing the other person's point of view."

Many workers feel more confident they could "get the job done" at work than at home. One study found that only 59 percent of workers feel their "performance" in the family is "good or unusually good," while 86 percent rank their performance on the job this way.

Forces at work and at home are simultaneously reinforcing this "reversal." This lure of work has been enhanced in recent years by the rise of company cultural engineering—in particular, the shift from Frederick Taylor's principles of scientific management to the Total Quality principles originally set out by W. Edwards Deming. Under the influence of a Taylorist world view, the manager's job was to coerce the worker's mind and body, not to appeal to the worker's heart. The Taylorized worker was de-skilled, replaceable and cheap, and as a consequence felt bored, demeaned and unappreciated.

Using modern participative management techniques, many companies now train workers to make their own work decisions, and then set before their newly "empowered" employees moral as well as financial incentives. At Amerco, the Total Quality worker is invited to feel recognized for job accomplishments. Amerco regularly strengthens the familylike ties of co-workers by holding "recognition ceremonies" honoring particular workers or self-managed production teams. Amerco employees speak of "belonging to the Amerco family" and proudly wear their "Total Quality" pins or "High Performance Team" T-shirts, symbols of their loyalty to the company and of its loyalty to them.

The company occasionally decorates a section of the factory and serves refreshments. The production teams, too, have regular get-togethers. In a New Age recasting of an old business slogan—"The Customer Is Always Right"—Amerco proposes that its workers "Value the Internal Customer." This means: Be as polite and considerate to co-workers inside the company as you would be to customers outside it. How many recognition ceremonies for competent performance are being offered at home? Who is valuing the internal customer there?

Amerco also tries to take on the role of a helpful relative with regard to employee problems at work and at home. The education-and-training division offers employees free courses (on company time) in "Dealing With Anger," "How to Give and Accept Criticism," "How to Cope With Difficult People."

At home, of course, people seldom receive anything like this much help on issues basic to family life. There, no courses are being offered on "Dealing With Your Child's Disappointment in You" or "How to Treat Your Spouse Like an Internal Customer."

If Total Quality calls for "re-skilling" the worker in an "enriched" job environment, technological developments have long been de-skilling parents at home. Over the centuries, store-bought goods have replaced homespun cloth, homemade soup and home-baked foods. Day care for children, retirement homes for the elderly, even psychotherapy are, in a way, commercial substitutes for jobs that a mother once did at home. Even family-generated entertainment has, to some extent, been replaced by television, video games and the VCR. I sometimes watched Amerco families sitting together after their dinners, mute but cozy, watching sitcoms in which television mothers, fathers and children related in an animated way to one another while the viewing family engaged in relational loafing.

The one "skill" still required of family members is the hardest one of all—the emotional work of forging, deepening or repairing family relationships. It takes time to develop this skill, and even then things can go awry. Family ties are complicated.

People get hurt. Yet as broken homes become more common—and as the sense of belonging to a geographical community grows less and less secure in an age of mobility—the corporate world has created a sense of "neighborhood," of "feminine culture," of family at work. Life at work can be insecure; the company can fire workers. But workers aren't so secure at home, either. Many employees have been working for Amerco for 20 years but are on their second or third marriages or relationships. The shifting balance between these two "divorce rates" may be the most powerful reason why tired parents flee a world of unresolved quarrels and unwashed laundry for the orderliness, harmony and managed cheer of work. People are getting their "pink slips" at home.

Amerco workers have not only turned their offices into "home" and their homes into workplaces; many have also begun to "Taylorize" time at home, where families are succumbing to a cult of efficiency previously associated mainly with the office and factory. Meanwhile, work time, with its ever longer hours, has become more hospitable to sociability—periods of talking with friends on e-mail, patching up quarrels, gossiping. Within the long workday of many Amerco employees are great hidden pockets of inefficiency while, in the far smaller number of waking weekday hours at home, they are, despite themselves, forced to act increasingly time-conscious and efficient.

The Averys respond to their time bind at home by trying to value and protect "quality time." A concept unknown to their parents and grandparents, "quality time" has become a powerful symbol of the struggle against the growing pressures at home. It reflects the extent to which modern parents feel the flow of time to be running against them. The premise behind "quality time" is that the time we devote to relationships can somehow be separated from ordinary time. Relationships go on during quantity time, of course, but then we are only passively, not actively, wholeheartedly, specializing in our emotional ties. We aren't "on." Quality time at home becomes like an office appointment. You don't want to be caught "goofing off around the water cooler" when you are "at work."

Quality time holds out the hope that scheduling intense periods of togetherness can compensate for an overall loss of time in such a way that a relationship will suffer no loss of quality. But this is just another way of transferring the cult of efficiency from office to home. We must now get our relationships in good repair in less time. Instead of nine hours a day with a child, we declare ourselves capable of getting "the same result" with one intensely focused hour.

Parents now more commonly speak of time as if it is a threatened form of personal capital they have no choice but to manage and invest. What's new here is the spread into the home of a financial manager's attitude toward time. Working parents at Amerco owe what they think of as time debts at home. This is because they are, in a sense, inadvertently "Taylorizing" the house—speeding up the pace of home life as Taylor once tried to "scientifically" speed up the pace of factory life.

Advertisers of products aimed at women have recognized that this new reality provides an opportunity to sell products, and have turned the very pressure that threatens to explode the home into a positive attribute. Take, for example, an ad promoting Instant Quaker Oatmeal: it shows a smiling mother ready for the office in her square-shouldered suit, hugging her happy son. A caption reads: "Nicky is a very picky eater. With Instant Quaker Oatmeal, I can give him a terrific hot breakfast in just 90 seconds. And I don't have to spend any time coaxing him to eat it!" Here, the modern mother seems to have absorbed the lessons of Frederick Taylor as she presses for efficiency at home because she is in a hurry to get to work.

Part of modern parenthood seems to include coping with the resistance of real children who are not so eager to get their cereal so fast. Some parents try desperately not to appease their children with special gifts or smooth-talking promises about the future. But when time is scarce, even the best parents find themselves passing a system-wide familial speed-up along to the most vulnerable workers on the line. Parents are then obliged to try to control the damage done by a reversal of worlds. They monitor mealtime, homework time, bedtime, trying to cut out "wasted" time.

In response, children often protest the pace, the deadlines, the grand irrationality of "efficient" family life. Children dawdle. They refuse to leave places when it's time to leave. They insist on leaving places when it's not time to leave. Surely, this is part of the usual stop-and-go of childhood itself, but perhaps, too, it is the plea of children for more family time and more control over what time there is. This only adds to the feeling that life at home has become hard work.

Instead of trying to arrange shorter or more flexible work schedules, Amerco parents often avoid confronting the reality of the time bind. Some minimize their ideas about how much care a child, a partner or they themselves "really need." They make do with less time, less attention, less understanding and less support at home than they once imagined possible. They *emotionally downsize* life. In essence, they deny the needs of family members, and they themselves become emotional ascetics. If they once "needed" time with each other, they are now increasingly "fine" without it.

Another way that working parents try to evade the time bind is to buy themselves out of it—an approach that puts women in particular at the heart of a contradiction. Like men, women absorb the work-family speed-up far more than they resist it; but unlike men, they still shoulder most of the workload at home. And women still represent in people's minds the heart and soul of family life. They're the ones—especially women of the urban middle and upper-middle classes—who feel most acutely the need to save time, who are the most tempted by the new "time saving" goods and services—and who wind up feeling the most guilty about it. For example, Playgroup Connections, a Washington-area business started by a former executive recruiter, matches playmates to one another. One mother hired the service to find her child a French-speaking playmate.

In several cities, children home alone can call a number for "Grandma, Please!" and reach an adult who has the time to talk with them, sing to them or help them with their homework. An ad for Kindercare Learning Centers, a for-profit child-care chain, pitches its appeal this way: "You want your child to be active, tolerant, smart, loved, emotionally stable, self-aware, artistic and get a two-hour nap. Anything else?" It goes on to note that Kindercare accepts children 6 weeks to 12 years old and provides a number to call for the Kindercare nearest you. Another typical service organizes children's birthday parties, making out invitations ("sure hope you can come") and providing party favors, entertainment, a decorated cake and balloons. Creative Memories is a service that puts ancestral photos into family albums for you.

An overwhelming majority of the working mothers I spoke with recoiled from the idea of buying themselves out of parental duties. A bought birthday party was "too impersonal," a 90-second breakfast "too fast." Yet a surprising amount of lunchtime conversation between female friends at Amerco was devoted to expressing complex, conflicting feelings about the lure of trading time for one service or another. The temptation to order flash-frozen dinners or to call a local number for a homework helper did not come up because such services had not yet appeared at Spotted Deer Child-Care Center. But many women dwelled on the question of how to decide where a mother's job began and ended, especially with regard to babysitters and television. One mother said to another in the breakroom of an Amerco plant: "Damon doesn't settle down until 10 at night, so he hates me to wake him up in the morning and I hate to do it. He's cranky. He pulls the covers up. I put on cartoons. That way I can dress him and he doesn't object. I don't like to use TV that way. It's like a drug. But I do it."

The other mother countered: "Well, Todd is up before we are, so that's not a problem. It's after dinner, when I feel like watching a little television, that I feel guilty, because he gets too much TV at the sitter's."

As task after task falls into the realm of time-saving goods and services, questions rise about the moral meanings attached to doing or not doing such tasks. Is it being a good mother to bake a child's birthday cake (alone or together with one's partner)? Or can we gratefully save time by ordering it, and be good mothers by planning the party? Can we save more time by hiring a planning service, and be good mothers simply by watching our children have a good time? "Wouldn't that be nice!" one Amerco mother exclaimed. As the idea of the "good mother" retreats before the pressures of work and the expansion of motherly services, mothers are in fact continually reinventing themselves.

The final way working parents tried to evade the time bind was to develop what I call "potential selves." The potential selves that I discovered in my Amerco interviews were fantasy creations of time-poor parents who dreamed of living as time millionaires.

One man, a gifted 55-year-old engineer in research and development at Amerco, told how he had dreamed of taking his daughters on a camping trip in the Sierra Mountains: "I bought all the gear three years ago when they were 5 and 7, the tent, the sleeping bags, the air mattresses, the backpacks, the ponchos. I got a map of the area. I even got the freeze-dried food. Since then the kids and I have talked about it a lot, and gone over what we're going to do. They've been on me to do it for a long time. I feel bad about it. I keep putting it off, but we'll do it, I just don't know when."

Banished to garages and attics of many Amerco workers were expensive electric saws, cameras, skis and musical instruments, all bought with wages it took time to earn. These items were to their owners what Cassie's fudge bar was to her—a substitute for time, a talisman, a reminder of the potential self.

Obviously, not everyone, not even a majority of Americans, is making a home out of work and a workplace out of home. But in the working world, it is a growing reality, and one we need to face. Increasing numbers of women are discovering a great male secret—that work can be an escape from the pressures of home, pressures that the changing nature of work itself are only intensifying. Neither men nor women are going to take up "family-friendly" policies, whether corporate or governmental, as long as the current realities of work and home remain as they are. For a substantial number of time-bound parents, the stripped-down home and the neighborhood devoid of community are simply losing out to the pull of the workplace.

There are several broader, historical causes of this reversal of realms. The last 30 years have witnessed the rapid rise of women in the workplace. At the same time, job mobility has taken families farther from relatives who might lend a hand, and made it harder to make close friends of neighbors who could help out. Moreover, as women have acquired more education and have joined men at work, they have absorbed the views of an older, male-oriented work world, its views of a "real career," far more than men have taken up their share of the work at home. One reason women have changed more than men is the world of "male" work seems more honorable and valuable than the "female" world of home and children.

So where do we go from here? There is surely no going back to the mythical 1950s family that confined women to the home. Most women don't wish to return to a full-time role at home—and couldn't afford it even if they did. But equally troubling is a workaholic culture that strands both men and women outside the home.

For a while now, scholars on work–family issues have pointed to Sweden, Norway and Denmark as better models of work–family balance. Today, for example, almost all Swedish fathers take two paid weeks off from work at the birth of their children, and about half of fathers and most mothers take additional "parental leave" during the child's first or second year. Research shows that men who take family leave when their children are very young are more likely to be involved with their children as they grow older. When I mentioned this Swedish record of paternity leave to a focus group of American male managers, one of them replied, "Right, we've already heard about Sweden." To this executive, paternity leave was a good idea not for the U.S. today, but for some "potential society" in another place and time.

Meanwhile, children are paying the price. In her book *When the Bough Breaks: The Cost of Neglecting Our Children*, the economist Sylvia Hewlett claims that "compared with the previous generation, young people today are more likely to underperform at school; commit suicide; need psychiatric help; suffer a severe eating disorder; bear a child out of wedlock; take drugs; be the victim of a violent crime." But we needn't dwell on sledgehammer problems like heroin and suicide to realize that children like those at Spotted Deer need more of our time. If other advanced nations with two-job families can give children the time they need, why can't we?

College Athletes
and Role Conflict

Peter Adler and Patricia A. Adler

introduction ∎ ∎ ∎ ∎ ∎

In earlier societies, there was no separate social institution called education. There were no special buildings called schools, and no people who earned their living as teachers. Instead, as an integral part of growing up, children learned what was necessary to get along in life. If hunting and cooking were the skills required for survival and taking on adult roles in their group, then people who already possessed those skills taught them to children. Socialization into adult roles by family and friends was education.

No longer is an informal system of passing on knowledge and skills adequate, and today a formal social institution known as education has become highly significant in social life. With each generation, the amount of education that young people are expected to attain has increased. A hundred years ago, graduating from the eighth grade was considered sufficient education for almost everyone—except for the few who went on to *higher* education in a place called *high* school. Today, in contrast, most young people are asked, "Where are you going to college?" This question is also asked of every top high school athlete, whom everyone presumes will be awarded a scholarship to college. Of the athletes who do get scholarships, many fail to graduate from college. Peter and Patricia Adler, a husband and wife team of sociologists, explore reasons for this.

Thinking Critically

As you read this selection, ask yourself:

1. Why is it common for athletes who receive college scholarships to fail to graduate from college? What part does the athlete subculture play in this?

2. What role conflict do college athletes experience? Why?

3. If you were the president of a Top 10 college and you wanted to dramatically increase the college graduation rate of your athletes, based on the findings in this selection, what would you do?

Athletes attend colleges and universities for the ostensible purpose of getting an education while they exercise and refine their athletic skills, but recent studies note that this ideal has become increasingly corrupted. Reports by journalists, former athletes, and social scientists note the commercialization of big-time college athletics, where the money and prestige available to universities have turned their athletic programs into business enterprises that emphasize winning at all costs, often neglecting the education goals of their institutions. The equality of the exchange between college athletes and their educational institutions has therefore been sharply questioned, with many critics leveling charges that universities have exploited their athletes by making excessive demands of them and failing to fulfill their educational promises to them. Several studies have suggested that these factors . . . result in [athletes] having lower grades and less chance of graduating than other students. . . . Drawing on four years of intensive participant observation with a major college basketball team, this article examines college athletes' academic experiences. . . .

■ ■ ■ METHODS AND SETTING

For four years the authors studied a major college basketball program via participant-observation. . . . The research was conducted at a medium-size private university with a predominantly white, suburban, and middle-class student body. The university's academic standards were demanding as it was striving to enhance its academic reputation. The athletic department, as a whole, had a recent history of success. Players were generally recruited from the region, were 70% black, and ranged from the lower to the middle classes. The basketball program fit what Coakley and Frey termed *big-time college athletics*. Although it could not compare to the really large universities, its recent success had compensated for its size and lack of historical tradition. The national ranking and past success of the basketball team and other teams in sending graduating members into the professional leagues imbued the entire athletic milieu with a sense of seriousness and purpose.

The basketball players' circle of significant others was largely predetermined by athletic environment. The role-set members fell into three main categories: athletic, academic, and social. Within the athletic realm, in addition to their teammates, athletes related primarily to the coaching staff, trainers, team managers, secretaries, and athletic administrators. Secondary role-set members included boosters, fans, and the news media. Within the academic realm, athletes' role-set members consisted of professors, tutors, classmates, and, to a lesser extent, academic counselors and administrators. Within the social realm, athletes related to girlfriends, local friends, and students (non-athletes), but most especially to their college athlete peers: the teammates and dormmates who were members of their subculture.

From Peter Adler and Patricia Adler, "Role Conflict and Identity Salience: College Athletics and the Academic Role." *The Social Science Journal,* Vol. 24, No. 4, pp. 443–455. Copyright © 1987 by Elsevier. Reprinted by permission of Elsevier.

■ ■ ■ **ROLE EXPECTATIONS**

Most incoming college athletes observed approached their academic role with initial feelings of idealism. They were surrounded by family and cultural messages that college would enhance their upward mobility and benefit their lives in many ways. They never doubted this assertion. Because of their academic experiences in high school, few athletes questioned their ability to succeed in college ("I graduated high school, didn't I?"). Athletes' idealism about their impending academic experience was further strengthened by the positive tone coaches had taken toward academics during the recruiting process. Entering freshmen commonly held the following set of prior expectations about their academic role: (1) they would go to classes and do the work (phrased as "putting the time in"); (2) they would graduate and get a degree, and (3) there would be no problems.

Approximately 47% ($N = 8$) of the entering athletes observed showed their initially high academic aspirations and expectations by requesting to be placed in a preprofessional major in the colleges of business, engineering, or arts and sciences. Despite warnings from coaches and older teammates about how difficult it would be to complete this coursework and play ball, they felt they could easily handle the demands. These individuals planned to use college athletics as a stepping-stone to career opportunities. As one freshman stated:

> I goin' to use basketball to get an education. Sure I'd like to make the NBA someday, but right now I've got to have something to fall back on if I don't.

Another group of freshmen, who had already accorded academics a less salient role (45%, $N = 17$), were enrolled by coaches in more "manageable" majors, such as physical education or recreation. Most of these individuals, though, believed that they too would get a degree. They had few prior expectations about academics, but assumed that they would make it through satisfactorily. Someone had taken care of these matters in high school, and they felt that college would be no different. Only a few individuals from the sample (8%, $N = 3$) entered college expecting to turn professional shortly thereafter. From the beginning these individuals disdained the academic role.

Much of this initial idealism was based on an inaccurate picture of college. Athletes did not anticipate the focus on analytical thinking and writing they would encounter, expecting that college courses would be an extension of their high school experiences. One sophomore reflected back on his expectations:

> I didn't think about it much, but when I did, I thought it'd be more or less the same here as it be back in high school, no big change. I be passin' all my courses there, but I still be goin' out every night.

In their first weeks on campus during their summer program, this early idealism was once again bolstered. Repeatedly the head coach stressed the importance of earning a degree. He cared about his players as people and wanted them to build a future out of their college experience. In fact, one of the main reasons athletes' parents encouraged their sons to attend this university was because of the head coach's integrity and good values. Once the school year began, athletes attended required nightly study halls, were told that tutors were available, and were constantly reminded by the coach to go to class. One freshman, interviewed during the preseason period, showed his idealism through his expectations and impressions:

> I'm here for two reasons: to get my degree and play basketball. I don't think it's goin' to be no problem to get my degree. I want to graduate in four years and I think I will. I think that's really important to Coach, too, because in practice he always mentions how important the degree is and everything.

Contrary to popular sentiment, most of the athletes observed began their college careers with a positive attitude toward academics. While their athletic role was unquestionably the most salient and their social role secondary, the academic role was still a critical dimension of their self-identity. Their behavior in the academic realm reflected this; they missed few classes, and turned in assignments regularly. For most this period lasted anywhere from one semester to two years.

■ ■ ■ ■ ROLE CONFLICT

After two semesters in school and a full basketball season, athletes began to realize that their academic expectations had not been entirely accurate. Their early naive idealism gave way to disappointment and cynicism. . . . A major change athletes encountered in shifting from high school to college basketball lay in their athletic role. In large part this was due to the professionalization process they underwent. As one junior remarked:

> In high school, basketball was fun and games, but now it's a job. We get to the gym, we gotta work. You gotta put your all into it no matter how you feelin' that day. 'Cause this is big business. There's a lotta money ridin' on us.

Compounding the professionalization was a dramatic increase in pressure. The basketball players were all public figures in the local area who received intense news coverage. They clearly knew how important winning was to the coaches, boosters, and fans.

The players' athletic role often encroached on their academic role. They soon discovered that handling both roles was not always possible. A primary reason was the time conflict: some courses they wanted or needed for their majors were only offered in the afternoons during practice time; road trips caused them to miss key lectures, examinations, or review sessions, and banquets and other booster functions (which occurred at least once a week) cut into their studying time. At some point during this freshman year, most athletes realized that they did not have the time to perform as well as they had originally hoped in the academic role. . . .

Athletes' perceptions of their athletic–academic role conflict was also influenced by the role model of their coaches. While the coaches sincerely cared about their players' academic responsibilities and achievements, they had their own priorities. Once the season began, they were too busy with their athletic work to pay much attention to academics. The pressures of recruiting, funding, and winning absorbed their energy. Despite their best preseason intentions, once practice officially began in October, the coaches became predominantly concerned with their players as athletes and ended up passing on the pressures of their organizational demands and constraints. Like their players, they were faced with a complex situation to which they often reacted, rather than acted. While they verbally stressed the importance of academics, they accorded athletic and team functions higher salience than school obligations: players' athletic time was strictly regulated, but their academic time was not. Players' behavior in practice, at games, at booster events, and on road trips was carefully monitored, yet their performance in class was not. Despite the coaches' concern about academics, the predominant message that athletes received was that, in contrast to academics, athletics had to be strictly adhered to because a powerful role-set member was always present.

ACADEMIC ROLE

During the school year, players began to notice other characteristics of their academic role that undercut their coaches' verbal emphasis on scholarship. One of the first was their lack of autonomy over their course (and sometimes major) selection. An assistant coach picked out classes and registered the athletes without consulting them. Assistant coaches bought their books, added and dropped courses for them, and contacted their professors if they had to be absent or were doing poorly in their work. By taking care of these academic matters for them, the coaches served as intermediaries between players and the academic realm. Consequently, most athletes failed to develop the knowledge, initiative, or the interest to handle these academic matters themselves, or to develop significant relationships with their professors or other academic role-set members. Thus, when the coaches were too busy to attend to these details, the players were unable to manage for themselves. As one senior remarked:

> Most of those guys don't even know how to fill out an add-drop card, so when they want to switch classes they just do it, and they tell the coaches to switch them. They figure it's not their job. But a lot of guys get Fs because the coaches never got around to it. The only reason I got through is that my girlfriend did it for me. I don't even know how to read a schedule of classes or where to get one.

Despite their occasional lapses, the fact that coaches managed these administrative matters gave athletes a false sense of security, a feeling that someone was always looking out for them academically and would make sure that they were given another chance. The athletes believed that they could fail to perform academically and not have to pay the consequences. They developed the perception that . . . they would be taken care of academically, and that they need not overly involve themselves in this arena. . . .

Concomitant with this lack of autonomy came a new freedom. Unlike high school, their attendance at classes was not compulsory. Being able to skip classes placed a greater responsibility for self-motivation on them. When their motivation waned, athletes developed a pattern of slipping behind in their attendance and classwork until their problems compounded. When athletes did attend class, they often encountered another set of difficulties or disillusionments. In the classroom athletes thought that many professors labeled them as jocks. This image was fostered by the fact that they were surrounded in their classes by other athletes (also placed there by assistant coaches), and that they were identified early in the semester to their professor as athletes (because assistant coaches called or sent out reports to monitor their academic progress). They therefore encountered different expectations and treatment than the general student body. Whether they were given greater tolerance (extra tutoring sessions, relaxed deadlines, relaxed academic standards) or less tolerance ("Those guys think they're entitled to special treatment because they're athletes, and I'm going to show them they're wrong"), they were treated as less than full adults. This special treatment reinforced the differentiation between these two roles and their perceptions of themselves as athletes more than students. When they returned to the dormitory rooms at night, exhausted and sore from practicing, it became easier for them to rationalize, procrastinate, and fritter away their time instead of studying.

Athletes also became disinterested in their academic role because of the content of their classes. The level of disinterest varied between the athletes enrolled in arts and sciences, business, or engineering courses, and those taking physical education or recreation courses. Many of those in the latter category had wanted and expected to take courses in college that were either entertaining, vocational, or in some way relevant to their everyday lives. This was not what they found. Instead, they were enrolled in courses that they considered comical and demeaning. One sophomore articulated the commonly held view:

> How could I get into this stuff? They got me taking nutrition, mental retardation, square dancing, and camp counseling. I thought I was goin' to learn something here. It's a bunch o' BS.

Players enrolled in more rigorous academic courses were often unequipped for the demanding calibre of the work. Many did not have the knowledge, interests, skills, or study habits to compete with other students. With their inadequate training, tight schedules, and waning motivation, athletes became frustrated, bored, and disinterested. Players often stopped going to classes they did not like, yet never officially withdrew from them. When they did poorly on the first test, they gave up on the course, figuring "to hell with it, I'm not gonna try." The positive feedback from their academic role that the athletes anticipated often was replaced by a series of disappointments. As a result they often spent their days lying around the dormitory rooms, watching television, and convincing each other not to go to class. Athletes' academic failures then brought them feelings of inadequacy and uncertainty, as one player described:

> When I first came here I thought I'd be goin' to class all the time and I'd study and that'd be it. But I sure didn't think it meant studyin' all the time. Back in high school you just be memorizin' things, but that's not what they want here. Back in high school I thought I be a pretty good student, but now I don't know.

Players' experiences in the classroom were very different from their preconceptions. The work was harder and they were not taken care of to the extent they had imagined. The intense competition of the athletic arena led them to be obsessed with success. Their frequent academic failures (or at best mediocre grades) led athletes to distance themselves from self-involvement in the academic role. It was better not to try than to try and fail. And they derived plenty of support for this tack within the peer subculture.

■ ■ ■ ■ SOCIAL ROLE

Athletes' social experiences at the university were predominantly with other athletes. Initially they had expected to derive both friendship and status recognition from other students as they had in high school. Instead they found themselves socially isolated. Geographically they were isolated by being housed in an athletic dormitory on a remote side of the campus. Temporally they were cut off by the demands of their practices, games, study halls, and booster functions. Culturally they were racially, socially, and economically different from the rest of the student body. Physically, they were different from other students in size and build, and many students, especially women, found them imposing or occasionally intimidating.

These factors left other athletes as their primary outlets for social relations. Housed together in a dormitory reserved almost exclusively for male athletes (primarily football and basketball players), they bonded together into a reference group and peer subculture. Relations within this group were made especially cohesive by the intensity of their living, playing, and traveling together. A junior described this living situation:

> Living in the jock dorm the privacy is limited. Everybody knows everythin' 'bout what you doin' and who you seein'. You got to live with these same faces twelve months out of the year, they like your brothers, and we all one big family, like it or not. You just got to fit in.

Within the dormitory, athletes briefed each other about what to expect from and think about various individuals, and how to handle certain situations. They formed generalized attitudes and beliefs about what things were important and what things were not. The peer subculture provided them with a set of norms that guided their interpretations of and actions within their various roles.

One of the peer subculture's strongest influences lay in its anti-intellectual and anti-academic character. Typically, dormitory conversation centered on athletic and social dimensions of their lives with little reference to academic, cultural, or intellectual pursuits. In fact, individuals who displayed too much interest, effort, or success in academics were often ridiculed, as one player described:

> When most of the other guys are making Ds or Fs, if I work hard and I get a B on a test, if I go back to the dorm and they all see I got a B, then they goin' "snap on" [make fun of] me. So most of the guys, they don't try. They all act like it's a big joke.

The athletes' peer subculture conflicted with their academic role in five ways: (1) by discouraging them from exerting effort in academics; (2) by providing them with distractions that made it harder for them to study; (3) by providing them with role models who appeared to be getting through college while according their academic role negligible identity salience; (4) by discouraging them from seeking out and associating with other students who could have provided greater academic role modeling; and (5) by providing excuses and justifications that legitimated their academic failures.

The conflict between their athletic, academic, and social roles pulled the athletes in too many directions. One junior expressed his continuing distress over this role conflict:

> When I think about it I get tense and frustrated, you just can't be everything they expect you to be and what you want to be. Something's gotta give. It's either cut off my social life, or flunk out of school, or not do the things I have to do to be able to make pro.

■ ■ ■ ROLE CONFLICT RESOLUTIONS

Athletes' expectations for their academic role were gradually replaced by feelings of anomie as they came to perceive the disparity between the recruiting and cultural rhetoric they had encountered and the reality of college life. In order to successfully negotiate their college experience they had to find some way to resolve this role conflict, which they did by realigning the expectations, priorities, and identity salience [the significance of a role, or how much one identifies with it] of their roles.

The biggest change in their core identity salience lay in the growth of their athletic role. While athletics had always been the first priority for most, it now engulfed them. This shift was brought about by the demands and expectations of their athletic role set and by their own desire to cling to their dreams of making it in the NBA. First, the head coach overwhelmed athletes by the intensity of his power and role demands. He expected them to place basketball before everything else. He influenced their view of their present and future life chances by framing these for them based on athletic priorities. He heard about everything they did and reprimanded them for violations of his behavior code. Yet it was the intensity of the athletic experience itself that ensured their self-immersion in this role. The glamour and excitement of playing for a big-time athletic program offered even the most marginal players their most fulfilling gratification and rewards. One player described the impossibility of maintaining any balance between his athletic and other roles:

> When I go to sleep at night what do you think I be thinking? History? Sociology? No way. I hear coach yelling in my ear, "Run, run, get on the ball, play defense, Robinson. Damn, Robinson, can you move your feet, son?" During the season I sleep, eat, and breathe basketball.

In addition, the athletic role pervaded and dominated the identity of their other roles in social and academic situations. On campus they were recognized as athletes first and students second. Off campus and even out of uniform, they were constantly responsible for "representing the program." Their appearance and demeanor reflected on their teammates, their coaches, their basketball program, and the entire university. They therefore had to relinquish a great deal of privacy and freedom.

The growth of the athletic role's identity salience was further endorsed by their peer subculture. Most of the athletes in their dormitory had reprioritized their roles and become engulfed by athletics. These significant others offered them a model of role conflict resolution that adopted the coach's perspective on the predominance of athletics, maintained the secondary importance of having a social life, and reshuffled academics to an even lower identity salience. All of the athletes realigned the identity salience of these roles in this manner, progressively detaching themselves from academics.

These changes in athletes' identities led to a series of pragmatic adjustments in their academic goals. Of the individuals who began with preprofessional majors, only one-fourth of them stayed with these all the way through college and graduated. They did so primarily without the academic care and concern they had originally anticipated. They ceased attending classes regularly, diminished their efforts to get to know professors, did not bother to get class notes or reading assignments until just before tests, and exerted the minimum amount of effort necessary to get by. More commonly, these individuals reassessed their academic goals and found that some adjustment was necessary. A second group (the remaining three-fourths of this original group) adjusted by both shifting their behavior and by changing from their preprofessional program to a more manageable major. While this shift meant that they had abandoned both their academic idealism and their earlier career goals, they still held to the goal of graduating. The predominant attitude changed to getting a diploma regardless of the major. As one player commented, "When you apply for a job all that matters is if you have that piece of paper. They don't care what you majored in." Many of the athletes in this group managed to graduate or keep on a steady course toward graduation. Much like Merton's innovators, they retained the socially approved goal but replaced their earlier means with a creative alternative.

Athletes who began their college careers with lower initial academic aspirations and who majored in physical education or recreation from the start made corresponding adjustments. Approximately one-fifth of these in this group originally held on to their initial goal and managed to graduate in one of these fields. Like the preprofessional majors, they did so with less concern than they had displayed on entering. The other four-fifths came to the realization, usually relatively late, that their chances for graduating from college were unrealistic. They therefore shifted their orientation toward maintaining their athletic eligibility. A junior's remarks illustrated how this shift to maintaining eligibility affected his attitude toward his academic role:

> I used to done thought I was goin' to school, but now I know it's not for real. . . . I don't have no academic goals. A player a coach is counting on, that's all he think about is ball. That's what he signed to do. So what you gotta do is show up, show your smilin' face. Try as hard as you can. Don't just lay over in the room. That's all the coach can ask. Or else you may not find yourself playing the next year. Or even that year.

By their senior year, when they had met their final eligibility requirements, many members of this last group abandoned the academic role entirely. They either anticipated going to one of the professional leagues, or they knew that their scholarships would soon expire and they would have to look for a job. In either case, wasting their time in class no longer seemed necessary.

▪ ▪ ▪ DISCUSSION

. . . In their academic role, many college athletes received poor or marginal grades and had to relinquish or readjust the academic goals they held on entering college. This perception awakened them to the conflict between their expectations that college would be much like high school and their realizations that the academic demands at the university were greater than they could achieve. Their emphasis on competition and winning, derived from their athletic role, made the failure especially difficult to accept.

When faced with extreme role conflict, individuals doing very poorly in their classes engaged in role distance, diminishing the importance of this role to their self-identity. Individuals from stronger academic backgrounds fared slightly better, however, and did not as greatly diminish their [identity with the] academic role. . . . As individuals assessed their relative strengths and weaknesses within given roles, they accorded higher salience to those in which they were evaluated positively and lower salience to those in which they were negatively evaluated. . . .

Most athletes' initial commitment to the academic role was induced by cultural expectations and by the encouragement of others, but that commitment was not firmly embedded in their self-conceptions. Once they got to college, their commitment to work hard academically was easily dislodged by their first few adverse experiences and by the peer culture's devaluation of academics. In contrast, their commitment to the athletic role was entrenched, because this was their dream since childhood. No matter how little playing time they received or how much the coach criticized them, they clung to the primary self-identification as athletes. . . .

As college athletes learned the nature of their new status they learned that they were seen as basketball players by nearly everyone they encountered. Their athletic identity pervaded and dominated the identity of their other roles in almost all other situations. This designation was true in their academic and social lives both on campus and off, and it grew more pervasive as they progressed through their playing careers and advanced to more visible team positions. . . . When people are constantly identified by one role to the near total exclusion of their others, they become increasingly committed to that role and it is likely to take precedence in influencing their self-conceptions. . . .

Athletes' position at the university was characterized by "institutional powerlessness," as their coaches had the ability to control all aspects of their lives. By influencing their personal time, academic schedules, and playing role on the team, coaches could dominate not only their athletic role, but their social and academic roles as well. Regardless of the players' own goals, expectations, or desires, they had to take into consideration the wishes and demands of the coach. Players also believed . . . that the coach could . . . keep them eligible to play if he wanted, even if they got into academic difficulty. The omnipotence of their athletic over their academic role influenced them to shift greater identity salience to the role where the apparent power lay. . . .

India's Sacred Cow

Marvin Harris

introduction ■■■■■

Although its form varies from one culture to another, religion is one of humanity's fundamental social institutions. A generation ago, some "experts" predicted that with the rise of science and rationality U.S. culture would become so secularized that religion would quietly fade into the background. Only in a few superstitious, backward corners of society would a remnant of religion remain. Events proved otherwise, of course, and today religion is as vital for Americans as it was in the past. As science has advanced, church membership has even grown, and it now is higher than at any time in U.S. history. Tens of millions of Americans seek guidance and solace in religion. They look to religion to answer many of the perplexing questions they face in life, ones for which science offers no answers.

Like the other social institutions, religion is interconnected with the other parts of society. When we refer to our own religion, however, it often is difficult to perceive these interconnections. What affects us directly, such as what occurs in our own congregation, synagogue, or mosque, gets our attention, not some abstract connections. In addition, the things we take for granted close our eyes and thinking. When we look at unfamiliar religions, in contrast, we are seeing practices that are far removed from our experiences, that are not part of our taken-for-granted assumptions. The unfamiliarity or "strangeness" of these religious practices prompts us to ask questions. For example, we might wonder why cows are allowed to wander India's city streets and country roads. Such wanderings match the background assumptions of Indians, and for them the sight of cows even in a city's heavy street traffic does not prompt questions. Similarly, we may wonder why deprived and hungry Indians don't eat these cattle. As Harris considers such matters, he makes the essential interconnections between religion and other aspects of culture more evident.

Thinking Critically

As you read this selection, ask yourself:

1. What interconnections are there between your religion (assuming you have one) and other aspects of your culture? Another way of asking this is: How do your religion and culture reinforce or influence one another?

News photographers that came out of India during the famine of the late 1960s showed starving people stretching out bony hands to beg for food while sacred cattle strolled behind undisturbed. The Hindu, it seems, would rather starve to death than eat his cow or even deprive it of food. The cattle appear to browse unhindered through urban markets eating an orange here, a mango there, competing with people for meager supplies of food.

By Western standards, spiritual values seem more important to Indians than life itself. Specialists in food habits around the world like Fred Simons at the University of California at Davis consider Hinduism an irrational ideology that compels people to overlook abundant, nutritious foods for scarcer, less healthful foods.

What seems to be an absurd devotion to the mother cow pervades Indian life. Indian wall calendars portray beautiful young women with bodies of fat white cows, often with milk jetting from their teats into sacred shrines.

Cow worship even carries over into politics. In 1966 a crowd of 120,000 people, led by holy men, demonstrated in front of the Indian House of Parliament in support of the All-Party Cow Protection Campaign Committee. In Nepal, the only contemporary Hindu kingdom, cow slaughter is severely punished. As one story goes, the car driven by an official of a United States agency struck and killed a cow. In order to avoid the international incident that would have occurred when the official was arrested for murder, the Nepalese magistrate concluded that the cow had committed suicide.

Many Indians agree with Western assessments of the Hindu reverence for their cattle, the zebu, or *Bos indicus,* a large-humped species prevalent in Asia and Africa. M. N. Srinivas, an Indian anthropologist, states: "Orthodox Hindu opinion regards the killing of cattle with abhorrence, even though the refusal to kill vast numbers of useless cattle which exist in India today is detrimental to the nation." Even the Indian Ministry of Information formerly maintained that "the large animal population is more a liability than an asset in view of our land resources." Accounts from many different sources point to the same conclusion: India, one of the world's great civilizations, is being strangled by its love for the cow.

The easy explanation for India's devotion to the cow, the one most Westerners and Indians would offer, is that cow worship is an integral part of Hinduism.

Religion is somehow good for the soul, even it if sometimes fails the body. Religion orders the cosmos and explains our place in the universe. Religious beliefs, many would claim, have existed for thousands of years and have a life of their own. They are not understandable in scientific terms.

But all this ignores history. There is more to be said for cow worship than is immediately apparent. The earliest Vedas, the Hindu sacred texts from the second millennium B.C., do not prohibit the slaughter of cattle. Instead, they ordain it as part of sacrificial rites. The early Hindus did not avoid the flesh of cows and bulls; they ate it at ceremonial feasts presided over by Brahman priests. Cow worship is a relatively recent development in India; it evolved as the Hindu religion developed and changed.

This evolution is recorded in royal edicts and religious texts written during the last 3,000 years of Indian history. The Vedas from the first millennium B.C. contain contradictory passages, some referring to ritual slaughter and others to a strict taboo on beef consumption. A. N. Bose, in *Social and Rural Economy of Northern India, 600 B.C.–200 A.D.*, concludes that many of the sacred-cow passages were incorporated into the texts by priests of a later period.

By 200 A.D. the status of Indian cattle had undergone a spiritual transformation. The Brahman priesthood exhorted the population to venerate the cow and forbade them to abuse it or to feed on it. Religious feasts involving the ritual slaughter and consumption of livestock were eliminated and meat eating was restricted to the nobility.

By 1000 A.D., all Hindus were forbidden to eat beef. Ahimsa, the Hindu belief in the unity of all life, was the spiritual justification for this restriction. But it is difficult to ascertain exactly when this change occurred. An important event that helped to shape the modern complex was the Islamic invasion, which took place in the eighth century A.D. Hindus may have found it politically expedient to set themselves off from the invaders, who were beefeaters, by emphasizing the need to prevent the slaughter of their sacred animals. Thereafter, the cow taboo assumed its modern form and began to function much as it does today.

The place of the cow in modern India is every place—on posters, in the movies, in brass figures, in stone and wood carvings, on the streets, in the fields. The cow is a symbol of health and abundance. It provides the milk that Indians consume in the form of yogurt and ghee (clarified butter), which contribute subtle flavors to much spicy Indian food.

This, perhaps, is the practical role of the cow, but cows provide less than half the milk produced in India. Most cows in India are not dairy breeds. In most regions, when an Indian farmer wants a steady, high-quality source of milk he usually invests in a female water buffalo. In India the water buffalo is the specialized dairy breed because its milk has a higher butterfat content than zebu milk. Although the farmer milks his zebu cows, the milk is merely a by-product.

More vital than zebu milk to South Asian farmers are zebu calves. Male calves are especially valued because from bulls come oxen, which are the mainstay of the Indian agricultural system.

Small, fast oxen drag wooden plows through late-spring fields when monsoons have dampened the dry, cracked earth. After harvest, the oxen break the grain from the stalk by stomping through mounds of cut wheat and rice. For rice cultivation in irrigated fields, the male water buffalo is preferred (it pulls better in deep mud), but for most other crops, including rainfall rice, wheat, sorghum, and millet, and for transporting goods and people to and from town, a team of oxen is preferred. The ox is the Indian peasant's tractor, thresher, and family car combined; the cow is the factory that produces the ox.

If draft animals instead of cows are counted, India appears to have too few domesticated ruminants, not too many. Since each of the 70 million farms in India require a draft team, it follows that Indian peasants should use 140 million animals in the fields. But there are only 83 million oxen and male water buffalo on the subcontinent, a shortage of 30 million draft teams.

In other regions of the world, joint ownership of draft animals might overcome a shortage, but Indian agriculture is closely tied to the monsoon rains of late spring and summer. Field preparation and planting must coincide with the rain, and a farmer must have his animals ready to plow when the weather is right. When the farmer without a draft team needs bullocks most, his neighbors are all using theirs. Any delay in turning the soil drastically lowers production.

Because of this dependence on draft animals, loss of the family oxen is devastating. If a beast dies, the farmer must borrow money to buy or rent an ox at interest rates so high that he ultimately loses his land. Every year foreclosures force thousands of poverty-stricken peasants to abandon the countryside for the overcrowded cities.

If a family is fortunate enough to own a fertile cow, it will be able to rear replacements for a lost team and thus survive until life returns to normal. If, as sometimes happens, famine leads a family to sell its cow and ox team, all ties to agriculture are cut. Even if the family survives, it has no way to farm the land, no oxen to work the land, and no cows to produce oxen.

The prohibition against eating meat applies to the flesh of cows, bulls, and oxen, but the cow is the most sacred because it can produce the other two. The peasant whose cow dies is not only crying over a spiritual loss but over the loss of his farm as well.

Religious laws that forbid the slaughter of cattle promote the recovery of the agricultural system from the dry Indian winter and from periods of drought. The monsoon, on which all agriculture depends, is erratic. Sometimes, it arrives early, sometimes late, sometimes not at all. Drought has struck large portions of India time and again in this century, and Indian farmers and the zebus are accustomed to these natural disasters. Zebus can pass weeks on end with little or no food and water. Like camels, they store both in their humps and recuperate quickly with only a little nourishment.

During drought the cows often stop lactating and become barren. In some cases the condition is permanent but often it is only temporary. If barren animals were summarily eliminated, as Western experts in animal husbandry have suggested, cows capable of recovery would be lost along with those entirely debilitated. By keeping alive the cows that can later produce oxen, religious laws against cow slaughter assure the recovery of the agricultural system from the greatest challenge it faces—the failure of the monsoon.

The local Indian governments aid the process of recovery by maintaining homes for barren cows. Farmers reclaim any animal that calves or begins to lactate. One police station in Madras collects strays and pastures them in a field adjacent to the station. After a small fine is paid, a cow is returned to its rightful owner when the owner thinks the cow shows signs of being able to reproduce.

During the hot, dry spring months most of India is like a desert. Indian farmers often complain they cannot feed their livestock during this period. They maintain the cattle by letting them scavenge on the sparse grass along the roads. In the cities the cattle are encouraged to scavenge near food stalls to supplement their scant diet. These are the wandering cattle tourists report seeing throughout India.

Westerners expect shopkeepers to respond to these intrusions with the deference due a sacred animal; instead, their response is a string of curses and the crack of a long bamboo pole across the beast's back or a poke at its genitals. Mahatma Gandhi was well aware of the treatment sacred cows (and bulls and oxen) received in India. "How we bleed her to take the last drop of milk from her. How we starve her to emaciation, how we ill-treat the calves, how we deprive them of their portion of milk, how cruelly we treat the oxen, how we castrate them, how we beat them, how we overload them" [Gandhi, 1954].

Oxen generally receive better treatment than cows. When food is in short supply, thrifty Indian peasants feed their working bullocks and ignore their cows, but rarely do they abandon the cows to die. When cows are sick, farmers worry over them as they would over members of the family and nurse them as if they were children. When the rains return and when the fields are harvested, the farmers again feed their cows regularly and reclaim their abandoned animals. The prohibition against beef consumption is a form of disaster insurance for all India.

Western agronomists and economists are quick to protest that all the functions of the zebu cattle can be improved with organized breeding programs, cultivated pastures, and silage. Because stronger oxen would pull the plow faster, they could work multiple plots of land, allowing farmers to share their animals. Fewer healthy, well-fed cows could provide Indians with more milk. But pastures and silage require arable land, land needed to produce wheat and rice.

A look at Western cattle farming makes plain the cost of adopting advanced technology in Indian agriculture. In a study of livestock production in the United States, David Pimentel of the College of Agriculture and Life Sciences at Cornell University, found that 91 percent of the cereal, legume, and vegetable protein suitable for human consumption is consumed by livestock. Approximately three quarters of the arable land in the United States is devoted to growing food for livestock. In the production of meat and milk, American ranchers use enough fossil fuel to equal more than 82 million barrels of oil annually.

Indian cattle do not drain the system in the same way. In a 1971 study of livestock in West Bengal, Stewart Odend'hal [1972] of the University of Missouri found that Bengalese cattle ate only the inedible remains of subsistence crops—rice straw, rice hulls, the tops of sugar cane, and mustard-oil cake. Cattle graze in the fields after harvest and eat the remains of crops left on the ground; they forage for grass and weeds on the roadsides. The food for zebu cattle costs the human population virtually nothing. "Basically," Odend'hal says, "the cattle convert the items of little direct human value into products of immediate utility."

In addition to plowing the fields and producing milk, the zebus produce dung, which fires the hearths and fertilizes the fields of India. Much of the estimated 800 million tons of manure produced annually is collected by the farmers' children as they follow the family cows and bullocks from place to place. And when the children see the droppings of another farmer's cattle along the road, they pick those up also. Odend'hal reports that the system operates with such high efficiency that the children of West Bengal recover nearly 100 percent of the dung produced by their livestock.

From 40 to 70 percent of all manure produced by Indian cattle is used as fuel for cooking; the rest is returned to the fields as fertilizer. Dried dung burns slowly, cleanly, and with low heat—characteristics that satisfy the household needs of Indian women. Staples like curry and rice can simmer for hours. While the meal slowly cooks over an unattended fire, the women of the household can do other chores. Cow chips, unlike firewood, do not scorch as they burn.

It is estimated that the dung used for cooking fuel provides the energy-equivalent of 43 million tons of coal. At current prices, it would cost India an extra 1.5 billion dollars in foreign exchange to replace the dung with coal. And if the 350 million tons of manure that are being used as fertilizer were replaced with commercial fertilizers, the expense would be even greater. Roger Revelle of the University of California at San Diego has calculated that 89 percent of the energy used in Indian agriculture (the equivalent of about 140 million tons of coal) is provided by local sources. Even if foreign loans were to provide the money, the capital outlay necessary to replace the Indian cow with tractors and fertilizers for the fields, coal for the fires, and transportation for the family would probably warp international financial institutions for years.

Instead of asking the Indians to learn from the American model of industrial agriculture, American farmers might learn energy conservation from the Indians. Every step in an energy cycle results in a loss of energy to the system. Like a pendulum that slows a bit with each swing, each transfer of energy from sun to plants, plants to animals, and animals to human beings involves energy losses. Some systems are more efficient than others; they provide a higher percentage of the energy inputs in a final, useful form. Seventeen percent of all energy zebus consume is returned in the form of milk, traction, and dung. American cattle raised on Western rangeland return only 4 percent of the energy they consume.

But the American system is improving. Based on techniques pioneered by Indian scientists, at least one commercial firm in the United States is reported to be building plants that will turn manure from cattle feedlots into combustible gas. When organic matter is broken down by anaerobic bacteria, methane gas and carbon dioxide are produced. After the methane is cleansed of the carbon dioxide, it is available for the same purposes as natural gas—cooking, heating, electric generation. The company constructing the biogasification plant plans to sell its product to a gas-supply company, to be piped through the existing distribution system. Schemes similar to this one could make cattle ranches almost independent of utility and gasoline companies; for methane can be used to run trucks, tractors, and cars as well as to supply heat and electricity. The relative energy self-sufficiency that the Indian peasant has achieved is a goal American farmers and industry are now striving for.

Studies of Odend'hal's understate the efficiency of the Indian cow, because dead cows are used for purposes that Hindus prefer not to acknowledge. When a cow dies, an Untouchable, a member of one of the lowest ranking castes in India, is summoned to haul away the carcass. Higher castes consider the body of the dead cow polluting; if they handle it, they must go through a rite of purification.

Untouchables first skin the dead animal and either tan the skin themselves or sell it to a leather factory. In the privacy of their homes, contrary to the teachings of Hinduism, untouchable castes cook the meat and eat it. Indians of all castes rarely acknowledge the existence of these practices to non-Hindus, but most are aware that beefeating takes place. The prohibition against beefeating restricts consumption by the higher castes and helps distribute animal protein to the poorest sectors of the population that otherwise would have no source of these vital nutrients.

Untouchables are not the only Indians who consume beef. Indian Muslims and Christians are under no restriction that forbids them beef, and its consumption is legal in many places. The Indian ban on cow slaughter is state, not national, law and not all states restrict it. In many cities, such as New Delhi, Calcutta, and Bombay, legal slaughterhouses sell beef to retail customers and to restaurants that serve steak.

If the caloric value of beef and the energy costs involved in the manufacture of synthetic leather were included in the estimate of energy, the calculated efficiency of Indian livestock would rise considerably. As well as the system works, experts often claim that its efficiency can be further improved. Alan Heston [et al., 1971], an economist at the University of Pennsylvania, believes that Indians suffer from an overabundance of cows simply because they refuse to slaughter the excess cattle. India could produce at least the same number of oxen and the same quantities of milk and manure with 30 million fewer cows. Heston calculates that only 40 cows are necessary to maintain a population of 100 bulls and oxen. Since India averages 70 cows for every 100 bullocks, the difference, 30 million cows, is expendable.

What Heston fails to note is that sex ratios among cattle in different regions of India vary tremendously, indicating that adjustments in the cow population do take place. Along the Ganges River, one of the holiest shrines of Hinduism, the ratio drops to 47 cows for every 100 male animals. This ratio reflects the preference for dairy buffalo in the irrigated sectors of the Gangetic Plains. In nearby Pakistan, in contrast, where cow slaughter is permitted, the sex ratio is 60 cows to 100 oxen.

Since the sex ratios among cattle differ greatly from region to region and do not even approximate the balance that would be expected if no females were killed, we can assume that some culling of herds does take place; Indians do adjust their religious restrictions to accommodate ecological realities.

They cannot kill a cow but they can tether an old or unhealthy animal until it has starved to death. They cannot slaughter a calf but they can yoke it with a large wooden triangle so that when it nurses it irritates the mother's udder and gets kicked to death. They cannot ship their animals to the slaughterhouse but they can sell them to Muslims, closing their eyes to the fact that the Muslims will take the cattle to the slaughterhouse.

These violations of the prohibition against cattle slaughter strengthen the premise that cow worship is a vital part of Indian culture. The practice arose to prevent the population from consuming the animal on which Indian agriculture depends. During the first millennium B.C., the Gange Valley became one of the most densely populated regions of the world.

Where previously there had been only scattered villages, many towns and cities arose and peasants farmed every available acre of land. Kingsley Davis, a population expert at the University of California at Berkeley, estimates that by 300 B.C. between 50 million and 100 million people were living in India. The forested Ganges Valley became a windswept semidesert and signs of ecological collapse appeared; droughts and floods became commonplace, erosion took away the rich topsoil, farms shrank as population increased, and domesticated animals became harder and harder to maintain.

It is probable that the elimination of meat eating came about in a slow, practical manner. The farmers who decided not to eat their cows, who saved them for procreation to produce oxen, were the ones who survived the natural disasters. Those who ate beef lost the tools with which to farm. Over a period of centuries, more and more farmers probably avoided beef until an unwritten taboo came into existence.

Only later was the practice codified by the priesthood. While Indian peasants were probably aware of the role of cattle in their society, strong sanctions were necessary to protect zebus from a population faced with starvation. To remove temptation, the flesh of cattle became taboo and the cow became sacred.

The sacredness of the cow is not just an ignorant belief that stands in the way of progress. Like all concepts of the sacred and the profane, this one affects the physical world; it defines the relationships that are important for the maintenance of Indian society.

Indians have the sacred cow, we have the "sacred" car and the "sacred" dog. It would not occur to us to propose the elimination of automobiles and dogs from our society without carefully considering the consequences, and we should not propose the elimination of zebu cattle without first understanding their place in the social order of India.

Human society is neither random nor capricious. The regularities of thought and behavior called culture are the principal mechanisms by which we human beings adapt to the world around us. Practices and beliefs can be rational or irrational, but a society that fails to adapt to its environment is doomed to extinction. Only those societies that draw the necessities of life from their surroundings without destroying those surroundings inherit the earth. The West has much to learn from the great antiquity of Indian civilization, and the sacred cow is an important part of that lesson.

REFERENCES

Gandhi, Mohandas K. 1954. *How to Serve the Cow.* Bombay: Navajivan Publishing House.

Heston, Alan, et al. 1971. "An Approach to the Sacred Cow of India." *Current Anthropology* 12, 191–209.

Odend'hal, Stewart. 1972. "Gross Energetic Efficiency of Indian Cattle in Their Environment." *Journal of Human Ecology* 1, 1–27.

Just Another Routine Emergency

Daniel F. Chambliss

introduction ▪ ▪ ▪ ▪

In social life, appearances may not be everything, but they certainly are essential for get-ting along. Just as buildings have façades—attractive front exteriors that are designed to give a good impression of what might be inside—so social groups and organizations have façades. Some organizations even hire public relations firms to put out favorable mes-sages to the public. To cultivate images of caring, others contribute to charitable causes. Oil companies that exploit the environment publish expensive, glossy ads and brochures to convince the public that they care more about the environment than does *Greenpeace* or *The Sea Shepherds*.

As mentioned in the introduction to Part II, some say that the first rule of sociol-ogy is that nothing is as it appears. If so, the first task of sociology is to look behind the scenes. Beneath the social façade put out for public consumption lies a different reality. As in the case of some oil companies, the reality may conflict greatly with their carefully cultivated public image. But in the typical case, the hidden reality has more to do with mundane matters: dissension within the group that leaders want to keep from the public or less dedication to the public welfare than the organization wants to reveal. At times, the façade may be designed to give an appearance of competence and order, while the hidden reality is a looming incompetence and disorder. As Chambliss takes us behind the social façade of the hospital, he reveals a reality unfamiliar to most of us.

Thinking Critically

As you read this selection, ask yourself:

1. How do hospital workers keep outsiders from seeing past their social façade?

2. What lies behind the scenes of hospitals?

3. From information in this reading, prove or disprove this statement: From their inap-propriate humor, we can see that doctors and nurses don't really care about their patients.

Every unit in the hospital . . . has its own normality, its own typical patients, number of deaths, and crises to be faced. But just as predictably, every unit has its emergencies that threaten the routine and challenge the staff's ability to maintain workaday attitudes and practices. Emergencies threaten the staff's ability to carry on as usual, to maintain their own distance from the patient's suffering, and to hold at bay their awe at the enormity of events. Occasionally breakdowns occur in unit discipline or the ability to do the required work.

Staff follow several strategies when trying to manage the threat of breakdowns: they will keep outsiders outside, follow routinization rituals, or use humor to distance themselves. Finally, even when all efforts fail, they will keep going, no matter what. Consider in turn each of these implicit maxims:

■ ■ ■ ■ 1. KEEP OUTSIDERS OUTSIDE

Every hospital has policies about visiting hours, designed not only to "let patients rest" but also to protect staff from outsiders' interference in their work. Visitors are limited to certain hours, perhaps two to a patient room for fifteen-minute visits; they may have to be announced before entering the unit or may be kept waiting in a room down the hall. No doubt many such policies are good for the patient. No doubt, too, they keep visitors out of the nurse's way, prevent too many obtrusive questions or requests for small services, and prevent curious laypersons from seeing the messier, less presentable sides of nursing care.

When visitors cannot be physically excluded, they can still be cognitively controlled, that is, prevented from knowing that something untoward is happening. Typically, the staff behave in such episodes as if everything were OK, even when it is not. This is similar to what Erving Goffman observed in conversations: when the shared flow of interaction is threatened by an accidental insult or a body failure such as a sneeze or flatulence, people simply try to ignore the break in reality and carry on as if nothing has happened. Such "reality maintenance" is often well-orchestrated, requiring cooperation on the part of several parties. For Goffman, normal people in normal interactions accept at face value each other's presentation of who they are:

> A state where everyone temporarily accepts everyone else's line is established. This kind of mutual acceptance seems to be a basic structural feature of interaction, especially the interaction of face-to-face talk. It is typically a "working" acceptance, not a "real" one.[1]

And when this routine breaks down, the immediate strategy is simple denial:

From *Beyond Caring: Hospitals, Nurses, and the Social Organization of Ethics* by Daniel F. Chambliss. Copyright © 1986 by Daniel F. Chambliss. Reprinted by permission of the University of Chicago Press.

When a person fails to prevent an incident, he can still attempt to maintain the fiction that no threat to face has occurred. The most blatant example of this is found where the person acts as if an event that contains a threatening expression has not occurred at all.[2]

In the hospital, the unexpected entrance of outsiders into a delicate situation can disrupt the staff's routine activities and create unmanageable chaos. To avoid this, the staff may pretend to outsiders that nothing special is happening; this pretense itself can be part of the routine. During a code (resuscitation) effort I witnessed, there were three such potential disruptions by outsiders: another patient calling for help, a new incoming patient being wheeled in, and the new patient's family members entering the unit. All three challenges were handled by the staff diverting the outsiders from the code with a show, as if nothing were happening:

> Code in CCU [Cardiac Care Unit] . . . woman patient, asystole [abnormal ventricle contractions]. Doc (res[ident]) pumping chest—*deep* pumps, I'm struck by how far down they push. Serious stuff. Matter of factness of process is striking. This was a surprise code, not expected. Patient was in Vtak [ventricular fibrillation], pulse started slowing, then asystole. N[urse]s pumping for a while, RT [Respiratory Therapist] ambu-bagging [pumping air into lungs]. Maybe 7–8 people in patient's room working. Calm, but busy. Occasionally a laugh.
>
> Pt in next room (no more than 10 feet away) called for nurse—a doc went in, real loose and casual, strolled in, pt said something; doc said, "There's something going on next door that's taking people's time; we'll get to you"—real easy, like nothing at all happening. Then strolls back to code room. Very calm. . . .
>
> Two N[urse]s came into unit wheeling a new patient. One said, "Uh, oh, bad time," very quietly as she realized, going in the door, that a code was on. Somebody said, "Close the door"—the outside door to the unit, which the Ns with the new pt were holding open. . . .
>
> When the new pt was brought in and rolled into his room, the family with him was stopped at unit door, told to stay in waiting room and "we'll call you" with a casual wave of hand, as if this is routine. [No one said a code was on. Patient lying on gurney was wheeled in, went right by the code room and never knew a thing.] [Field Notes]

This is a simple example of protecting the routine from the chaos of a panicking patient or a horrified family; the outsiders never knew that a resuscitation was occurring fifteen feet away. The staff's work was, in their own eyes, routine; their challenge was protecting that routine from outside disruption.

■ ■ ■ 2. FOLLOW ROUTINIZATION RITUALS

The staff's sense of routine is maintained by the protective rituals of hospital life. Under stress, one may use them more and more compulsively, falling back on the old forms to reconvince oneself that order is still present. Frantic prayers in the foxhole are the prototype cases.

Most prominent of such rituals in hospitals are "rounds," the standard ritual for the routine handling of patient disasters in the hospital. "Rounds" is the generic term for almost any organized staff group discussion of patients' conditions. "Walking rounds" refers to a physician walking through the hospital, usually trailed by various residents and interns, going from patient to patient and reviewing their condition. "Grand rounds" are large meetings of the medical staff featuring the presentation of an interesting case, with elaborate discussion and questions, for the purpose of education and review of standard practices. Nursing rounds usually consist of a meeting between the staff for one (outgoing) shift reporting to the staff of the next (incoming) shift on the condition of all patients on the floor. Here the staff collectively explains what has happened and why, bringing every case into the staff's framework of thinking, and systematically enforcing the system's capability for handling medical problems without falling to pieces. In rounds, the staff confirm to each other that things are under control. Once a week, for instance, the Burn Unit at one hospital holds rounds in their conference room with a group of residents, one or two attending, several nurses, the social workers, dieticians, and physical therapists. The patients here are in terrible shape; one can sometimes hear moans in the hallway outside as patients are taken for walks by the nurses. But rounds continue:

> Macho style of the docs very evident. . . . Resident will present a case, then the attendings take rapid-fire shots at what he [the resident] had done: wrong dressing, wrong feeding schedule, failure to note some abnormality in the lab results. Much of the talk was a flurry of physiological jargon, many numbers and abbreviations. The intensity of the presentation, the mercilessness of the grilling, is surprising. . . . Focus is on no errors made in situation of extreme pressure—i.e., both in patient treatment and then here in rounds presenting the case. Goal here is to be predictable, *controlled,* nothing left out. [Field Notes]

■ ■ ■ 3. USE HUMOR TO DISTANCE YOURSELF

Keeping outsiders away and following the standard rituals for maintaining normality can help, but sometimes the pathos of hospital life becomes psychologically threatening to staff members. One response is to break down, cry, and run out, but this is what they are trying to avoid; the more common reaction is the sort of black humor that notoriously characterizes hospitals and armies everywhere. Humor provides an outlet; when physical space is not available, humor is a way to separate oneself psychologically from what is happening. It says both that I am not involved and that this really isn't so important. (In brain surgery, when parts of that organ are, essentially, vacuumed away, one may hear comments like "There goes 2d grade, there go the piano lessons," etc.) With laughter, things seem less consequential, less of a burden. What has been ghastly can perhaps be made funny:

> Today they got a 600-gram baby in the Newborn Unit. When Ns heard [the baby] was in Delivery, they were praying, "Please God let it be under 500 grams"—because

that's the definite cutoff under which they won't try to save it—but the doc said admit it anyway. Ns unhappy.

I came in the unit tonight; N came up to me and said brightly, with a big smile, "Have you seen our fetus?" Ns on the Newborn Unit have nicknames for some. There's "Fetus," the 600-gram one; "Munchkin"; and "Thrasher," in the corner, the one with constant seizures. Grim humor, but common. ["Fetus" was born at 24 weeks, "Munchkin" at 28.] [Field Notes]

The functions of such humor for medical workers have been described in a number of classic works of medical sociology. Renée Fox, writing in her book *Experiment Perilous* about physicians on a metabolic research unit, says, "The members of the group were especially inclined to make jokes about events that disturbed them a good deal," and she summarizes that

by freeing them from some of the tension to which they were subject, enabling them to achieve greater detachment and equipoise, and strengthening their resolve to do something about the problems with which they were faced, the grim medical humor of the Metabolic Group helped them to come to terms with their situation in a useful and professionally acceptable way.[3]

Fox and other students of hospital culture (notably Rose Coser)[4] have emphasized that humor fills a functional purpose of "tension release," allowing medical workers to get on with the job in the face of trauma; their analyses usually focus on jokes explicitly told in medical settings. This analysis is correct as far as it goes, but in a sense I think it almost "explains away" hospital humor—as if to say that "these people are under a lot of strain, so it's understandable that they tell these gruesome jokes." It suggests, in a functionalist fallacy, that jokes are made because of the strain and that things somehow aren't "really" funny.

But they are. An appreciation of hospital life must recognize that funny things—genuinely funny, even if sometimes simultaneously horrible—do happen. Hospitals are scenes of irony, where good and bad are inseparably blended, where funny things happen, where to analytically excuse laughter as a defense mechanism is simultaneously to deny the human reality, the experience, that even to a non-stressed outsider *this is funny*.[5] The humor isn't found only in contrived jokes but in the scenes one witnesses; laughter can be spontaneous, and it's not always nervous. True, one must usually have a fairly normalized sense of the hospital to laugh here, but laugh one does.

Certainly, the staff make jokes:

In the OR [operating room]:
"This is his [pt's] 6th time [for a hernia repair]."
"After two, I hear you're officially disabled."
"Oh good, does that mean he gets a special parking place?"
[Field Notes]
In the ICU [Intensive Care Unit], two Ns—one male, one female—working on pt.
Nurse 1 (male): "This guy has bowel sounds in his scrotum."

> Nurse 2 (female): "In his scrotum?"
> Nurse 1: "Yeah, didn't you pick that up?"
> Nurse 2: "I didn't put my stethoscope there!" (Big laughs.) [Field Notes]

Sometimes jokes are more elaborate and are obviously derived from the tragedy of the situation:

> In another ICU, staff member taped a stick to the door of the unit, symbolizing (for them) "The Stake," a sign of some form of euthanasia [perhaps the expression sometimes used, "to stake" a patient, derives from the myth that vampires can only be killed by driving a stake through the heart]. Periodically word went around that a resident had just won the "Green Stake Award," meaning that he or she had, for the first time, allowed or helped a patient to die. [Field Notes]
>
> Some colorful balloons with "Get Well Soon" were delivered to a patient's room. The patient died the following night. Someone on the staff moved the balloons to the door of another patient's room; that patient died! Now the staff has put the balloons at the door of the patient they believe is "most likely to die next." [Field Notes]

But jokes have to be contrived; they are deliberate efforts at humor and so make a good example of efforts to distance oneself, or to make the tragic funny. But the inherent irony of the hospital is better seen in situations that spontaneously provoke laughter. These things are funny in themselves; even an outsider can laugh at them:

> Nurse preparing to wheel a patient into the OR tells him, "Take out your false teeth, take off your glasses . . . ," and continuing, trying to make a joke, "Take off your leg, take out your eyes." The patient said, "Oh, I almost forgot—" and pulled out his [false] eye! [Interview]

Or:

> Lady patient [Geriatric floor] is upset because she called home, there's no answer; she's afraid her husband has died. Sylvia [a nurse] told her he probably just went somewhere for lunch, but patient said he would have called. She's afraid.
>
> [Later] Sylvia went back in lady's room—she's crying. Husband called! Sylvia happy, smiling, "You should be happy!" "But," says the old lady, "he called to say he was out burying the dog!"
>
> Sylvia had to leave the room because she was starting to laugh; she and Janie laughing at this at the N's station, saying it's really sad but funny at the same time. [Field Notes]

Or:

> In looking at X-rays of a patient's colon, the resident explains to the team a shadow on the film: "Radiology says it could be a tumor, or it might just be stool." Jokes all around about how "helpful" Rays [Radiology] is. [Field Notes]

One needn't be under pressure to find such things funny. People do laugh to ease pressure or to distance oneself. But sometimes the distance comes first: laughter is made possible by the routinization that has gone before.

■ ■ ■ ■ 4. WHEN THINGS FALL APART, KEEP GOING

Sometimes routinization fails: outsiders come into the room and, seeing their dead mother, break down, screaming and wailing; or a longtime, cared-for patient begins irretrievably to "decompensate" and lose blood pressure, sliding quickly to death; or emergency surgery goes bad, the trauma shakes the staff, and there are other patients coming in from the ambulances. Any of these can destroy the staff's sense of "work as usual." In such cases, the typical practice seems to be, remarkably: just keep going. Trauma teams specialize in the psychological strength (or cold-bloodedness, perhaps) to continue working when the world seems to be falling apart. Finally, nurses and physicians are notable for continuing to work even, in the final case, after the patient is for almost all purposes dead, or will be soon.

> A resident said to the attending [physician] on one floor, discussing a terminal patient: "If we transfuse him, he might get hepatitis."
> Another resident: "By the time he gets hepatitis he'll be dead."
> Attending: "OK, so let's transfuse." [Field Notes]

Perseverance is a habit; it's also a moral imperative, a way of managing disaster as if it were routine.

In every unit there are nurses known for being good under pressure. These are people who, whatever their other skills (and, typically, their other skills are quite good), are able to maintain their presence of mind in any crisis. Whereas "being organized" is a key quality for nurses in routine situations, staying calm is crucial in emergency situations. Compare two nurses known for remaining calm (Mavis and Anna) to two others who are prone to alarm (Linda and Julie):

> Mavis [in Neonatal ICU] is cited as a good nurse (great starting IVs, e.g.) who doesn't get shook, even in a code, even if her pt is dying, she still keeps doing what you're supposed to do. Linda, by contrast, is real smart, very good technically, but can freak out, start yelling, etc., if things are going badly. [Field Notes]
> Julie [in Medical ICU], hurrying around, looks just one step ahead of disaster, can't keep up, etc. Doc says something about the patient in room 1. Julie says, walking past, "He's not mine," keeps going. But Anna, calm, walks in pt's room—pt with oxygen mask, wants something. Anna goes out, calmly, comes back in a minute w/cup of crushed ice, gives pt a spoonful to ease thirst. She *always* seems to be doing that little thing that others "don't have time for"—never flustered and yet seems to get more done than anyone else. [Field Notes, Interview]

But to "keep going" depends not so much on the individual fortitude of nurses such [as] Mavis and Anna, but on the professional and institutional habits of the nursing staff and the hospital. The continuance of care even in the face of obvious failure of efforts is itself a norm. Whatever one's personal disposition, one keeps working; the staff keep working, often when the patient is all but dead, or "dead" but not officially recognized as such:

> Dr. K., walking rounds with four residents, discussing a 30-year-old male patient, HIV-positive, gone totally septic [has bloodstream infection, a deadly problem], no hope at all of recovery—Dr. K. says this is a "100 percent mortality" case; so they decide how to proceed with minimal treatment, at the end of which Dr. K. says brightly, "And if he codes—code him!" [Field Notes]

Coding such a patient is an exercise in technique; there is no hope entailed, no optimism, no idea that he might be saved. There is only the institutional habit which substitutes for hope, which in many cases obviates the staff's pessimism or lack of interest. When standard procedure is followed, courage is unnecessary. It is one thing to be routinely busy, caring for vegetative patients; it happens every day. It is quite another to handle emergency surgery with no time and a life at stake. Sometimes such a case will challenge all the staff's resources—their personal fortitude, their habitualization of procedures, the self-protection offered by an indefatigable sense of humor. To maintain one's composure while under tremendous pressures of time and fatefulness requires all the courage a staff can muster.

One such case was that of emergency surgery on a thirty-five-year-old woman who came to Southwestern Regional hospital in severe abdominal pain; she was diagnosed with a ruptured ectopic [tubal] pregnancy estimated at sixteen weeks. The case provides us with a dramatic example of the pressure placed on the staff to retain their composure in the face of disaster.

The long description which follows is graphic. The scene was more than bloody; it was grotesque. More than one staff member—including one member of the surgical team itself—left the room during the operation, sickened. Other nurses, even very experienced ones, told me they have never witnessed such a scene and hope never to witness one. I include it here, in some detail, to exemplify both what health professionals face in their work and how, incredibly, some of them can carry on. The description is reconstructed from Field Notes (some written at the time on the inside of a surgical mask, some on sheets of paper carried in a pocket), and from interviews afterward with participants:

> Saturday night OR suite; hasn't been busy. Only one case so far, a guy who got beat up with a tire iron (drug deal), finished about 8:30 P.M. It's about 10:00. 2 Ns—the Saturday night staff—sitting around in the conference room, just chatting and waiting for anything that happens.
>   Call comes over intercom: ruptured tubal (pregnancy) just came in OR, bringing to the crash room. 35-year-old black woman, very heavy—250 pounds maybe—apparently pregnant for 16 weeks, which means she's been in pain for 10 weeks or more without coming in. Friends brought her to ER screaming in pain. Blood pressure is at "60 over palpable," i.e., the diastolic doesn't even register on the manometer. She's obviously bleeding bad internally, will die fast if not opened up. Ns run to OR

and set up fast. I've never seen people work so quickly here, no wasted motion at all. This is full speed *emergency*.

When patient is rolled in, fully conscious, there are more than a dozen staff people in the room, including three gynecological surgery residents, who will operate; all three are women. The surgeons are scrubbed and gowned and stand in a line, back from the table, watching without moving, the one in charge periodically giving orders to the nurses who are setting up. At one point there are twelve separate people working on the patient—IVs going into both arms, anesthesiologist putting mask on pt to gas, nurse inserting a Foley [bladder] catheter, others tying pt's arms to the straightout arms of the table, others scrubbing the huge belly, an incredible scene. The patient is shaking terribly, in pain and fear. Her eyes are bugging out, looking around terribly fast. She's whimpering, groaning as needles go in, crying out softly. No one has time even to speak to her; one nurse briefly leans over and speaks into her ear something like "try not to worry, we're going to take care of you," but there is no time for this. I've never seen anyone so afraid, sweating and crying and the violent shaking.

As soon as they have prepped her—the belly cleansed and covered with Opsite, in a matter of minutes, very, very fast, the anesthesiologist says, "All set?" And someone says "yes," and they gas her. I'm standing right by her head, looking to the head side of the drape which separates her head from her body; the instant that her eyes close, I look to the other side—and the surgeon has already slit her belly open. No hesitation at all, maybe before the patient was out.

What happened next, more extraordinary than the very fast prep, was the opening. Usually in surgery the scalpel makes the skin cut, then slowly scissors are used, snipping piece by piece at muscle, the Bovie cauterizing each blood vessel on the way, very methodical and painstaking. This was nothing like that. It was an entirely different style. They cut fast and deep, sliced her open deep, just chopped through everything, in a—not a panic, but something like a "blitzkrieg," maybe—to get down into the Fallopian tube that had burst and was shooting blood into the abdomen.

When they first got into the abdominal cavity, usually there would be some oozing blood; here as they opened blood splattered out all over the draping on the belly. It was a godawful mess, blood everywhere. They had one surgeon mopping up with gauze sponges, another using a suction pump, a little plastic hose, trying to clean the way. Unbelievable. They got down to the tubes, reaching down and digging around with their hands. And then they found it—suddenly out of this bloody mess down in the abdomen, with the surgeons groping around trying to feel where things were, out of this popped up, right out of the patient and, literally, onto the sheet covering her, the 16-week fetus itself. Immediately one surgeon said mock-cheerfully, "It's a boy!" "God, don't do that," said the scrub tech, turning her head away.

The scrub tech then began to lose it, tears running down her cheeks. Two other people on the team—there were maybe six around the table—said about the same time, nearly together, "Damien!" and "Alien!" recalling recent horror movies, "children of the devil" themes. The fetus lay on the sheet just below the open abdomen for a few moments. The head surgery resident, working, just kept working. The scrub tech should have put the fetus into a specimen tray, but she was falling to pieces fast, crying, and starting to have trouble handing the proper tools to the surgeon, who said something like, "What are you doing?" At this point the circulating nurse, a man, said, "If nobody else will do it," picked up the fetus and put it in a specimen tray, which he then covered with a towel and put aside. He then told another nurse to help him into a gown—he wasn't scrubbed. This violates sterile technique badly, for him to start handling tools, but the scrub tech was becoming a problem. The circulating nurse then quickly gowned and gloved, gently pulled the scrub tech aside and said, "I'll do it." The scrub tech ran out of the room in tears. And the circulating nurse began passing tools to the surgeons himself. It is the circulating nurse's responsibility to handle problems this way, and he did. Another nurse had gone out to scrub properly, and when she came back, maybe ten minutes later, she gowned and gloved and relieved him; so he (the circulating nurse) went back to his regular job of charting the procedure, answering the phone, etc.

By this time, things were under control; the bleeding was stopped, the tube tied off. The other tube was OK and left alone so the pt can get pregnant again. The blood in the abdomen was cleaned up—over 1500 cc's were lost, that's just under a half-gallon of blood. The pt would have died fast if they hadn't gotten in there.

Within two hours after the patient had first rolled in, the room was quiet, only three staff members left, two surgeons and the scrub nurse closing up and talking quietly. Most of the mess—the bloody sponges, the used tools, and all—was gone, cleared away, and all the other staff people, including the chief surgeon, had left. Very calm. The patient, who two hours ago was on the end of a fast terrible death, will be out of the hospital in two days with no permanent damage beyond the loss of one Fallopian tube. [Field Notes, Interviews]

In this situation, we can see two somewhat distinct problems in maintaining the routine order of things: first, the challenge simply in getting the work done; and second, the challenge of upholding the moral order of the hospital.[6] The first issue was resolved by replacing the scrub tech so the operation could continue. The second issue is trickier. The scrub tech's response appeared to be set off not by the horror of what she saw—the bloody fetus—but by the reaction of the assisting surgeon—"It's a boy!" I can only guess that the joke was too much for her. In continuing to work without her, and continuing without noticeable change of demeanor, the surgical team was asserting not only the imperative to protect the operational routine but also, I think, to protect the moral order of emergency surgery as well. That order includes:

1. The job comes first, before personal reactions of fear or disgust.
2. Cynicism is an acceptable form of expression if it helps to maintain composure and distance.
3. The medical team is rightfully in charge and above what may be happening in the OR [operating room].
4. Preserving life is the central value; others (such as niceties of language or etiquette) fall far behind.

There is clearly a morality here. Just as clearly, it is not the morality of everyday life.

NOTES

1. Erving Goffman, "On Face-Work," in *Interaction Ritual: Essays on Face-to-Face Behavior* (New York: Pantheon Books, 1967), p. 11.

2. Ibid., pp. 17–18.

3. Renée C. Fox, *Experiment Perilous* (New York: Free Press, 1959; reprint ed., Philadelphia: University of Pennsylvania Press, 1974), pp. 80–82.

4. Rose Laub Coser, "Some Social Functions of Laughter," in Lewis Coser, *The Pleasures of Sociology*, edited and with an introduction and notes by Lewis Coser (New York: New American Library, 1980), pp. 81–97.

5. The genius of Shem's *House of God* is that it accepts this fact and presents it honestly.

6. I am indebted to Robert Zussman, who suggested these in his review of the manuscript.

V Social Change

Like it or not, we are destined to live in the midst of rapid social change. Social change is so extensive that little remains the same from one generation to the next. Social change is so swift that it even threatens to maroon us in a previous era. We have to learn new skills—and relearn old ones. U.S. physicians, for example, receive a top notch education and are familiar with the latest developments in their profession. If they fail to continue taking courses in their specialties, however, in a short time they fall woefully behind.

Some changes are small and of little consequence for our lives. A fast food outlet opens where a gas station used to be. The new models of cars sprout new lines—ever so slightly. Computers appear in new colors. Our college adds a course and drops another. A band, singer, or actor becomes an overnight sensation, then quickly drops from sight.

Other changes are broader, and have greater impact on us. Cities grow so large that they expand into one another, and no longer can you tell where one ends and the other leaves off. Increasingly, these megacities influence U.S. culture, changing the way we view life. Latinos immigrate to the United States in such vast numbers that they become our largest minority group. Upset about some social condition, people band together in social movements, their protests echoing through the culture.

In their consequences, some changes are huge. As the globalization of capitalism sweeps millions of jobs away from us, transplanting them into parts of the world where labor is cheaper, our own economic future may become uncertain. The mass media grow more powerful, increasingly shaping public opinion and placing the affairs of the nation in fewer hands. Computers change the way we work, are educated, have our illnesses diagnosed, and how we fight wars. They even change the way we think, although this fundamental impact is so recent—and so subtle—that we currently have little understanding of it.

To conclude this book, then, we shall consider social change. Farai Chideya opens this final part by giving us a background for understanding the major changes that Latino immigration is bringing. Social movements are also in the forefront of change, and in the following selection James Jasper and Dorothy Nelkin analyze the animal rights movement. Reinforcing the analyses of Reading 9 ("Life on the Global Assembly Line") and Reading 14 ("The McDonaldization of Society"), we again turn our focus on what is perhaps the most sweeping social change the world is currently experiencing: the globalization of capitalism. Benjamin Barber examines the growing uniformity and integration that he calls McWorld, as well as the violent opposition that this change is engendering. In the selection that closes this final part, written by a team of researchers, we consider changes in the sex lives of Americans.

Border Blues: The Dilemma of Illegal Immigration

Farai Chideya

introduction ■ ■ ■ ■ ■

Although they ordinarily seem remote, something occurring at a distance that has little relevance for our own lives, changes in urbanization and population are two of the most significant events that the world is experiencing. They are so significant that it is difficult to exaggerate their impact not only on society but also on our own future. As our society has urbanized—as increasing numbers of people have moved from village and farm to the city—the city has expanded its influence. Today, U.S. culture so revolves around urban life that even rural life has been urbanized. To say *U.S. culture* is to say *urban culture*. Similarly significant are changes in population, which sociologists call *demographic shifts*. On a global level, population growth and population shrinkage affect the welfare of nations. They set up conditions for vast migrations, bringing ethnic changes that transform nations—and conflicts that reverberate around the world.

A demographic shift that is having a major impact on the United States is migration from Mexico and South America. This migration has been so extensive in the past decade that Latinos have replaced African Americans as the largest ethnic group in the country. It is too early to tell what changes this demographic shift will bring to U.S. social institutions and to popular culture, but we can be certain that they will be extensive. In this selection, Farai Chideya provides a background for understanding this fundamental shift in our population, as well as an insider's perspective into some of the experiences of illegal immigrants.

Thinking Critically

As you read this selection, ask yourself:

1. Why is this vast migration occurring? Look for both social and personal factors.

2. What changes to U.S. social institutions and culture is this demographic shift likely to bring?

3. What solutions would you propose to solving the problem of illegal immigration? What problems would your solution solve? What problems would it create? In formulating your answer, be sure to take the main points of this article into consideration.

The land around El Paso, Texas, is an imposing desert scene painted in tones of ochre and red clay—stark mountains, vast sky, arid plains. It's so far west that it's the only major Texas city in the mountain, rather than the central, time zone. Atop a nearby mountain is the massive Christo Rey—an imposing figure of Jesus hewn out of tons of stone. It seems like a peaceful vista, but this land is the staging ground for a colossal dash of cultures—the meeting of Mexico and the United States at the border. The biggest dash is not between Mexico and the United States per se, but between many competing visions of what Mexican immigration means to the United States. Mexican immigration has been decried as an "illegal alien invasion," an erosion of America's job base, even the beginnings of a plot to return the Southwest to Mexican hands. And sometimes Mexican Americans themselves are perceived with suspicion, in the belief their allegiance is pledged to Mexico, not the United States.

What's the reality behind these perceptions? And what's life on the border like?. . . I've spent virtually my whole life living on the East Coast, where the Latino communities are dominated by Puerto Ricans, Dominicans, Cubans. I groove to Latin hip-hop and Afro-Cuban sounds, but I hadn't heard much Mexican-American music like ranchero and Tejano. I know a good plate of *pernil* when I eat one, but I couldn't tell you from *tortas*. And I've heard more opinions over whether Puerto Rico should become independent than I've heard firsthand accounts of life on the border. In other words, when I came to El Paso I was starting at ground zero. Why did I choose El Paso? Well, first, this border city has been the site of a well-publicized crackdown on illegal immigration. Second, it's been deeply impacted by government policies like NAFTA. But third, and most important to me, El Paso is not majority Anglo but 70 percent Latino and Mexican American, a place where there are bound to be differences of opinion between members of the Latino community. . . .

[W]hile trade with Mexico has been good for Texas in general, the NAFTA free trade treaty has hit El Paso's economy hard. The city already has an unemployment rate double the national average. Now plants that used to pay workers five dollars an hour in El Paso can pay them five dollars a day just across the border in Juarez—and not pay duty on the goods shipped back to the United States. Among the issues I want to explore here in El Paso are not just questions of Mexican-American identity—how they see themselves—but also how they see their (real or distant) cousins across the border. Do the residents of El Paso look upon the Mexicans as brothers, economic competitors—or a bit of both?

One of the first people I meet in El Paso gives me a hint of the differences in opinion about border issues. Nora is chic, almost out of place in the grungy alternative bar we're both sitting in, with high cheekbones, light skin, and curly black hair cut in a bob. "I hate to say it, but I agree with him," she says. "They need to learn English." The "him" Nora is talking about is a black city councilman who chewed out a citizen who addressed a town hall meeting in Spanish. The "they"—an implicit "they"—are recent Mexican immigrants. Nora, who used to model in New York and now works in the local clothing industry, takes the councilman's side. But some local cartoonists lampooned the politician's outrage, and many residents wrote letters of protest to the newspaper.

Many El Paso residents are from first- or second-generation immigrant families, people who remember life in Mexico and have direct family ties across the border. But it's a mistake to think that they encompass all of El Paso's Latinos. A large proportion of El Paso families, like Nora's, are *Tejano,* a term which means that her forebears have lived in Texas for generations—i.e., even before it was part of the United States. (As many Tejanos like to say, "We didn't cross the border. The border crossed us.") The unique Tex-Mex culture of the Tejanos gave rise to one of the biggest Latina singing sensations, Selena, whose premature death in 1995 woke America up to the size of the Latino community. And one lesson America has yet to learn about the Latino community is how many different cultural and political perspectives there are—even within a single group, like Mexican Americans.

Those different perspectives come into direct conflict when it comes to an issue as controversial as the border. I focused on two groups of people familiar with El Paso: the enforcers who try to keep people out, and the border crossers desperate to stay in America.

■ ■ ■ THE ENFORCERS

Melissa Lucio gets the radio call at noon on a scorching summer day. An electric sensor just inside the U.S. border's been tripped; agents are looking around but they haven't found anyone yet. She heads for the sensor's coordinates and pulls up alongside a couple of agents. They're beating the bushes around a splotch of water halfway between a pond and a puddle. After a minute, a guy about thirty-five years old steps out of a thicket with a resigned look on his face and a satchel slung over his shoulder. A Mexican worker who's crossed illegally into the States, he also happens to be wearing an OFFICIAL U.S. TAXPAYER baseball cap. When I laughingly point this out to Melissa, she goes me one better. "We had a guy who walked in with a Border Patrol hat the other day. We asked him where he got it and he said he found it on the bank of the river. The officer's name was still written on the inside—he'd lost it over a year ago."

Melissa's just one of the thousands of U.S. Border Patrol agents charged with the thankless (and some would say impossible) task of keeping illegal immigrants out of America and catching them once they come in. A Mexican-American El Paso native, she's also the wife of another Mexican-American Border Patrol agent. Just thirty years old, she's also the mother of five sons. With her thick black hair pulled back in a neat French braid, her brown uniform replete with two-way radio and gun, Melissa rides the Texas–Mexico–New Mexico border tracking and detaining border crossers. Sometimes she gets help from the electronic signals of hidden sensors, but much of the time she relies on her own eyes, scanning the horizon and bending toward the earth to interpret "signs"—the scant marks and footprints in the dry earth which she reads for vital clues of time and direction. The day is hot and clear. Recent rains have made it easier to track signs—and have also put desert flowers into bloom. Melissa's comments as she navigates the covered-cab truck around bumps and gullies are punctuated with interjections about the wildlife—"Beautiful bird!" "Really cool lizard!" "Check out that jackrabbit!" But her ear is always tuned to the radio, and she's tough when she has to be. If her truck gets stuck, she breaks off branches and digs it out; if a suspect in a vehicle takes off into a residential area, she pursues and radios the local police. As we traverse highways, dirt roads, and long stretches of pristine desert, we don't run into any other female agents out in the field.

The man Melissa has just picked up doesn't protest when she puts him in the covered back area of the truck. In fact, he reaches into his satchel, pulls out a newspaper, and starts to read. At my request, she asks him where he was going and what he was going to do.

"*¿Para dónde vas?*" she asks.

"*Para Coronado,*" he answers.

Coronado is an affluent area, replete with a country club, where he was headed to cut yards. "He was actually closer to the east side of Juarez," Melissa translates, "and I asked him why he didn't cross over there. And he said there's a lot of *cholos* [bandits] stealing and robbing in that area. He says it's easier to cross over here. He says he doesn't come often, but every once in a while when he needs money."

One stereotype of illegal immigrants is that they're a bunch of welfare cheats. But this crosser, and most of the ones that Melissa picks up, are coming in strictly to work—sometimes to stay for the day and go back that night. The economics are clear cut. The starting wage in the *maquiladoras,* or twin plants—so named because they're owned by U.S. corporations who maintain both Mexican factories and their "twins" across the border—is about five dollars a day. The wages for yard work are far, far higher. "If they have their own tools, they could make sixty bucks a day," Melissa says. "If not, it could be thirty or forty." In other words, one day per week of work in the United States earns more than an entire week's labor in Mexico. Of course, there'd be no point crossing the border if U.S. employers weren't willing, even eager, to give undocumented workers jobs. If a border crosser makes it in every day, the payoff is good even relative to U.S. workers. "If you think about minimum wage, four sixty per hour with taxes taken out, [the border crossers] are going to make more," she says. "Even the Mexican police officers, some of them make four hundred dollars per month if they're lucky."

I ask Melissa if the people she picks up ever give her flack for being Mexican American and picking up Mexicans. "I've only had one person say, 'Don't you think you're being mean?'" she says. "And I say, if you had a job, you would do it to the best of your ability, right? They say 'Yeah.'"—she draws the word out to give it a dubious inflection. "And I say that's just what I'm doing. I've got five children. I want to maintain my household. And they understand."

"Like this education issue," she continues. "Let's say you educate them, and then what? They're illegal in the United States so they can't obtain work. Or let's say they become legal, then they're going to be competing against my children or me for a job that could have very well been mine." She's no fan of NAFTA, which she believes has knocked the wind out of an already weakened local economy. "Not a month goes by that you don't hear about a local company that's up and relocating to Mexico," she says. "It may be a good law, but not for the people who live paycheck to paycheck."

We drop our passenger off at the Paso Del Norte processing station, a short-term holding area that seems appropriately located in the middle of nowhere. Inside the plain building is a bullpen of officers at their desks, surrounded by large cells where individuals are sorted by gender, age, and area of origin. Locals—people from Juarez and nearby border areas—are the easiest to process and return. People from the interior of Mexico, farther south, are interviewed by Mexican officials and given bus fare home. And last of all are detainees from Central America, some of whom have traveled hundreds upon hundreds of miles from Honduras and points south, only to be caught on the final leg of their journey. There are men and women, old and young—really young. One of the kids in the pen, who flashes me an impish grin when I check him out, looks about twelve.

"Oh, we get kids who are eight, nine, ten. I ask them, 'Your Mom, doesn't she worry about you?' And some of their parents do, but they really run wild. If they know a lady at a bakery [in the United States] will give them sweet-breads, stuff like that, they'll come. Some of them have friends they come to goof off with. This is what they do. This is recreation."

By the time they're sixteen—which is the age of the next border crosser we pick up—they're usually crossing to work. The teenager has tan skin and hair bleached nearly blond by the sun; he's carrying yard tools.

"*¿Con qué te posito entro los Estados Unidos?*" Melissa asks.

"*Trabajo.*"

"*¿Qué clase trabajo?*"

"*En yardas,*" he answers. He was headed to Coronado as well.

An Economic Judgment

Melissa Lucio is not only a Border Patrol agent, but a mother and a taxpayer as well. She believes the influx of illegal immigrants could curtail her children's chances at prosperity. "When people talk about immigration issues as being racial," she says, "you have Hispanics as well as Anglos as well as other ethnic groups that will say the same thing: 'We need to be strong on immigration issues.' Why should my tax dollars and my anything be funding someone else?"

Melissa's family immigrated from Mexico a couple of generations ago. "My grandma jokes that I'm going to send her back over the border," Melissa says. She had what she describes as a typical, happy coming of age in El Paso. She met her first love, Rick, who's also Mexican American, in high school, and married him right after she graduated. Like several members of both of their families, Rick went into law enforcement, joining the Border Patrol. Melissa dreamed about the same thing for ten years before she decided to take the plunge. "I had thought about going to college and to the FBI behavioral science department, to pursue some forensics. But the more and more children I started having, I just started to see that dream being pushed further and further away," she says.

Melissa found out the Border Patrol was hiring when Rick told her about a career day he was coordinating—but he tried to discourage her from trying out. It was an arduous process. First she had to take a written test to get admitted to the academy. Then she had to get in shape. After seven years of bearing and raising five sons (Daniel, David, Derek, Dario, and Andrew—"we ran out of Ds," she says), she was two hundred and twenty pounds. She quit her job and lost forty before going into the academy, and another ten once she was there. When it came time for the induction ceremony, she received her badge from an officer who'd specially requested the honor—her husband "As he's pinning me he whispers in my ear, 'Oh Melissa, I never thought you would make it. You've never made me so proud.'" She beams. "It was absolutely great. It was amazing."

Now Melissa works just past the El Paso line in the Christo Rey area of New Mexico. Standing atop the hill that supports the huge statue of Christ, you can see Mexico, New Mexico, and Texas in panorama. You can also see the latest attempts to keep the border clamped down. Along the length of the border, construction crews are putting up an immense fence designed to eventually cover the entire U.S.-Mexico line. But Melissa for one is skeptical it will stop the crossings. "They'll just have to walk a little further," she says, to where mesas break the fence line.

Her division, which contains forty to sixty agents per day depending on scheduling, picks up about a hundred and fifty people per day, a thousand per week. It's labor-intensive work, particularly given the nature of the terrain. The El Paso Border Patrol region gained prominence in 1991 when Silvestre Reyes, the chief at the time, implemented a policy he called Operation Hold the Line. Instead of chasing border crossers after they walked over train tracks or through the Rio Grande (at the Juarez–El Paso border, the river is little more than a trickle in a concrete culvert), Reyes posted agents in vehicles along large stretches of the border. Their presence dropped the number of crossers at that juncture from eight thousand a day to virtually zero. But that meant more Mexicans who wanted to come to Texas chose to go through the New Mexico mountains. "You can't do that here. You'd have to have a ton of agents to watch every side of every hill. We have to be mobile," Melissa says.

It seems like an awful lot of work for each agent on an eight-hour shift to pick up the equivalent of three border jumpers a day. But the political stakes are far higher than those numbers would suggest. Tensions about immigration characterize the turn of this century as deeply as they marked the turn of the last one. But instead of Italians, Irish, and Jews who received a lukewarm welcome disembarking at Ellis Island in the late 1800s and early 1900s, Mexican Americans crossing into the border for points as far flung as New York and the Midwest are the immigrants under scrutiny today. . . .

The pickups don't always go smoothly. Some of the border crossers have passed out and nearly died from heat stroke or dehydration as they're being taken in; other times agents just find the bodies. (One agent tells me a gruesome, perhaps apocryphal tale of finding a body whose eyes had literally popped out of the scorched head.) Sometimes people resist or carry weapons. The agents also have to watch out for *cholos*—gang members who can come from either side of the border, and who often prey on those crossing the border to work. In a Wild West twist, some of the *cholos* rob trains passing through the region. "A bandit will board the trains out West and pilfer through first, and say, 'The Nike tennis shoes are here.' Then they have their buddies, twenty or thirty or forty guys, shunt the track so the little computer tells the train to stop. As soon as it stops, these guys start throwing the stuff down. They don't care if the nine hundred ninety-nine dollar television cracks open because the good ones will land somewhere and they will grab it and sell it. Or on the other hand, in the next two weeks you'll arrest a bunch of people that are all wearing brand new Nike tennis shoes."

Sometimes they prey on the individuals working along the border fence line. As our day together draws to a close, Melissa gets a radio call from one of the men erecting the new fence. He's worried because four men are approaching and he's alone. "Ten-four. Horse patrol and myself will thirteen over there and check it out," Melissa radios back. As we approach, two men on powerful horses gallop parallel, about twenty yards away. "I'm on the list for horseback," Melissa says. "I think it's so cool." She surveys the situation as we approach. "These guys are definitely up to no good." I ask how she can tell. "They don't have any bags, which means they're not crossing. They don't have any water and they're just hanging around with no attempt to go north." They might have wanted to get their hands on some of the construction supplies, she figures.

Every eight weeks Melissa and the other agents change shift—days, evenings, overnights (which start at midnight). Now she's working days and her husband is working evenings, making it easy for him to take the kids to and from school. They try to avoid both doing the evening shift, "because we've noticed that our kids' grades drop."

To help out, Rick and Melissa have hired a live-in housekeeper, which is a drama in and of itself. "I advertised for a housekeeper two years ago, [and] the first thing off the bat was, 'Are you a U.S. citizen or a legal resident? If not, I work for immigration and I can't hire you: And half the people would hang up. A quarter of the people would say, 'I'm a border crosser,' but they were not permitted to work. The lady we hired, she's late forties, great with the kids, teaching the kids Spanish, and she's a legal resident, so it worked out really, really, well."

"So what's funny, a neighbor came up and said, 'Do you realize your house is under surveillance?' I was like 'Excuse me?'" One day, when both husband and wife were gone, an agent came to the home and asked their housekeeper for documents. Neighbors came out to watch, and she waved right back at them to say "I'm still here because I'm legal," Melissa says. The couple learned why the Immigration and Naturalization Service suspected them when they talked the matter over with their chief. A neighbor had phoned in with an elaborate tale how the housekeeper, supposedly illegal, had begged up and down the street for work and found it with the Lucios. "It's just someone being vindictive. I thought, that is really terrible," Melissa says. "At the time we lived in the Coronado Country Club area. They were really unhappy about Hold the Line because their maids couldn't come in illegally." As we head back into the station, I think again about the economics of the illegal immigration debate. The reality is that for every undocumented immigrant who finds low-wage work in America, there is somebody willing to hire that person. And some of the same people benefiting from below-market labor loudly decry illegal immigration at the same time.

The Politics of the Border

America likes to think its immigration laws are tough. And while they're arguably harsh on people who cross the border, most penalties on the businesses that hire illegal immigrants are modest. And people like the border crossers Melissa Lucio picked up often don't work for "businesses" at all, but everyday U.S. citizens who usually suspect the person they've hired to cut their lawn or babysit their kids doesn't hold a green card. America decries the waves of illegal immigration. But some Americans on the border and throughout the United States profit from the cheap labor these immigrants provide.

The economics of the border are full of conflict and duplicity, people who profit, people who lose, and people who lie about which camp they're in. Most important, the economics are deeply intertwined. Downtown El Paso, an unremarkable collection of modest office buildings and low-priced shops, is tethered by a bridge to downtown Juarez, Mexico. The Mexicans who cross the bridge come to work, visit, and shop. The Anglos going the other way often buy cheap groceries and pharmaceuticals (you can purchase Valium and Prozac without a prescription there), and college students hit the bars, where the words "drinking age" are meaningless. What happens when the Border Patrol cracks down on illegal crossings? Many downtown El Paso businessmen say their shops suffer, deprived of the day workers that used to buy clothes and consumer goods.

Many Mexican residents of Juarez aren't happy about the increasingly fortified border, either. El Paso and Juarez are separated by an unimpressive trickle of water that, amazingly enough, is part of the mighty Rio Grande river. A cement aqueduct, fenced on both sides, contains the water and separates the people. Painted on the concrete are signs decrying the border fortifications:

One reads OJO MIGRA (eyes are painted into the o's) ¡¡YA BASTA!!

Another says: POR CADA ILEGAL QUE NOS MALTRATEN EN LOS ESTADOS UNIDOS DE N. A. VAMOS A MALTRATAR UN VISITANTE GAVACHO. BIENVENIDOS LOS PAISANOS.

Their translations: "Look, Immigration—enough already!" and "For every illegal they mistreat in the United States, we are going to mistreat a visiting gringo. Welcome, countrymen."

It sounds like a bit of useless bravado, the "welcome, countrymen" sign. But the history of the Southwest is the history of what Mexico founded and America fought to win—not particularly fairly, either. Writes biographer Hugh Pearson:

> In 1845, hewing to the strictures of Manifest Destiny we annexed the Republic of Texas, which had been part of Mexico. Its American settlers decided to introduce slavery into the territory, which was illegal in Mexico. Then, as gratitude for the Mexican government's inviting them to settle the territory and because they wanted to keep their slaves, they fought for independence. As former President and Gen. Ulysses S. Grant wrote in his memoirs, "The occupation, separation and annexation were, from the inception of the movement to its final consummation, a conspiracy to acquire territory out of which slave states might be formed for the American union."
>
> After accepting the Texas republic's petition to be annexed by the United States, a dispute between the United States and Mexico ensued, regarding where the exact boundary of Texas lay. Mexican and U.S. patrols clashed somewhere along the disputed territory and the Unified States declared war on Mexico. In the process of fighting the war, U.S. troops captured from Mexico what is now New Mexico and

what the Mexicans called Upper California. As conditions for surrender, Mexico was forced to cede all of the captured territory north of the Rio Grande River, and an agreed upon jagged imaginary line that now separates California, Arizona and New Mexico from Mexico. So today, Mexicans crossing into U.S. California are treated as illegal aliens if they don't go through the proper channels for entering territory that was originally theirs.

I didn't learn any of this in high school, and I'd wager that many Americans don't know it today. What happened doesn't change the fact that America has the right to control its borders, but it does cast into sharper relief the interconnectedness of these two nations. Texas was birthed from Mexico. But—defying the stereotypes that pervade much of the news coverage about the border—many Mexican Americans are now the ones guarding the border.

Silvestre Reyes headed the Border Patrol for the entire El Paso region. . . . I meet the solid, handsome fifty-year-old in the offices where he's running his campaign [for U.S. Congress] with the help of his twenty-five-year-old daughter. Even in his civilian clothes, he's got the demeanor of a law enforcement officer. Reyes grew up in a small farming town where his high school graduating class was made up of just twenty-six students. When he was a child, he served as a lookout against *la migra*—the Border Patrol—in the fields where Mexicans worked. He served in Vietnam, then worked as a Border Patrol agent for over twenty-five years. He believes that people's opinions about the border don't have anything to do with ethnic loyalty, but quality of life. "Hispanics, like every ethnic group in the country, have an expectation to be safe and secure in their neighborhoods," he says. "A Hispanic no more than anybody else appreciates undocumented people flowing through their backyards, creating a chaotic situation."

Still, Reyes says he'd like to find a way to benefit both Mexicans and Americans at the same time. "Mexican citizens don't want to come up here," he says. "They would rather stay home. But they stay home, they starve. We've got forces down in Mexico that want jobs, and people up here that want them to come up here. But the whole problem is, let's find a system that does it legally."

Despite its adverse effect on the El Paso economy, Reyes supports NAFTA as a way of increasing employment opportunities in Mexico. If things don't get better there, he reasons, illegal immigration will never stop. "Mexico has a surplus of manpower. I think 60 percent of Mexican citizens are under the age of twenty, if I remember my statistics right," he says. . . .

One policy he doesn't support is California's Proposition 187, which voters passed in 1994 in an effort, among other things, to prevent illegal immigrants from receiving government medical care or public education. Reyes calls the measure "illegal and unconstitutional. . . . Should we amend the Constitution in order to deny children born in this country their citizenships? I think we're crazy," he says. "What's gonna keep someone from going back retroactively and saying, 'You know, your father was born to illegal parents back in 1924. Therefore he was illegal, therefore you're illegal.'" (Such logic recalls a joke by Mexican-American comedian Paul Rodriguez, who says he supports making deportations for illegal immigration retroactive and shipping the Anglos back home.) The idea of barring education to undocumented children is "insanity running amok. The way that people enslave whole segments of our society is by keeping them ignorant. . . . To me it doesn't matter whether it's black or Hispanics or Chinese or whites or who it is. I think it's just wrong for any country to guarantee a subculture of ignorance. And that's what you're doing when you don't educate the kids."

The wording of California's Proposition 187 was also openly militaristic, reading:

> WE CAN STOP ILLEGAL ALIENS. If the citizens and the taxpayers of our state wait for the politicians in Washington and Sacramento to stop the incredible flow of ILLEGAL ALIENS, California will be in economic and social bankruptcy. We have to act and ACT NOW! On our ballot, Proposition 187 will be the first giant stride in ultimately ending the ILLEGAL ALIEN invasion.

Some advocates say the border has already become militarized, infringing upon the rights of citizens and legal immigrants. El Paso's Border Rights Coalition says that . . . half of the individuals who complained to their group about mistreatment by the Border Patrol, Immigration and Naturalization Service, and U.S. Customs were U.S. citizens, not legal or illegal immigrants. The group helped students at El Paso's Bowie High School file a class action suit. They alleged that Border Patrol agents were routinely harassing individuals on and near campus—in one case, arresting a group of students, U.S. citizens, who were driving to school. Today, the Border Patrol is operating under a settlement that requires they meet higher standards before detaining individuals, and limits searches at schools and churches.

Of course, the ultimate military-style solution would be to create a physical wall between Mexico and the United States. Reyes strongly disagrees with such a plan. "That's impractical, you know. The Berlin wall didn't seal, and that was using mines and barbed wire and guards and concrete, and all of that, and still people got out of there," he says. Yet as Reyes and I talk, construction on just such a wall is happening along the border near El Paso. While I'm out with Melissa Lucio, she shows me the early stages of the construction site. It's impossible to cover the whole border, of course. But . . . several miles of what Reyes calls the "impractical" solution stand completed.

■ ■ ■ ■ **THE BORDER CROSSERS**

A Family Full of Contradictions

Gilberto, an eighteen-year-old undocumented immigrant from Chihuahua, has few marketable skills but one strong advantage on his side. He has family legally in the United States who are willing to help him. Gilberto is the brother-in-law of a naturalized U.S. citizen who emigrated from Hong Kong. Chiu, who went to college in the United States, met his wife Lorena, in a Juarez nightclub. Now they have two children, baby Jenny Anna and Andy, who turned three the day after I spoke with them. Both attend the University of Texas at El Paso, and they earn a living by running a home care facility for the elderly.

Gilberto helps out with the home care, meaning he's guaranteed a job as well as a place to stay far from the eyes of the Border Patrol. Like virtually all illegal immigrants, he's an unskilled laborer. Like many Mexicans, he finished the "secondario" level of schooling at fifteen and then started working. His first job was in a junkyard—hot, heavy work for very little money. Still, like a teenager, he used the remaining money he had to party rather than save. Asked if he's worried *la migra* will find him—something they did once before, as he was out and about—he shakes his head confidently, "No."

Chiu and Lorend's generous brick house is nestled in a pristine, upper-middle-class enclave undergoing rapid development. Bold and self-assured, Chiu strongly opposes illegal immigration, a position it's hard not to think deeply about when you see Gilberto sitting sheepishly on the other side of the table. "My brother-in-law, he's an illegal alien. He come and go whenever he wants. When you're talking about Hold the Line, it's only to make the government look good," Chiu scolds. "Washington, D.C., will furnish a lot of money for this project because it's very successful—you catch ten billion illegal aliens. Oh great job!" he sneers. "Now they have this Hold the Line thing, OK, and then they say, 'Nobody coming across.' But in the reality it's not true. In Mexico, if the people over there are making three to five dollars a day and if they cannot support their kids, do you think they would just sit there and die?"

Gilberto isn't in the dire straits many border crossers are. In fact, he originally entered not to stay but to fulfill teenage longings. "All the boys, they have the same dream: you know, they wanted to come and get some money and buy a truck, a nice truck," his sister Lorena translates, "and then go back to Mexico and spend one or two months or whatever on the money they saved up. Then after that, they come back to the United States again and work and get some more money. That's the way they think." Now Gilberto's changed his mind. He wants to stay in the United States and become a nurse. "It's very important to learn to speak English, otherwise there's no way to find a job—well, maybe in El Paso a very low job. But I want to go further," he says. He's enrolled in a local high school, where his legal status proved no problem. "As a matter of fact, they are not allowed to ask you whether you have papers or not or whether you have a Social Security number or not, because if they do that they have violated federal law." Chiu says. "So they have to let him register although he's an illegal alien." In a clear example of how self-interest overrides politics, Chiu says that he's happy his brother-in-law can be enrolled, but that he is opposed to educating undocumented children. "When they do that they are inviting illegal immigrants to come to school here, you see. I would say no illegal immigrants to go to school in this country for free."

Neither Mexican nor American

A pensive seventeen-year-old named Diana finds herself in the opposite situation from Gilberto: with her near-perfect English and years of schooling in the

United States, she seems culturally American, but this undocumented immigrant has no one to advocate for her or protect her. She's been caught between two worlds most of her life. Four years ago, Diana crossed into the United States at the Juarez–El Paso bridge that symbolizes the border so well. Now she's a senior at Fremont High School in Oakland, California. . . . Before crossing the Rio Grande, she spent her junior high school years near Durango, Mexico. And before that, from the ages of two until nine, she lived in the United States—attending American schools, playing with American toys, speaking both English and Spanish. Without a green card or citizenship, but with a keen understanding of American culture and her precarious position in it, she is neither fully American nor fully Mexican.

Diana remembers the day her family crossed over from Juarez to El Paso. "We used a raft to get across. It was really sunny that day. People were on the bridge watching us. They were like 'Oh look!'" she says. "I remember I saw this man with a little boy in his arms pointing at us." Once they got to El Paso, her family tried to blend in with the rest of the crowds in the downtown shopping area. "We crossed the street right in front of a Border Patrol car," Diana remembers. "The car stopped so we could cross the street! My Mom was praying and I was like, 'Mom, they're not going to do anything to us now.' They didn't."

While her experience in crossing the Rio Grande was a common one until recently, Diana's reasons for going back and forth between the United States and Mexico are personal and complex. Like most families who cross over from Mexico, Diana's came to work and make a better life for their children. Her father has a green card, so he was able to live and work legally; but he brought Diana, her mother, and Diana's older brother into the country without papers. Diana's father began drinking too much, and after living in the United States for several years, he decided to move the family back to Mexico and pull himself together. But there's little work near Durango, so he ended up going back to the United States to earn a living (taking Diana's teenage brother along with him) and sending money to the family back home. It was only once her father had stopped drinking that he decided to reunite the family, arranging for a "coyote"—or someone who smuggles people across the border—to bring Diana and the rest of the family north through Mexico, on a raft over the Rio Grande, and by truck out of Texas.

Diana was too young to remember the first time she crossed the border. She was only two years old, and friends of the family who had papers for their own toddler smuggled her in as their child. "People told me I kept saying, 'I want my mother.' They needed me to be quiet," she says. From two on, Diana lived in Chico, California, as a normal Mexican-American kid—almost. When I ask her if she knew she was an "illegal immigrant," she says, "That question really bothered me and came into my head in, I think, the second grade. Most of my friends would go to Mexico on their summer vacations to see their grandparents, and I would ask, 'Why aren't we going to Mexico?' My mother would say, 'We can't.' Then," she continues, "one time in school I said, 'Um, I'm illegal.' And my teacher said, 'Honey, don't say that out loud. You could get your parents in a lot of trouble.' That's when I started feeling a little inferior to other kids."

Sometimes she still does. "Not because of who I am but because of what I can't do," she says, quietly breaking into tears. One thing she can't do is apply to college, even though she's a solid student. Without legal residence papers, she has little hope of attending school or getting anything but the most menial of jobs. Her older brother tried enrolling in college, but after they repeatedly asked him for a Social Security number, he simply left. Now he plays in a band. "I want to get a green card so I can work, so I can go to school, so I don't need to worry about getting deported and everything. But we have to pay a lawyer seven hundred dollars for each person applying for the green card," money her struggling family doesn't have. After she gets a green card, she wants to become a citizen "because I would like to be heard in this country. I would like to vote and be part of the process."

The most wrenching part of her experience is that Diana knows she could have been a legal resident by now. In 1987, she says, "we could have gotten our papers through the National Amnesty Program," a one-shot chance for illegal immigrants to declare themselves to officials in exchange for a green card. "My mother applied for us, but my Dad [who was drinking] felt that if we went back to Mexico, everything would be for the best." She remembers the day they left the United States. "I had to leave all my friends and the things I had. We left everything: the furniture, my toys, my Barbies. I had to practically leave my life there."

Yet Diana credits the time she spent in Mexico with helping her reconnect with her heritage. She became close with her grandmother, was in the Mexican equivalent of junior ROTC, and won dramatic speaking contests, reciting poetry. "In Mexico, I always wanted to be the one with the best grades—always wanted to be the center of attention," she says. "Maybe because I believed in myself and what I did," she says. That sense of confidence is lacking in Diana today. But if she had stayed in Mexico, it would have been difficult for her to continue her education considering how little money her family had. Most of the girls Diana knew stopped going to school at fourteen or fifteen, got married to a farmer or laborer, and started a family.

So, in one sense, Diana feels she was lucky to return to the United States. But when she first arrived, she had a difficult time readjusting. She returned in time for ninth grade, which in Oakland at the time was still a part of junior high school. Teachers put her in an English as a second language program, probably because her shyness inhibited her from talking much. "It wasn't very helpful," she says. Luckily, as soon as one of her teachers found out how good Diana's English really was, Diana was moved into the regular track.

But Diana was dealing not only with educational displacement but ethnic culture shock. "In the ninth grade, there was only my Mexican friends . . . and we felt a little inferior to the rest." In her opinion, the Mexican kids broke down into two cliques: the "Mexican Mexicans," or hard-working immigrants, and the "little gangsters," or tough, Americanized teens. She hung out with the former—until tenth grade, when she went to Fremont and joined the Media Academy. There she made friends of several races. "When I got to Fremont there was African Americans, Asians, and Mexicans and everybody hangs out together and it was cool," she says.

What is heartbreaking to Diana today is that, though she loves school, she has little hope of continuing her education. She remembers a time that her teacher was leading them through an exercise in filling out college applications. "Everybody was like: 'Oh, I want to go to this place and I wanna go such and such and oh, my grades are good and everything.' My teacher was like, 'Aren't you going to fill out your applications?' And I was like, 'What for?'" Another girl in the class asked the question Diana was desperate to, but just couldn't. "What if you're not a legal resident?" Her teacher said to leave the Social Security number slot blank, but Diana says, dejected, "I didn't want to continue it.". . .

Still, "Regardless of all the barriers that are put between you and other people, America *is* the Land of Opportunity," says Diana. "No matter where you go, you will never find another place where even when you're not legal you can still get a job that pays you. There's no other place like it. In Mexico you can't even get a job. You depend on the crops on your land and live on what grows. There's nowhere for you to go, no McDonald's for you to hang out at. To me, it's better in America."

■ ■ ■ ■ MEXICANIZING AMERICA?

The unspoken fear that underlies much of our policy about the border is that an influx of immigrants will "Mexicanize" America. But my journey through El Paso illustrates the complex culture of Mexican Americans, and just how unfounded the fears about "Mexicanization" are. Those living on the U.S.-Mexican border face some difficult political and economic questions: whether Americans can compete with the low-wage workers in Mexico; whether Washington lawmakers can truly understand the issues facing Americans on the border; and, for Mexican Americans in particular, whether they should feel some connection to the problems facing Mexicans, or simply focus on their own issues. The influence of Mexican culture on America's should be seen as part of a continuum. Just as every immigration wave has shaped this country, so will the rise of the Latino population. In a best-case scenario, border towns like El Paso would help foster a rich appreciation for Mexican culture as *part* of American-style diversity.

The Animal Rights Crusade

James M. Jasper and Dorothy Nelkin

introduction

People tend to assume that their own values are good, right, and even moral. The more we are committed to a value, the more its arbitrariness recedes from sight and the more that we assume its "rightness." An excellent example is attitudes toward animals. In tribal and agricultural societies, people view animals instrumentally; that is, they think of animals as instruments to help them. A cow is to give milk, plow fields, and be eaten. A deer is to be hunted. A horse is for riding or to pull a plow or wagon. A dog is to pull a sleigh, to retrieve game, or to protect the home. The assumption—considered good, right, and moral—is that animals should be put into the service of humans.

Such societies—and their ideas—are remote from our own life situation. Because we face different circumstances, we have developed a different set of attitudes about animals. Our attitudes are so changed that we tend to see previous generations as misguided, even cruel and evil. For us, animals are to be loved and cuddled and cared for. They are to be taken to vets for shots and even surgery. They are to be fed a nourishing and "balanced" diet. They are to be bathed and groomed—even their teeth should be brushed and their nails clipped. Animals are sensitive and need to be protected: for the failures, we even train animal psychologists. Like the assumptions about animals held in earlier societies, these assumptions of reality, too, are presumed to belong to some fundamental, universal morality. With attitudes toward animals still changing, coming generations may see ours as misguided, even bizarre. In the forefront of today's changing attitudes is the animal rights movement, the topic of this selection by Jasper and Nelkin.

Thinking Critically

As you read this selection, ask yourself:

1. How are historical changes in attitudes toward animals related to urbanization?

2. What are your attitudes toward animals? Do you think that the treatment we give to an ant should be less than that we give to a dog, cat, or horse? Why? What is the *social* origin of your attitudes?

3. In what sense is the animal rights movement similar to a religion?

Changes in beliefs about animals extend back to the growth of towns and mercantile values in the midst of the aristocratic, agrarian societies of sixteenth- and seventeenth-century Europe. A new urban middle class appeared, and by the nineteenth century it had changed daily life in Western Europe. The "civilizing process" that discouraged the new bourgeoisie from spitting on the floor, wiping their noses on their sleeves, and eating with their hands, represented an increased concern for the feelings and sensibilities of others. . . .

As urbanization removed many people from their direct dependence on animals as a resource, except as a means of transportation, close experience with animals other than pets declined. The bourgeois wife in town had fewer chickens to feed or cows to milk, so that her appreciation of animals came from her pet dogs. By 1700, people were naming their pets, often with human names (especially in England); pets appeared regularly in paintings; and some even received legacies when their owners died. When pets died, they (unlike farm animals) were never eaten; often they were buried in style, with epitaphs written by their owners. As the family home and its members became privatized and idealized, so did the family pet.

This new attitude toward animals had a distinct basis in social class, as Robert Darnton's description in *The Great Cat Massacre* dramatically suggests. The massacre occurred in the 1730s at a Paris printing shop where the wife of the master printer was "impassioned" of several pet cats. They were fed at the table with the family, while the printer's apprentices ate table scraps—the cat food of the time—in the kitchen. In symbolic rebellion, the apprentices and workers captured sacksful of pet and stray cats, held a mock trial, and hanged them all. Torturing cats was an old European tradition: a favorite pastime at many holidays was to set cats on fire, largely to hear their terrible "caterwauling." The apprentices' action dramatized the conflict between the traditional view of animals and the emerging sensibility of the wealthy classes. The new moral sensitivity began in the rising middle classes, but quickly conquered much of the aristocracy, and eventually—although not widely until the twentieth century—the laboring classes. In each case, its apostles were mainly women, priests, and the occasional philosopher who articulated the changing beliefs.

Before the nineteenth century, only a few individuals had expressed a heightened moral sensitivity toward animals. Margaret Cavendish, Duchess of Newcastle, wrote extensively in the 1650s and 1660s about the human tendency to tyrannize other species. Considered highly eccentric by her peers, she criticized the hunting of song birds and claimed that "the groans of a dying beast strike my soul." In the eighteenth century, pastors and poets such as Alexander Pope, John Gay, and William Blake attacked cruelty to animals, reinterpreting the biblical acknowledgment of man's dominion over nature to mean thoughtful stewardship rather than ruthless exploitation. As the age of democratic revolutions ushered in new standards of respect and dignity for the rights of individuals, new attention was paid to the treatment of animals. In the often-quoted words of Jeremy Bentham in 1789, the question to ask about animals ". . . is not Can they *reason*? nor Can they *talk*? but, Can they *suffer*?" Here was a new criterion, one that placed humans and animals in the same circle rather than drawing a boundary between them. . . .

The nineteenth-century expansion of industry and cities in Britain and America accelerated the speed of bourgeois moral sensibilities, including sympathy for animals, across all social classes. The realities of nature had little bearing on the lives of those in cities, who were free to project onto nature a pleasant, pastoral image that overlooked its cruelties and dangers. They could forget the violent, precarious lives of animals in the wild and exaggerate their innocence and goodness. The romanticization of nature was largely a reaction to industrial society and the passing of rural life. . . .

Animal rights activists act as moral entrepreneurs, igniting and then building on moral outrage. They appeal to widespread beliefs about the similarities between humans and animals, the love of pets as part of the family, and anxieties about encroaching instrumentalism. And they use shocking images of common practices that violate deeply held sentiments about decency and justice to convert people to the cause.

Shocking visual images are perhaps their most powerful tool. Monkeys in restraining devices, furry raccoons in steel traps, kittens with their eyes sewn shut, and other images of constrained mammals appeal to anthropomorphic sympathies. People's worst fears of a science and a technology out of control seem justified by photographs of animals probed with scientific devices—rats with syringes down their throats, cats with electrodes planted on their heads. A bright patch of red blood on a black-and-white poster catches the eye. . . .

Most moral shocks inform the viewer about what others—scientific researchers, circus trainers, cosmetics companies—do to animals. Some, like New Age consumer efforts, try to shock viewers into thinking about their own actions—their own contribution to animal cruelty. Where did the hamburger in the neat Styrofoam container come from? What was the original animal like? How did it live and how did it die? "Meat's no treat for those you eat!" What animal died to make your fur? "Are you wearing my mother on your back?" We are forced to think of animals, not as commodities, but as living beings with a point of view that we are invited to share.

Moral shocks are recruiting tools for protest movements, but the power of a shocking image is not by itself sufficient to build a movement. Membership generally requires time for activities, discretionary income to contribute, and a conviction that participants can make a difference. But shocks can be so persuasive that even people with no prior political experience become "converts." Moral crusades are often filled with recruits who have not been in other movements; the anti-abortion movement is one example. . . .

Moral truth requires missionary zeal. Those who believe they know the truth are often loud and shrill in their attacks. Fundamentalists hurl venomous labels at those who abuse animals. Scientists are "sadists," meat-eaters are "cannibals,"

factory farmers are "fascists," and furriers are "criminals." But even those who simply disagree with the fundamentalists become targets. At a public forum, Michael W.
Fox of the Humane Society of the United States was asked whether there were any
circumstances in which he would accept animal experimentation. He replied, "Just
to ask that question indicates you are a speciesist and probably a sexist and a racist."
Such labeling inevitably precludes further dialogue. . . .

The smug zeal of moral crusades is familiar. Seeing the moral world in black
and white, many activists, especially those drawn into activism for the first time, are
politically naïve and dismissive of majority sensibilities. In addition to saying that "A
rat is a pig is a dog is a boy," PETA's [People for the Ethical Treatment of Animals]
Ingrid Newkirk declared in a controversial statement, "Six million people died in
concentration camps, but six billion broiler chickens will die this year in slaughterhouses." Others compare the plight of today's animals with that of African-American
slaves before the Civil War. Those willing to grant moral rights to chickens easily
make comparisons that offend mainstream tastes.

In the Gulf of St. Lawrence, the ice was said to have a red tinge after the seal hunt
every March, when 100,000 seals were killed for their pelts. Most prized of all were
the babies, which, for the first three weeks of life, have furry white coats. With their
large eyes, they could bring out sentimental anthropomorphism in almost anyone. A
Canadian film crew—expecting only to film seals in their natural habitat—caught part
of the 1964 hunt, and the sight of baby seals being clubbed and spiked in the head
caused outrage throughout the industrialized world and generated a major contro-
versy, attracting the attention of both environmentalists and animal welfarists.

Brian Davies, then executive-secretary of the New Brunswick SPCA, merged
his welfare perspective with the political arguments of environmentalists: "I discovered that an over-capitalized sealing industry was intent on killing the last seal pup
in order to get a return on its equipment, and that those who profited from the seals
gave not one thought to their suffering." Davis buttressed this critique of instrumentalism with an explicit anthropomorphic description: "Their hind flippers were like
two hands crossed in prayer, and again, the five fingernails. I can well imagine why
many biologists consider sea mammals the most advanced form of nonhuman life."
Whether for anthropomorphic or other reasons, whales, dolphins, seals, and other
sea mammals have aroused tremendous sympathies.

Davies later described the first baby seal he saw killed. "He was a little ball
of white fur with big dark eyes and a plaintive cry . . . *he was only ten days old.* He
went to meet, in a curious, friendly, and playful way, the first human he had ever seen
and was . . . by the same human . . . clubbed on the head and butchered on the spot.
He was skinned alive. I saw the heart in a body without a skin pumping frantically.
From that very moment . . . ending the commercial whitecoat hunt was a cause that
consumed me." As in a religious conversion, he knew his life would henceforth be
devoted to what he called a "crusade against cruelty."

Those who believe that animals have absolute rights demand the elimination
of all animal research. Condemning the instrumental rationality of science, they find

it morally unacceptable to reduce animals to the status of raw materials, in pursuit of human benefit: "We don't consider animals to be a tool, the test tube with legs." Improving conditions is not enough, for as one poster puts it, "Lab animals never have a nice day."

Anti-vivisectionists insist that immoral methods can never be used to support even the most worthy goals. They support their impassioned argument by comparing laboratories to Nazi death camps: "For animal researchers, the ends justify the means. This argument has a familiar ring: Hitler used it when he allowed experiments to be done on Jews."

Farms have changed in recent decades. In 1964, British writer Ruth Harrison coined the term "Factory Farming" in her book *Animal Machines*. Describing the highly regimented conditions of slaughterhouses and the transport of animals by meat packing companies, she questioned the right of humans to place economic criteria over ethical considerations in the use of animals for food. Efficiency rules today's large farms. Chickens, which Americans consume at the rate of several billion a year, spend their lives in windowless buildings. They are subjected to intense light when they are young, because that stimulates rapid growth. They are kept in increasing darkness later in their seven-week lives, because this reduces their fighting with each other. Their beaks are cut off soon after they are born, so that they will do less damage to each other as they grow and fight. Each broiler chicken has about one half a square foot of space. Laying hens have the same space, but live longer, up to eighteen months, at which time they are sent to be slaughtered. Not just chickens, but pigs, veal calves, turkeys, and most other food animals are confined in small areas, often in darkness. Beef cattle spend their first six months in pastures, but then are shipped to cramped feedlots. These techniques have made American agriculture extremely efficient. . . .

Those who believe in the rights of animals as sentient beings support modest reforms, but only as a temporary measure, for their ultimate goal is to abolish altogether the production and consumption of meat. These groups have organized demonstrations and boycotts, picketed restaurants on Mother's Day, attacked turkey farms on Thanksgiving, and liberated restaurant lobsters. The ALF [Animal Liberation Front, a radical organization] has gone further, leaving butchers and slaughterhouses with broken windows and graffiti. Even remote ranches have had water systems broken, fences cut, and equipment damaged.

Both abolitionist and reformist organizations document the immorality of factory farming in brochures and magazines filled with gruesome photographs and ghoulish descriptions of cruelty in slaughterhouses and farms. These documents show contorted hens living their entire lives confined in wire cages so cramped that their toes grow around the wire. They describe the stressful conditions that cause pecking and cannibalism. Bulls are branded and castrated. Rabbits are "living machines" forced to produce eight to ten litters each year. Animals are crammed into trucks and shipped long distances to packing plants.

To highlight the immorality of industrial practices, the animal rights literature describes animals about to be killed for food or fun in human terms. Easily personified, veal calves are a favorite target of activists. Babies with large eyes, they are separated from their mothers ("yanked from their mothers' sides"), confined in stalls ("crated and tortured"), and kept anemic to produce lighter meat. Even lobsters are anthropomorphized: "They have a long childhood and an awkward adolescence. . . . They flirt. Their pregnancies last nine months and they can live to be over one hundred years old." They also have feelings and scramble frantically to escape the pot, "much the way I suppose I would sound were I popped into a pot and boiled alive.". . .

Animal activists direct their moral outrage primarily against large corporations. Their rhetoric is couched in terms of *we* and *they,* two sides separated by a vast moral chasm. Fur and meat producers are depicted as villains, profiteering without regard to pain, and willing to place economic over moral value. Agribusiness thrives "on the backs of the least empowered groups in our social structure: farm workers, future generations, and, of course, farm animals." Animal activists exploit a long tradition of rhetoric against capitalism and the factory system to link animal rights with other social and political issues like exploitation and deprivation for profit.

A Trans-Species brochure describes "New MacDonald's Farm" as a full-scale factory in which animals are enslaved, becoming machines to produce meat. John Robbins—author of *Diet for a New America,* heir to the Baskin Robbins Ice Cream Company, and the president of Earthsave—eulogizes pigs in "The joy and Tragedy of Pigs," noting their high IQs, superior problem-solving abilities, and "sophisticated and subtle relationships with their human companions." Having described the human qualities of pigs, Robbins naturally criticizes "pork production engineers," who treat pigs like "machines." He quotes a trade journal, *Hog Farm Management:* "Forget the pig is an animal. Treat him just like a machine in a factory. Schedule treatment like you would lubrication. Breeding season like the first step in an assembly line. And marketing like the delivery of finished goods." The critique of factory farms, in which machines dominate the production process with no regard for animals, follows Karl Marx's nineteenth-century attack on the treatment of human labor in factories. Factory life turns living beings—humans or animals—into cogs in a relentless machine.

The campaign against furs has had far greater impact—especially on the attitudes of consumers. A New York City lawyer tells a reporter that she feels "very conflicted" about owning a fur, as her own son tells her she is doing something immoral. A fashion agent has no desire to wear her mink coat, for "it's asking for trouble." A travel consultant says she is "a little nervous about walking down a street and being pelted with eggs or paint." A business executive says that when she bought her mink coat it did not occur to her to think about how animals are bred or killed. "Now I am aware of the brutality of trapping an animal, and I would not wear a trapped fur."

Environmentalists and animal protectionists had once attacked the fur industry primarily because of the cruelty involved in trapping wild animals. This view still dominated their discourse in 1979, when the Animal Welfare institute published and widely distributed an exposé, *Facts on Furs,* that focused on leg-hold traps. But animal rightists equally condemn the ranching of fur animals, which now accounts for roughly 80 percent of furs sold. Although most ranched animals die from gas or lethal injection, critics claim that many foxes are still electrocuted by means of a clip on their lip and a probe in their anus. Such practices are seen as brutal and unwarranted, a blight on civilized society. . . .

Perhaps because protestors have had little success with ranchers, current anti-fur campaigns are aimed at those who wear furs more than at trappers, making department stores and fur salons the sites of protest. In 1987, Bob Barker, a popular television game show host, publicly refused to participate in a Miss U.S.A. pageant in which the women were to parade out in furs and remove them to reveal swim suits. One prize was to be a fur coat. The following year Barker attracted further media attention as the head of the Fur-Free Friday march in New York; he seemed to encourage demonstrators to spit on passersby wearing furs by saying that this tactic had been effective in changing public attitudes toward fur in Europe.

Demonstrators have picketed, spray-painted, and smashed the windows of fur stores, distributed the names and home addresses of furriers, harassed women by shouting or spitting on them, placed advertisements on subways and city buses, and sponsored fashion shows with the message "Real People Wear Fake Furs" and "Fake People Wear Real Furs." They have organized rock concerts, liberated beavers from fur farms, and held public memorial services for animals killed for furs. Graphic slogans provide effective moral shocks: "Somewhere There Are Animals Missing Their Paws," and "Wear the Bloody Side Out!" Like the anti-meat crusade, anti-fur films and photos dwell on the cruelty and pain inflicted on vulnerable and sensitive beings. A photograph of a rack of pelts is captioned: "A few moments ago, these were live, vulnerable beings capable of fear, happiness, hope, and pain." A sign on a New York City bus encourages empathy by portraying a trapped animal: "Get a Feel for Fur. Slam your hand in a car door." Some activists even oppose the wearing of wool, combining arguments based on pain (sheep may be nicked during shearing or may be cold once shorn) with rights talk (sheep should not be used for human ends).

Furriers launched a multimillion-dollar campaign against the animal protection movement. The movement has had even greater influence in European countries, where fur sales have drastically declined (fur sales have dropped 90 percent in the Netherlands, 75 percent in Britain and Switzerland since the early eighties), and Harrods, once boasting it sold every existing product, has abandoned its sale of fur coats. The industry defends itself as catering to consumer choice and protecting fundamental freedoms. A radio commercial by the fur industry asks the listener to imagine enjoying a steak dinner in a nice restaurant: "Suddenly there's a commotion. People are around your table jostling you. Shouting. Pointing at your steak and screaming that you are a killer." Ads in major newspapers proclaim, "Today fur. Tomorrow leather. Then wool. Then meat. . . ." The American Fur Industry/Fur Information Council of America ends with an appeal to American individualism: "The decision to wear fur is a personal one. We support the freedom of individuals to buy and wear fur. This freedom is not just a fur industry issue—it's everybody's issue." This defense of consumer choice as a fundamental freedom is as close to the high moral ground as the fur industry can come.

Furriers routinely label all animal activists as terrorists. Even the audience [members] at a "Rock Against Fur" concert were "supporting terrorism." When Beauty Without Cruelty published ads with a list of celebrities under the caption "Say NO to furs—They did," the Fur Retailers Council wrote to each person listed. It implied they were being used by terrorist groups, and warned them to "review the enclosed material recently sent to police chiefs and sheriffs throughout the U.S. calling attention to violence and revenue-producing campaigns that often have very little relationship to animal care." The materials included lists of break-ins and animal thefts. Labeling the movement the "Animal Rights Protection Industry," the Council also provided information on the net worth of various organizations such as Greenpeace and the ASPCA (American Society for the Prevention of Cruelty to Animals). Both animal rightists and their opponents denounce each other as large, powerful, and ruthless.

Amidst the moral confusions of contemporary culture, animal rightists offer a clear position based on a set of compelling principles. They offer moral engagement and commitment in a secular society with few opportunities to sort out one's values, appealing especially to those who reject organized religion as a source of moral tenets. Animals are a perfect outlet for moral impulses, for—unlike people—they seem incapable of duplicity, infidelity, or betrayal. Like children, they are innocent victims unable to fight for their own interests. Thus, protecting animals sometimes inspires the shrill tone, the sense of urgency, and the single-minded obsession of a fundamentalist crusade. Its members become missionaries, defining the world in terms of the treatment of animals. They see the world as good or evil, and the villain—the person who exploits animals—becomes a model of malice. . . . Convinced of the truth of their moral mission, many animal rights activists feel justified in using radical tactics as well as revolutionary rhetoric to serve their cause of abolishing all animal exploitation. . . .

Animal rights is but one of many controversies that have grown out of a clash of basic moral values, of competing world views. Unlike conflicts based on interests, such controversies cannot be fully resolved. Yet, raising basic questions that reflect widespread social and political concerns, moral crusades can never be dismissed. To stubbornly defend current practices is to encourage further polarization. To denounce the movement as irrational, kooky, or terrorist is to miss the popular appeal of its moral intuitions and political beliefs. If a solution is possible in such rancorous conflict, it will require good faith from both sides to ensure the dialogue and compromise basic to a democratic conversation.

22▪▪▪ ▪▪▪▪▪▪▪▪▪▪▪▪▪▪▪▪▪▪▪▪▪▪▪▪▪▪▪▪▪▪

Jihad vs. McWorld

Benjamin R. Barber

introduction ▪ ▪ ▪ ▪ ▪

We tend to take the social changes that swirl around us for granted. Although our way of life is vastly different from those of earlier generations, it seems to be natural and right. We live in a world of fast-food restaurants, frozen dinners, and instant oil changes. We know what to expect when we step inside a Burger King, a Taco Bell, a Wendy's, an Olive Garden, a Chic-fil-A, a Popeye's, a Cracker Barrel, or, of course, a McDonald's. We know what the décor will look like, what the employees will be wearing and what they will say to us. We know what items will be on the menu, and, no matter what meal we order, we know its precise taste. Rationalization, reviewed in Reading 14, has led to almost identical experiences, whether we visit one of these restaurants in Paris or in Muncie, Indiana. In short, we now live in a McWorld, a uniformity and integration driven by the globalization of capitalism that is making societies the world over similar to one another.

Despite the powerful imperatives that underlie McWorld, oppositional forces have been unleashed. The primary opposition can be called *culturism*, the attempt by small groups that feel united by a culture to preserve their way of life in the face of global social change, or their attempt to make their way of life dominant in some region. Unlike McWorld, culturism represents traditional ways of doing social life. To those who hold their traditional cultures so dear, McWorld is ominous, threatening: If allowed to proceed, McWorld will dominate, engulf, and obliterate their culture. The response of culturism (or, as termed in this selection, *Jihad* or *retribalization*) has been so forceful and violent that it has led to small-scale wars around the globe.

With these powerful forces in conflict, what will the future bring? As Barber makes clear, there can be no uniting of McWorld and culturism, for they are oppositional forces. The victory of the one can come only with the defeat of the other.

Thinking Critically

As you read this selection, ask yourself:

1. What is McWorld? What are the social forces (called *imperatives* in this reading) that are driving McWorld?

2. What is the primary opposition that McWorld is coming up against, according to the analysis in this selection? What social forces drive this opposition?

3. How does the author think that the conflict will be resolved? Do you agree?

Just beyond the horizon of current events lie two possible political futures—both bleak, neither democratic. The first is a retribalization of large swaths of humankind by war and bloodshed: a threatened Lebanonization of national states in which culture is pitted against culture, people against people, tribe against tribe—a Jihad in the name of a hundred narrowly conceived faiths against every kind of interdependence, every kind of artificial social cooperation and civic mutuality. The second is being borne in on us by the onrush of economic and ecological forces that demand integration and uniformity and that mesmerize the world with fast music, fast computers, and fast food—with MTV, Macintosh, and McDonald's, pressing nations into one commercially homogenous global network: one McWorld tied together by technology, ecology, communications, and commerce. The planet is falling precipitantly apart *and* coming reluctantly together at the very same moment. . . .

The tendencies of what I am here calling the forces of Jihad and the forces of McWorld operate with equal strength in opposite directions, the one driven by parochial hatreds, the other by universalizing markets, the one re-creating ancient subnational and ethnic borders from within, the other making national borders porous from without. They have one thing in common: neither offers much hope to citizens looking for practical ways to govern themselves democratically. If the global future is to pit Jihad's centrifugal whirlwind against McWorld's centripetal black hole, the outcome is unlikely to be democratic—or so I will argue.

■ ■ ■ ■ McWORLD, OR THE GLOBALIZATION OF POLITICS

Four imperatives make up the dynamic of McWorld: a market imperative, a resource imperative, an information-technology imperative, and an ecological imperative. By shrinking the world and diminishing the salience of national borders, these imperatives have in combination achieved a considerable victory over factiousness and particularism, and not least of all over their most virulent traditional form—nationalism. It is the realists who are now Europeans, the utopians who dream nostalgically of a resurgent England or Germany, perhaps even a resurgent Wales or Saxony. Yesterday's wishful cry for one world has yielded to the reality of McWorld.

The Market Imperative

Marxist and Leninist theories of imperialism assumed that the quest for ever-expanding markets would in time compel nation-based capitalist economies to push

Published originally in *The Atlantic Monthly*, March 1992, as an introduction to the *Jihad vs. McWorld* (Ballantine paperback, 1996), a volume that discusses and extends the themes of the original article.

against national boundaries in search of an international economic imperium. Whatever else has happened to the scientistic predictions of Marxism, in this domain they have proved farsighted. All national economies are now vulnerable to the inroads of larger, transnational markets within which trade is free, currencies are convertible, access to banking is open, and contracts are enforceable under law. In Europe, Asia, Africa, the South Pacific, and the Americas such markets are eroding national sovereignty and giving rise to entities—international banks, trade associations, transnational lobbies like OPEC and Greenpeace, world news services like CNN and the BBC, and multinational corporations that increasingly lack a meaningful national identity—that neither reflect nor respect nationhood as an organizing or regulative principle.

The market imperative has also reinforced the quest for international peace and stability, requisites of an efficient international economy. Markets are enemies of parochialism, isolation, fractiousness, war. Market psychology attenuates the psychology of ideological and religious cleavages and assumes a concord among producers and consumers—categories that ill fit narrowly conceived national or religious cultures. Shopping has little tolerance for blue laws, whether dictated by pub-closing British paternalism, Sabbath-observing Jewish Orthodox fundamentalism, or no-Sunday-liquor-sales Massachusetts puritanism. In the context of common markets, international law ceases to be a vision of justice and becomes a workaday framework for getting things done—enforcing contracts, ensuring that governments abide by deals, regulating trade and currency relations, and so forth.

Common markets demand a common language, as well as a common currency, and they produce common behaviors of the kind bred by cosmopolitan city life everywhere. Commercial pilots, computer programmers, international bankers, media specialists, oil riggers, entertainment celebrities, ecology experts, demographers, accountants, professors, athletes—these compose a new breed of men and women for whom religion, culture, and nationality can seem only marginal elements in a working identity. Although sociologists of everyday life will no doubt continue to distinguish a Japanese from an American mode, shopping has a common signature throughout the world. Cynics might even say that some of the recent revolutions in Eastern Europe have had as their true goal not liberty and the right to vote but well-paying jobs and the right to shop (although the vote is proving easier to acquire than consumer goods). The market imperative is, then, plenty powerful; but, notwithstanding some of the claims made for "democratic capitalism," it is not identical with the democratic imperative.

The Resource Imperative

Democrats once dreamed of societies whose political autonomy rested firmly on economic independence. The Athenians idealized what they called autarky, and tried for a while to create a way of life simple and austere enough to make the polis genuinely self-sufficient. To be free meant to be independent of any other community or polis. Not even the Athenians were able to achieve autarky, however: human nature, it turns out, is dependency. By the time of Pericles, Athenian politics was inextricably bound up with a flowering empire held together by naval power and commerce—an empire that, even as it appeared to enhance Athenian might, ate away at Athenian independence and autarky. Master and slave, it turned out, were bound together by mutual insufficiency.

The dream of autarky briefly engrossed nineteenth-century America as well, for the underpopulated, endlessly bountiful land, the cornucopia of natural resources, and the natural barriers of a continent walled in by two great seas led many to believe that America could be a world unto itself. Given this past, it has been harder for Americans than for most to accept the inevitability of interdependence. But the rapid depletion of resources even in a country like ours, where they once seemed inexhaustible, and the maldistribution of arable soil and mineral resources on the planet, leave even the wealthiest societies ever more resource-dependent and many other nations in permanently desperate straits.

Every nation, it turns out, needs something another nation has; some nations have almost nothing they need.

The Information-Technology Imperative

Enlightenment science and the technologies derived from it are inherently universalizing. They entail a quest for descriptive principles of general application, a search for universal solutions to particular problems, and an unswerving embrace of objectivity and impartiality.

Scientific progress embodies and depends on open communication, a common discourse rooted in rationality, collaboration, and an easy and regular flow and exchange of information. Such ideals can be hypocritical covers for power-mongering by elites, and they may be shown to be wanting in many other ways, but they are entailed by the very idea of science and they make science and globalization practical allies.

Business, banking, and commerce all depend on information flow and are facilitated by new communication technologies. The hardware of these technologies tends to be systemic and integrated—computer, television, cable, satellite, laser, fiber-optic, and microchip technologies combining to create a vast interactive communications and information network that can potentially give every person on earth access to every other person, and make every datum, every byte, available to every set of eyes. If the automobile was, as George Ball once said (when he gave his blessing to a Fiat factory in the Soviet Union during the Cold War), "an ideology on four wheels," then electronic telecommunication and information systems are an ideology at 186,000 miles per second—which makes for a very small planet in a very big hurry. Individual cultures speak particular languages; commerce and science increasingly speak English; the whole world speaks logarithms and binary mathematics.

Moreover, the pursuit of science and technology asks for, even compels, open societies. Satellite footprints do not respect national borders; telephone wires penetrate the most closed societies. With photocopying and then fax machines having infiltrated Soviet universities and *samizdat* literary circles in the eighties, and computer modems having multiplied like rabbits in communism's bureaucratic warrens thereafter, *glasnost* could not be far behind. In their social requisites, secrecy and science are enemies.

The new technology's software is perhaps even more globalizing than its hardware. The information arm of international commerce's sprawling body reaches out and touches distinct nations and parochial cultures, and gives them a common face chiseled in Hollywood, on Madison Avenue, and in Silicon Valley. Throughout the 1980s one of the most-watched television programs in South Africa was *The Cosby Show*. The demise of apartheid was already in production. Exhibitors at the 1991 Cannes film festival expressed growing anxiety over the "homogenization" and "Americanization" of the global film industry when, for the third year running, American films dominated the awards ceremonies. America has dominated the world's popular culture for much longer, and much more decisively. In November of 1991 Switzerland's once insular culture boasted best-seller lists featuring *Terminator 2* as the No. 1 movie, *Scarlett* as the No. 1 book, and Prince's *Diamonds and Pearls* as the No. 1 record album. No wonder the Japanese are buying Hollywood film sudios even faster than Americans are buying Japanese television sets. This kind of software supremacy may in the long term be far more important than hardware superiority, because culture has become more potent than armaments. What is the power of the Pentagon compared with Disneyland? Can the Sixth Fleet keep up with CNN? McDonald's in Moscow and Coke in China will do more to create a global culture than military colonization ever could. It is less the goods than the brand names that do the work, for they convey life-style images that alter perception and challenge behavior. They make up the seductive software of McWorld's common (at times much too common) soul.

Yet in all this high-tech commercial world there is nothing that looks particularly democratic. It lends itself to surveillance as well as liberty, to new forms of manipulation and covert control as well as new kinds if participation, to skewed, unjust market outcomes as well as greater productivity. The consumer society and the open society are not quite synonymous. Capitalism and democracy have a relationship, but it is something less than a marriage. An efficient free market after all requires that consumers be free to vote their dollars on competing goods, not that citizens be free to vote their values and beliefs on competing political candidates and programs. The free market flourished in junta-run Chile, in military-governed Taiwan and Korea, and, earlier, in a variety of autocratic European empires as well as their colonial possessions.

The Ecological Imperative

The impact of globalization on ecology is a cliché even to world leaders who ignore it. We know well enough that the German forests can be destroyed by Swiss and Italians driving gas-guzzlers fueled by leaded gas. We also know that the planet can be asphyxiated by greenhouse gases because Brazilian farmers want to be part of the twentieth century and are burning down tropical rain forests to clear a little land to plough, and because Indonesians make a living out of converting their lush jungle into toothpicks for fastidious Japanese diners, upsetting the delicate oxygen balance and in effect puncturing our global lungs. Yet this ecological consciousness has meant not only greater awareness but also greater inequality, as modernized nations try to slam the door behind them, saying to developing nations, "The world cannot afford *your* modernization; ours has wrung it dry!"

Each of the four imperatives just cited is transnational, transideological, and transcultural. Each applies impartially to Catholics, Jews, Muslims, Hindus, and Buddhists; to democrats and totalitarians; to capitalists and socialists. The Enlightenment dream of a universal rational society has to a remarkable degree been realized—but in a form that is commercialized, homogenized, depoliticized, bureaucratized, and, of course, radically incomplete, for the movement toward McWorld is in competition with forces of global breakdown, national dissolution, and centrifugal corruption. These forces, working in the opposite direction, are the essence of what I call Jihad.

■ ■ ■ ■   JIHAD, OR THE LEBANONIZATION OF THE WORLD

OPEC, the world bank, the united nations, the International Red Cross, the multinational corporation . . . there are scores of institutions that reflect globalization. But they often appear as ineffective reactors to the world's real actors: national states and, to an ever greater degree, subnational factions in permanent rebellion against uniformity and integration—even the kind represented by universal law and justice. The headlines feature these players regularly: they are cultures, not countries; parts, not wholes; sects, not religions; rebellious factions and dissenting minorities at war not just with globalism but with the traditional nation-state. Kurds, Basques, Puerto Ricans, Ossetians, East Timoreans, Quebecois, the Catholics of Northern Ireland, Abkhasians, Kurile Islander Japanese, the Zulus of Inkatha, Catalonians, Tamils, and, of course, Palestinians—people without countries, inhabiting nations not their own, seeking smaller worlds within borders that will seal them off from modernity.

A powerful irony is at work here. Nationalism was once a force of integration and unification, a movement aimed at bringing together disparate clans, tribes, and cultural fragments under new, assimilationist flags. But as Ortega y Gasset noted more than sixty years ago, having won its victories, nationalism changed its strategy. In the 1920s, and again today, it is more often a reactionary and divisive force, pulverizing the very nations it once helped cement together. The force that creates nations is "inclusive," Ortega wrote in *The Revolt of the Masses*. "In periods of consolidation, nationalism has a positive value, and is a lofty standard. But in Europe everything is more than consolidated, and nationalism is nothing but a mania. . . ."

This mania has left the post–Cold War world smoldering with hot wars; the international scene is little more unified than it was at the end of the Great War, in Ortega's own time. There [are] more than thirty wars in progress [in some years], most of them ethnic, racial, tribal, or religious in character, and the list of unsafe regions doesn't seem to be getting any shorter. Some new world order!

The aim of many of these small-scale wars is to redraw boundaries, to implode states and resecure parochial identities: to escape McWorld's dully insistent imperatives. The mood is that of Jihad: war not as an instrument of policy but as an emblem of identity, an expression of community, an end in itself. Even where there is no shooting war, there is fractiousness, secession, and the quest for ever smaller communities. Add to the list of dangerous countries those at risk: In Switzerland and Spain, Jurassian and Basque separatists still argue the virtues of ancient identities, sometimes in the language of bombs. Hyperdisintegration in the former Soviet Union may well continue unabated—not just a Ukraine independent from the Soviet Union but a Bessarabian Ukraine independent from the Ukrainian republic; not just Russia severed from the defunct union but Tatarstan severed from Russia. Yugoslavia makes even the disunited, ex-Soviet, nonsocialist republics that were once the Soviet Union look integrated, its sectarian fatherlands springing up within factional motherlands like weeds within weeds within weeds. Kurdish independence would threaten the territorial integrity of four Middle Eastern nations. Well before the current cataclysm Soviet Georgia made a claim for autonomy from the Soviet Union, only to be faced with its Ossetians (164,000 in a republic of 5.5 million) demanding their own self-determination within Georgia. The Abkhasian minority in Georgia has followed suit. Even the good will established by Canada's once promising Meech Lake protocols is in danger, with Francophone Quebec again threatening the dissolution of the federation. In South Africa the emergence from apartheid was hardly achieved when friction between Inkatha's Zulus and the African National Congress's tribally identified members threatened to replace Europeans' racism with an indigenous tribal war. After thirty years of attempted integration using the colonial language (English) as a unifier, Nigeria is now playing with the idea of linguistic multiculturalism—which could mean the cultural breakup of the nation into hundreds of tribal fragments. Even Saddam Hussein has benefited from the threat of internal Jihad, having used renewed tribal and religious warfare to turn last season's mortal enemies into reluctant allies of an Iraqi nationhood that he nearly destroyed.

The passing of communism has torn away the thin veneer of internationalism (workers of the world unite!) to reveal ethnic prejudices that are not only ugly and deep-seated but increasingly murderous. Europe's old scourge, anti-Semitism is back with a vengeance, but it is only one of many antagonisms. It appears all too easy to throw the historical gears into reverse and pass from a Communist dictatorship back into a tribal state.

Among the tribes, religion is also a battlefield. ("Jihad" is a rich word whose generic meaning is "struggle"—usually the struggle of the soul to avert evil. Strictly applied to religious war, it is used only in reference to battles where the faith is under assault, or battles against a government that denies the practice of Islam. My use here is rhetorical, but does follow both journalistic practice and history.) Remember the Thirty Years War? Whatever forms of Enlightenment universalism might once have come to grace such historically related forms of monotheism as Judaism, Christianity, and Islam, in many of their modern incarnations they are parochial rather than cosmopolitan, angry rather than loving, proselytizing rather than ecumenical, zealous rather than rationalist, sectarian rather than deistic, ethnocentric rather than universalizing. As a result, like the new forms of hypernationalism, the new expressions of religious fundamentalism are fractious and pulverizing, never integrating. This is religion as the Crusaders knew it: a battle to the death for souls that if not saved will be forever lost.

The atmospherics of Jihad have resulted in a breakdown of civility in the name of identity, of comity in the name of community. International relations have sometimes taken on the aspect of gang war—cultural turf battles featuring tribal factions that were supposed to be sublimated as integral parts of large national, economic, postcolonial, and constitutional entities.

■ ■ ■ ■ **THE DARKENING FUTURE OF DEMOCRACY**

These rather melodramatic tableaux vivants do not tell the whole story, however. For all their defects, Jihad and McWorld have their attractions. Yet, to repeat and insist, the attractions are unrelated to democracy. Neither McWorld nor Jihad is remotely democratic in impulse. Neither needs democracy; neither promotes democracy.

McWorld does manage to look pretty seductive in a world obsessed with Jihad. It delivers peace, prosperity, and relative unity—if at the cost of independence, community, and identity (which is generally based on difference). The primary political values required by the global market are order and tranquillity, and freedom—as in the phrases "free trade," "free press," and "free love." Human rights are needed to a degree, but not citizenship or participation—and no more social justice and equality than are necessary to promote efficient economic production and consumption. Multinational corporations sometimes seem to prefer doing business with local oligarchs, inasmuch as they can take confidence from dealing with the boss on all crucial matters. Despots who slaughter their own populations are no problem, so long as they leave markets in place and refrain from making war on their neighbors (Saddam Hussein's fatal mistake). In trading partners, predictability is of more value than justice.

The Eastern European revolutions that seemed to arise out of concern for global democratic values quickly deteriorated into a stampede in the general direction of free markets and their ubiquitous, television-promoted shopping malls. East Germany's Neues Forum, that courageous gathering of intellectuals, students, and workers which overturned the Stalinist regime in Berlin in 1989, lasted only six months in Germany's mini-version of McWorld. Then it gave way to money and markets and monopolies from the West. By the time of the first all-German elections, it could scarcely manage to secure three percent of the vote. Elsewhere there is growing evidence that *glasnost* will go and *perestroika*—defined as privatization and an opening of markets to Western bidders—will stay. So understandably anxious are the new rulers of Eastern Europe and whatever entities are forged from the residues of the Soviet Union to gain access to credit and markets and technology—McWorld's flourishing new currencies—that they have shown themselves willing to trade away democratic prospects in pursuit of them: not just old totalitarian ideologies and command-economy production models but some possible indigenous experiments with a third way between capitalism and socialism, such as economic cooperatives and employee stock-ownership plans, both of which have their ardent supporters in the East.

Jihad delivers a different set of virtues: a vibrant local identity, a sense of community, solidarity among kinsmen, neighbors, and countrymen, narrowly conceived. But it also guarantees parochialism and is grounded in exclusion. Solidarity is secured through war against outsiders. And solidarity often means obedience to a hierarchy in governance, fanaticism in beliefs, and the obliteration of individual selves in the name of the group. Deference to leaders and intolerance toward outsiders (and toward "enemies within") are hallmarks of tribalism—hardly the attitudes required for the cultivation of new democratic women and men capable of governing themselves. Where new democratic experiments have been conducted in retribalizing societies, in both Europe and the Third World, the result has often been anarchy, repression, persecution, and the coming of new, noncommunist forms of very old kinds of despotism. During the past year, Havel's velvet revolution in Czechoslovakia was imperiled by partisans of "Czechland" and of Slovakia as independent entities. India seemed little less rent by Sikh, Hindu, Muslim, and Tamil infighting than it was immediately after the British pulled out, more than forty years ago.

To the extent that either McWorld or Jihad has a *natural* politics, it has turned out to be more of an antipolitics. For McWorld, it is the antipolitics of globalism: bureaucratic, technocratic, and meritocratic, focused (as Marx predicted it would be) on the administration of things—with people, however, among the chief things to be administered. In its politico-economic imperatives McWorld has been guided by laissez-faire market principles that privilege efficiency, productivity, and beneficence at the expense of civic liberty and self-government.

For Jihad, the antipolitics of tribalization (have) been explicitly antidemocratic: one-party dictatorship, government by military junta, theocratic fundamentalism—often associated with a version of the *Führerprinzip* that empowers an individual to rule on behalf of a people. Even the government of India, struggling for decades to model democracy for a people who will soon number a billion, longs for great leaders; and for every Mahatma Gandhi, Indira Gandhi, or Rajiv Gandhi taken from them by zealous assassins, the Indians appear to seek a replacement who will deliver them from the lengthy travail of their freedom.

■ ■ ■ THE CONFEDERAL OPTION

How can democracy be secured and spread in a world whose primary tendencies are at best indifferent to it (McWorld) and at worst deeply antithetical to it (Jihad)? My guess is that globalization will eventually vanquish retribalization. The ethos of material "civilization" has not yet encountered an obstacle it has been unable to thrust aside. Ortega may have grasped in the 1920s a clue to our own future. . . .

> Everyone sees the need of a new principle of life. But as always happens in similar crises—some people attempt to save the situation by an artificial intensification of the very principle which has led to decay. This is the meaning of the "nationalist" outburst of recent years. . . . Things have always gone that way. The last flare, the

longest; the last sigh, the deepest. On the very eve of their disappearance there is an intensification of frontiers—military and economic.

Jihad may be a last deep sigh before the eternal yawn of McWorld. On the other hand, Ortega was not exactly prescient; his prophecy of peace and internationalism came just before blitzkrieg, world war, and the Holocaust tore the old order to bits. Yet democracy is how we remonstrate with reality, the rebuke our aspirations offer to history. And if retribalization is inhospitable to democracy, there is nonetheless a form of democratic government that can accommodate parochialism and communitarianism, one that can even save them from their defects and make them more tolerant and participatory: decentralized participatory democracy. And if McWorld is indifferent to democracy, there is nonetheless a form of democratic government that suits global markets passably well—representative government in its federal or, better still, confederal variation.

With its concern for accountability, the protection of minorities, and the universal rule of law, a confederalized representative system would serve the political needs of McWorld as well as oligarchic bureaucratism or meritocratic elitism is currently doing. As we are already beginning to see, many nations may survive in the long term only as confederations that afford local regions smaller than "nations" extensive jurisdiction. Recommended reading for democrats of the twenty-first century is not the U.S. Constitution or the French Declaration of Rights of Man and Citizen but the Articles of Confederation, that suddenly pertinent document that stitched together the thirteen American colonies into what then seemed a too loose confederation of independent states but now appears a new form of political realism, as veterans of Yeltsin's new Russia and the new Europe created at Maastricht will attest.

By the same token, the participatory and direct form of democracy that engages citizens in civic activity and civic judgment and goes well beyond just voting and accountability—the system I have called "strong democracy"—suits the political needs of decentralized communities as well as theocratic and nationalist party dictatorships have done. Local neighborhoods need not be democratic, but they can be. Real democracy has flourished in diminutive settings: the spirit of liberty, Tocqueville said, is local. Participatory democracy, if not naturally apposite to tribalism, has an undeniable attractiveness under conditions of parochialism.

Democracy in any of these variations will, however, continue to be obstructed by the undemocratic and antidemocratic trends toward uniformitarian globalism and intolerant retribalization which I have portrayed here. For democracy to persist in our brave new McWorld, we will have to commit acts of conscious political will—a possibility, but hardly a probability, under these conditions. Political will requires much more than the quick fix of the transfer of institutions. Like technology transfer, institution transfer rests on foolish assumptions about a uniform world of the kind that once fired the imagination of colonial administrators. Spread English justice to the colonies by exporting wigs. Let an East Indian trading company act as the vanguard to Britain's free parliamentary institutions. Today's well-intentioned quick-fixers in the National Endowment for Democracy and the Kennedy School of Government, in the unions and foundations and universities zealously nurturing contacts in Eastern Europe and the Third World, are hoping to democratize by long distance. Post Bulgaria a parliament by first-class mail. Fed Ex the Bill of Rights to Sri Lanka. Cable Cambodia some common law.

Yet Eastern Europe has already demonstrated that importing free political parties, parliaments, and presses cannot establish a democratic civil society; imposing a free market may even have the opposite effect. Democracy grows from the bottom up and cannot be imposed from the top down. Civil society has to be built from the inside out. The institutional superstructure comes last. Poland may become democratic, but then again it may heed the Pope, and prefer to found its politics on its Catholicism, with uncertain consequences for democracy. Bulgaria may become democratic, but it may prefer tribal war. The former Soviet Union may become a democratic confederation, or it may just grow into an anarchic and weak conglomeration of markets for other nations' goods and services.

Democrats need to seek out indigenous democratic impulses. There is always a desire for self-government, always some expression of participation, accountability, consent, and representation, even in traditional hierarchical societies. These need to be identified, tapped, modified, and incorporated into new democratic practices with an indigenous flavor. The tortoises among the democratizers may ultimately outlive or outpace the hares, for they will have the time and patience to explore conditions along the way, and to adapt their gait to changing circumstances. Tragically, democracy in a hurry often looks something like France in 1794 or China in 1989.

It certainly seems possible that the most attractive democratic ideal in the face of the brutal realities of Jihad and the dull realities of McWorld will be a confederal union of semi-autonomous communities smaller than nation-states, tied together into regional economic associations and markets larger than nation-states—participatory and self-determining in local matters at the bottom, representative and accountable at the top. The nation-state would play a diminished role, and sovereignty would lose some of its political potency. The Green movement adage "Think globally, act locally" would actually come to describe the conduct of politics.

This vision reflects only an ideal, however—one that is not terribly likely to be realized. Freedom, Jean-Jacques Rousseau once wrote, is a food easy to eat but hard to digest. Still, democracy has always played itself out against the odds. And democracy remains both a form of coherence as binding as McWorld and a secular faith potentially as inspiriting as Jihad.

How Many Sexual Partners Do Americans Have?

Robert T. Michael, John H. Gagnon,
Edward O. Laumann, and Gina Kolata

introduction ▪ ▪ ▪ ▪ ▪

Human sexual behavior is one of the many fascinating aspects of social life that sociologists study. Sexuality is one of the most significant aspects of humans, for it involves not only behaviors and social relationships, but also it is central to our personal identity—to our feelings of self, of who we are. Yet when sociologists investigate this vital area of human behavior, they meet resistance and suspicion. Resistance comes from people who feel that human sexuality is solely a private matter and no prying sociologist should examine it. Suspicion is generalized, coming from a great number of people who feel that the sociologists' motives are somehow impure. If sociologists do research on teenage sexuality, they are thought to harbor secret fantasies. If they do research on prostitutes, they are thought to visit prostitutes under cover of night. If they gather data on homosexual behavior, they are thought to be closet homosexuals. No matter what area of sexual behavior sociologists investigate, they are suspected of harboring inappropriate fantasies and secret desires, or of hiding other dark secrets about their own sexual selves.

This risk to reputation and relationships (which is often accompanied by snide remarks and smirks) is not faced by sociologists who do research on how people vote or on how their food preferences are changing. Researchers who study these other areas of human behavior do not come under suspicion that they covertly want to undermine the political system or that they may be harboring secret longings for some particular food. Because of negative reactions to research on human sexual behavior, few sociologists investigate this area of social life, despite its significance for understanding people. Some researchers do forge ahead despite the risk, however, and in this selection Michael, Gagnon, Laumann, and Kolata provide an update on our changing sexual behavior.

Thinking Critically

As you read this selection, ask yourself:

1. In the introduction to this selection, the editor says that unlike those who do research on political behavior, sociologists who study human sexual behavior risk damage to their reputations and relationships. Why do you think this is so?

2. This selection underscores the significance and influence of marriage. What evidence do you find for this statement?

3. Based on this reading, how has the sexual behavior of Americans changed?

*S*ometimes, the myths about sex contain a grain of truth. The common perception is that Americans today have more sexual partners than they did just a decade or two ago. That, it turns out, is correct. A third of Americans who are over age fifty have had five or more sexual partners in their lifetime. But half of all Americans aged thirty to fifty have had five or more partners even though being younger, they had fewer years to accumulate them.

Still, when we ask older or younger people how many partners they had in the past year, the usual reply is zero or one. Something must have changed to make younger people accumulate more partners over a lifetime, yet sustain a pattern of having no partners or only one in any one year. The explanation is linked to one of our most potent social institutions and how it has changed.

That institution is marriage, a social arrangement so powerful that nearly everyone participates. About 90 percent of Americans have married by the time they are thirty, and a large majority spends much of their adulthood as part of a wedded couple. And marriage, we find, regulates sexual behavior with remarkable precision. No matter what they did before they wed, no matter how many partners they had, the sexual lives of married people are similar. Despite the popular myth that there is a great deal of adultery in marriage, our data and other reliable studies do not find it. Instead, a vast majority are faithful while the marriage is intact. . . .

So, yes, many young people probably are having sexual intercourse with a fair number of partners. But that stops with marriage. The reason that people now have more sexual partners over their lifetimes is that they are spending a longer period sexually active, but unmarried. The period has lengthened from both ends and in the middle. The average age at which people have their first sexual intercourse has crept down and the average age at which people marry for the first time has edged up. And people are more likely to divorce now, which means they have time between marriages when they search for new partners once again.

To draw these conclusions, we looked at our respondents' replies to a variety of questions. First, we asked people when they first had heterosexual intercourse. Then, we asked what happens between the time when people first have intercourse and when they finally marry. How many partners do they have? Do they have more than one partner at any one time or do they have their partners in succession, practicing serial monogamy? We asked how many people divorced and how long they remained unmarried. Finally, we asked how many partners people had in their lifetimes.

In our analyses of the numbers of sex partners, we could not separately analyze patterns for gay men and lesbians. That is because homosexuals are such a small percentage of our sample that we do not have enough people in our survey to draw valid conclusions about this aspect of sexual behavior.

If we are going to look at heterosexual partners from the beginning, from the time that people first lose their virginity, we plunge headfirst into the maelstrom of teenage sex, always a turbulent subject, but especially so now, in the age of AIDS.

While society disputes whether to counsel abstinence from sexual intercourse or to pass out condoms in high schools, it also must grapple with a basic question: Has sexual behavior among teenagers changed? Are more having sexual intercourse and at younger ages, or is the overheated rhetoric a reaction to fears, without facts? The answer is both troubling and reassuring to the majority of adults who prefer teenagers to delay their sexual activity—troubling because most teenagers are having intercourse, but reassuring because sexual intercourse tends to be sporadic during the teen years.

We saw a steadily declining age at which teenagers first had sexual inter-course. Men and women born in the decade 1933–1942 had sex [for the first time] at an average age of about eighteen. Those born twenty to thirty years later have an

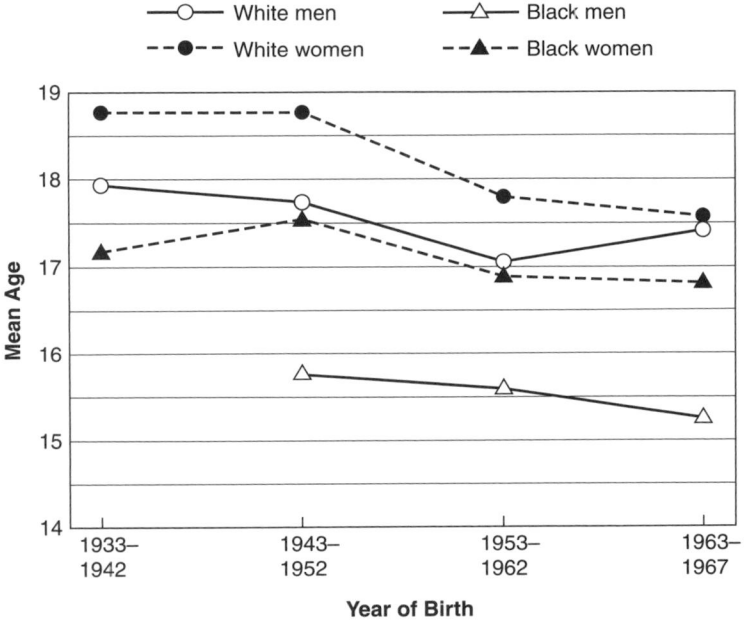

FIGURE 1   Mean Age at First Intercourse

Note: This includes respondents who had vaginal intercourse no later than age twenty-five and who have reached their twenty-fifth birthday by the date of the interview. [There were an] insufficient number of cases [to show Hispanics]. Whites computed from cross-section sample; blacks computed from cross-section and the over-sample.

average age at first intercourse that is about six months younger, as seen in Figure 1. The figure also indicates that the men report having sex at younger ages than the women. It also shows that blacks report a younger age at first intercourse than whites.

Another way to look at the age at first intercourse is illustrated in Figure 2. The figure shows the proportions of teenagers and young adults who experienced sexual intercourse at each age from twelve to twenty-five. To see at what age half the people had intercourse, for example, follow the . . . horizontal line that corresponds to a cumulative frequency of 50 percent. It shows that half of all black men had intercourse by the time they were fifteen, half of all Hispanic men had intercourse by the time they were about sixteen and a half, half of all black women had intercourse by the time they were nearly seventeen, and half the white women and half the Hispanic women had intercourse by the time they were nearly eighteen. By age twenty-two, about 90 percent of each group had intercourse.

The patterns are crystal clear. About half the teenagers of various racial and ethnic groups in the nation have begun having intercourse with a partner in the age range of fifteen to eighteen, and at least four out of five have had intercourse by the time their teenage years are over. Since the average age of marriage is now in the mid-twenties, few Americans wait until they marry to have sex. . . .

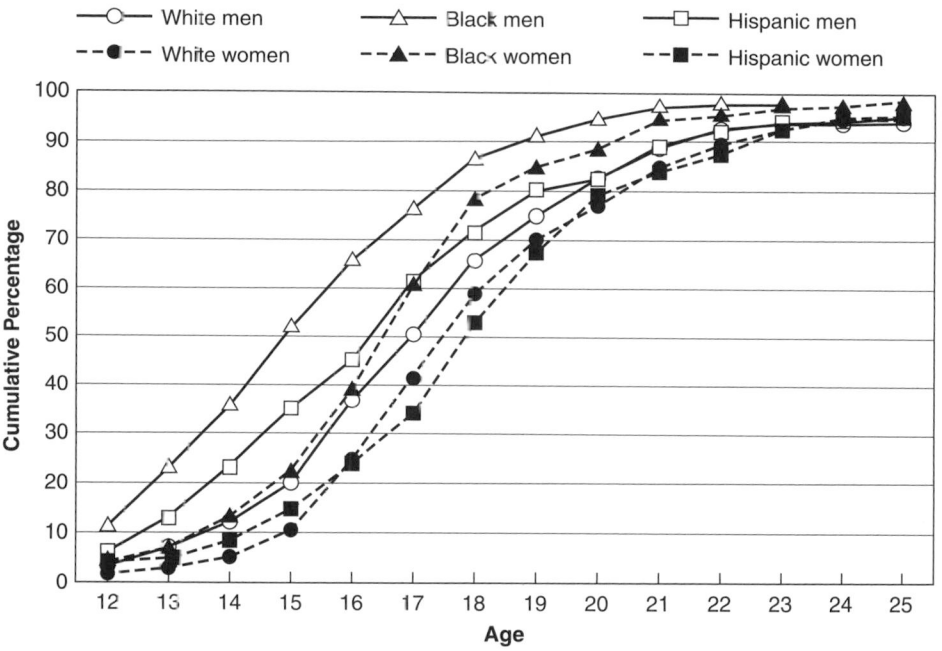

FIGURE 2 Cumulative Percentage Who Have Had Intercourse [by Age 25]

Note: Cumulative percentage indicates the proportion of respondents of a given group at a given age. This figure only includes respondents who have reached their twenty-fifth birthday by the date of the interview.

It's a change that built up for years, making it sometimes hard to appreciate just how profound it is. Stories of what sex among the unmarried was like decades ago can be startling. Even people who were no longer teenagers, and who were engaged, felt overwhelming social pressure to refrain from intercourse before marriage. . . .

In addition to having intercourse at younger ages, many people also are marrying later—a change that is the real legacy of the late 1960s and early 1970s. This period was not, we find, a sexual revolution, a time of frequent sex with many partners for all. Instead, it was the beginning of a profound change in the sexual life course, providing the second reason why Americans have accumulated more partners now than in decades past.

Since the 1960s, the route to the altar is no longer so predictable as it used to be. In the first half of the twentieth century, almost everyone who married followed the same course: dating, love, a little sexual experimentation with one partner, sometimes including intercourse, then marriage and children. It also was a time when there was a clear and accepted double standard—men were much more likely to have had intercourse with several women before marrying than women were to have had intercourse with several men.

. . . [W]e are left with a nation that still has this idealized heterosexual life course but whose actual course has fragmented in the crucial years before marriage. Some people still marry at eighteen, others at thirty, leading to very different numbers of sexual partners before marriage. Social class plays a role, with less-educated people marrying earlier than better-educated people. Blacks tend to marry much later than whites, and a large number of blacks do not marry at all.

But a new and increasingly common pattern has emerged: affection or love and sex with a number of partners, followed by affection, love, and cohabitation. This cycles back to the sexual marketplace, if the cohabitation breaks up, or to marriage. Pregnancy can occur at any of these points, but often occurs before either cohabitation or marriage. The result is that the path toward marriage, once so straight and narrow, has begun to meander and to have many side paths, one of which is being trodden into a well-traveled lane.

That path is the pattern of living together before marriage. Like other recent studies, ours shows a marked shift toward living together rather than marriage as the first union of couples. With an increase in cohabitation, the distinctions among having a steady sexual partner, a live-in sexual partner, and a marriage have gotten more fuzzy. This shift began at the same time as talk of a sexual revolution. Our study shows that people who came of age before 1970 almost invariably got married without first living together, while the younger people seldom did. But, we find, the average age at which people first move in with a partner—either by marrying, or living together—has remained nearly constant, around age twenty-two for men and twenty for women. The difference is that now that first union is increasingly likely to be a cohabitation. . . .

With the increase in cohabitation, people are marrying later, on average. The longer they wait, however, the more likely they are to live with a sexual partner in the meantime. Since many couples who live together break up within a short time and seek a new partner, the result has been an increase in the average number of partners that people have before they marry. . . .

Finally, we can look at divorce rates, another key social change that began in the 1960s and that has led to increasing numbers of partners over a lifetime. . . . For example, we can look at how likely it is that a couple will be divorced by the tenth anniversary of their marriage. For people born between 1933 and 1942, the chance was about one in five. For those born between 1943 and 1952, the chance was one in three. For those born between 1953 and 1962, the chance was closer to 38 percent. Divorced people as a group have more sexual partners than people who remain married and they are more likely, as a group, to have intercourse with a partner and live with a partner before they marry again.

These three social trends—earlier first intercourse, later marriage, and more frequent divorce—help explain why people now have more sexual partners over their lifetimes.

To discern the patterns of sexual partnering, we asked respondents how many sexual partners they had. We could imagine several scenarios. People could find one partner and marry. Or they could have sex with several before marrying. Or they could live with their partners first and then marry. Or they could simply have lots of casual sex, never marrying at all or marrying but also having extramarital sex.

Since our respondents varied in age from eighteen to fifty-nine, the older people in the study, who married by their early twenties, would have been married by the time the turbulent 1960s and 1970s came around. Their premarital behavior would be a relic from the past, telling us how much intercourse people had in the days before sex became so public an issue. The younger people in our study can show us whether there is a contrast between the earlier days and the decades after a sexual revolution was proclaimed. We can ask if they have more partners, if they have more than one sexual partner at a time, and if their sexual behavior is markedly different from that of the older generations that preceded them.

Most young people today show no signs of having very large numbers of partners. More than half the men and women in America who were eighteen to twenty-four in 1992 had just one sex partner in the past year and another 11 percent had none in the last year. In addition, studies in Europe show that people in the United Kingdom, France, and Finland have sexual life courses that are virtually the same as the American life course. The picture that emerges is strikingly different from the popular image of sexuality running out of control in our time.

In fact, we find, nearly all Americans have a very modest number of partners, whether we ask them to enumerate their partners over their adult lifetime or in the past year. The number of partners varies little with education, race, or religion. Instead, it is determined by marital status or by whether a couple is living together. Once married, people tend to have one and only one partner, and those who are unmarried and living together are almost as likely to be faithful.

Our data for the United States are displayed in Table 1.

The right-hand portion of Table 1 tells how many sexual partners people had since they turned eighteen. Very few, just 3 percent, had no partners, and few, just 9 percent, had a total of more than twenty partners.

TABLE 1 Number of Sex Partners in Past Twelve Months and since Age Eighteen

| | SEX PARTNERS PAST TWELVE MONTHS | | | | SEX PARTNERS SINCE AGE EIGHTEEN | | | | | |
	0	1	2 to 4	5+	0	1	2 to 4	5 to 10	10 to 20	21+
Total	12%	71%	14%	3%	3%	26%	30%	22%	11%	9%
Gender										
Men	10	67	18	5	3	20	21	23	16	17
Women	14	75	10	2	3	31	36	20	6	3
Age										
18–24	11	57	24	9	8	32	34	15	8	3
25–29	6	72	17	6	2	25	31	22	10	9
30–34	9	73	16	2	3	21	29	25	11	10
35–39	10	77	11	2	2	19	30	25	14	11
40–44	11	75	13	1	1	22	28	24	14	12
45–49	15	75	9	1	2	26	24	25	10	14
50–54	15	79	5	0	2	34	28	18	9	9
55–59	32	65	4	0	1	40	28	15	8	7
Marital status										
Never married, noncohabiting	25	38	28	9	12	15	29	21	12	12
Never married, cohabiting	1	75	20	5	0	25	37	16	10	13
Married	2	94	4	1	0	37	28	19	9	7
Divorced, separated, widowed, noncohabiting	31	41	26	3	0	11	33	29	15	12
Divorced, separated, widowed, cohabiting	1	80	15	3	0	0	32	44	12	12
Education										
Less than high school	16	67	15	3	4	27	36	19	9	6
High school graduate or equivalent	11	74	13	3	3	30	29	20	10	7
Some college, vocational	11	71	14	4	2	24	29	23	12	9
Finished college	12	69	15	4	2	24	26	24	11	13
Master's/advanced degree	13	74	10	3	4	25	26	23	10	13
Current Religion										
None	11	68	13	7	3	16	29	20	16	16
Mainline Protestant	11	73	13	2	2	23	31	23	12	8
Conservative Protestant	13	70	14	3	3	30	30	20	10	7
Catholic	12	71	13	3	4	27	29	23	8	9
Jewish	3	75	18	3	0	24	13	30	17	17
Other religion	15	70	12	3	3	42	20	16	8	13
Race/Ethnicity										
White	12	73	12	3	3	26	29	22	11	9
Black	13	60	21	6	2	18	34	24	11	11
Hispanic	11	69	17	2	4	35	27	17	8	9
Asian	15	77	8	0	6	46	25	14	6	3
Native American	12	76	10	2	5	28	35	23	5	5

Note: Row percentages total 100 percent.

The oldest people in our study, those aged fifty-five to fifty-nine, were most likely to have had just one sexual partner in their lifetimes—40 percent said they had had only one. This reflects the earlier age of marriage in previous generations and the low rate of divorce among these older couples. Many of the men were married by age twenty-two and the women by age twenty.

The left-hand portion of Table 1 shows the number of sexual partners that people had in the past twelve months. These are the data that show how likely people are to remain faithful to their sexual partner, whether or not they are married. Among married people, 94 percent had one partner in the past year. Couples who were living together were almost as faithful. Seventy-five percent of people who had never married but were living together had one partner in the past year. Eighty percent of people who were previously married and were cohabiting when we questioned them had one partner in the past year. Two-thirds of the single people who were not living with a partner had no partners or only one in the past year. Only a few percent of the population had as many as five partners for sexual intercourse in the past year, and many of these were people who were never married and were not living with anyone. They were mostly young and mostly male.

One way to imagine the patterns of sexual partners is to think of a graph, with the vertical axis showing numbers of partners and the horizontal axis showing a person's age. The graph will be a series of blips, as the person finds partners, interspersed with flat regions where the person has no partners or when the person has just one steady partner. When the person marries, the line flattens out at a height of one, indicating that the individual has only one partner. If the marriage breaks up, the graph shows a few more blips until the person remarries, and then it flattens out again.

For an individual, the graph is mostly flat, punctuated by a few areas of blips. But if we superimposed everyone's graph on top of each other, we would have a sort of supergraph that looked like it was all blips. That, in essence, is what has led to the widespread impression that everyone is having lots of partners. We see the total picture—lots of sex in the population—without realizing that each individual spends most of his or her life with only one partner.

These findings give no support to the idea of a promiscuous society or of a dramatic sexual revolution reflected in huge numbers of people with multiple casual sex partners. The finding on which our data give strong and quite amazing evidence is not that most people do, in fact, form a partnership, or that most people do, in fact, ultimately get married. That fact also was well documented in many previous studies. Nor is it news that more recent marriages are much less stable than marriages that began thirty years ago. That fact, too, was reported by others before us. But we add a new fact, one that is not only important but that is striking.

Our study clearly shows that no matter how sexually active people are before and between marriages, no matter whether they lived with their sexual partners before marriage or whether they were virgins on their wedding day, marriage is such a powerful social institution that, essentially, married people are nearly all alike—they are faithful to their partners as long as the marriage is intact. It does not matter if the couple were high-school sweethearts who married after graduation day or whether they are in their thirties, marrying after each had lived with several others. Once married, the vast majority have no other sexual partner; their past is essentially erased. Marriage remains the great leveler.

We see this, for example, when we ask about fidelity in marriage. More than 80 percent of women and 65 to 85 percent of men of every age report that they had no partners other than their spouse while they were married. . . .

The marriage effect is so dramatic that it swamps all other aspects of our data. When we report that more than 80 percent of adult Americans age eighteen to fifty-nine had zero or one sexual partner in the past year, the figure might sound ludicrous to some young people who know that they and their friends have more than one partner in a year. But the figure really reflects the fact that most Americans in that broad age range are married and are faithful. And many of the others are cohabiting, and they too are faithful. Or they are without partners altogether, a situation that is especially likely for older women. . . . We find only 3 percent of adults had five or more partners in the past year. Half of all adult Americans had three or fewer partners over their lifetimes.

Name Index

Subject Index